Spain's Empire In The New World

Spain's Empire
In The New World
THE ROLE OF IDEAS IN INSTITUTIONAL
AND SOCIAL CHANGE

Colin M. MacLachlan

UNIVERSITY OF CALIFORNIA PRESS
Berkeley   Los Angeles   London

University of California Press
Berkeley and Los Angeles, California

University of California Press, Ltd.
London, England

Copyright © 1988 by The Regents of the University of California

Library of Congress Cataloging-in-Publication Data
MacLachlan, Colin M.
  Spain's empire in the New World.
  Includes index.
  1. Spain—Colonies—America—Administration.
2. Spain—Colonies—America—Constitutional history.
3. Spain—Colonies—America—Social policy. I. Title.
JV4062.M32 1988   325'.31'46   87-18156
ISBN 0-520-05697-3 (alk. paper)

Printed in the United States of America

1 2 3 4 5 6 7 8 9

Contents

Acknowledgments

During the research and writing of this book I have received the help and encouragement of many friends and colleagues. It is a pleasure to acknowledge these intellectual debts. Jaime E. Rodríguez O., as always, proved an inexhaustible source of bibliographical knowledge and intelligent criticism. Many of my ideas have been worked out, or perhaps steamed out, in his jacuzzi. William Sater read the entire manuscript and provided valuable suggestions. Long conversations with Chris Archer, Linda Arnold, Mark A. Burkholder, Brian Hamnett, John Hart, Phil B. Johnson, Allen Kuethe, Peggy Liss, and Paul Vanderwood provided useful insights. Roberto Moreno de los Arcos and María Refugio González have supported my efforts for a number of years and their own scholarship is evident in the bibliography of this work. E. Bradford Burns read a preliminary essay and urged me on to a more complete study. James W. Wilkie provided suggestions along with his usual wit and humor.

At Tulane, Ralph Lee Woodward read the complete draft and made helpful comments. Many other Tulane colleagues and friends offered books, intellectual stimulation, and genial conversation. Among those I want to mention Samuel C. Ramer, Eric Mack, John Glenn, Robert Cook, Michael Boardman, Gerald Snare, and Paul H. Lewis. James Davidson made brief remarks concerning university governance that set me off in an enjoyable and fruitful direction. Charles Davis suggested appropriate works as well as provided amusing observations that made my task lighter. Leisurely and informative lunches at the UCLA Faculty Club with Jim Kubeck, now retired from the University of California Press, are remembered with pleasure.

Doubtless, many others along the way have contributed ideas and perceptions that I have incorporated. If I can neither name nor specifically recall them all here, they nevertheless contributed to shaping my philosophical matrix.

The Latin American Institute at the University of Texas, Austin, and its director William Glade generously provided a professional home for me as a visiting scholar at the institute during the academic year 1981-82.

Many librarians helped me immeasurably. Thomas Niehaus, director of the Latin American Library of Tulane University, offered energetic and prompt assistance. His own work also appears in the bibliography. The Nettie Lee Benson Library of the University of Texas, Austin, provided the rich resources needed for a study of this type. Nettie Lee Benson herself offered straight to the point comments and insights that helped define the book. Library Director Laura G. de Witt and her staff welcomed me and saw to it that I had a comfortable place to work. Joan A. Hughes, Mildred Covert, and Sandra Haro provided the secretarial skills needed to produce this study. Ramona Michaeles then applied her skills to do her usual excellent job of copy-editing. My thanks to them all.

COLIN M. MACLACHLAN
New Orleans

Introduction

THE BROADENING OF THE SPANISH world to embrace a new continent required an intellectual reordering of reality.[1] Castile's conquest of the New World, by means of force and culture, enabled it to insist on the general shape of the new colonial empire. Europeans drew the major components of their imperial invention from their own rich philosophical and historical experience. In the bestiary of Western European civilization, philosophers-theorists already had grappled with an amazing array of actors and realities both mythical and real. Europe's intellectual geography included the pagan genius of ancient Greece, a romanticized, idealized Roman Empire, and a Christian utopia. At one time or another pagans, barbarians, Romans, Ethiopians, Africans, Moors, prophets, prelates, popes, and others populated the mental landscape. Small wonder credulous Europeans, excitedly exploring seemingly fabulous new continents, reported Amazon women, Indians with inverted feet for running backward, and other amazing New World curiosities. The imaginative and intellectual heritage of Spain proved equal to the task of colonial invention.

A common fund of philosophical notions facilitated political exchange and empire building. All sides manipulated ideas to support their particular interests. In the end the most powerful group prevailed, yet at the same time found itself restricted by philosophical principles. The manipulation of ideas justified and legitimized but also modified and restrained. Consequently, in the Spanish world intellectuals functioned at the very heart of the sociopolitical system.

The relative importance of the ideas that formed the philosophical foundations cannot be established. Although the contribution of major theoretical notions may be distinguished, the combined mass of ideas is too complex to separate and evaluate. Moreover, demonstrating the influence of individual philosophers is an inconclusive endeavor. It is possible only to reconstruct the general philosophical matrix that determined the nature of the monarchy and society. (For the purpose of this study, the term *philosophical matrix* denotes a combination of ideas, not easy to separate or define, that embodies the expectations of society as to how it should function.)[2]

Empire building constituted an intellectual task as well as one of force. The New World fell before a small group of enterprising conquistadores, yet force alone could not construct an empire. In the end, ideas relegated the conquerors to subordinate positions, and organized a vast and varied aboriginal population of different historical, cultural, and political traditions under royal control. The ideas that underpinned the Castilian monarchy proved adaptable to the needs of the aboriginal peasantry. Traditional Indian societies relied upon rules and customs in a manner similar to Spain. Their psychological needs blended with European philosophical notions.[3] Ideas supplied a sense of mission and the mutual confidence that an accommodation between different cultures could be achieved.

Royal officials and political theorists understood that domination depended on the manipulation of ideas rather than on force. Humanist Juan de Mal Lara (1524-1571) thus confidently asserted that a mind represented the most worthy offering one could make a monarch because an empire depended upon knowledge. Mal Lara's belief that philosophical notions had folk roots also implied the socially unifying function of ideas.[4] Intellectual debate created, legitimized, and institutionalized authority and provided the means to balance competing interests.[5]

Acceptance of the notion of natural law as the knowable reflection of celestial legislation placed a weighty and important burden on those charged with deciphering it. Theorists earnestly sought to discover how political needs fitted into the divine order. Sixteenth and seventeenth-century casuistry should not be confused with a self-serviing and open-ended justification of necessity. The casuists labored within a philosophical structure that required attention to the principles of common good, beneficence, and spiritual-ethical considerations. The often used term *unwritten constitution* thus appears too narrow to convey the broad nature and impact of ideas that extended far beyond the political realm.

Legislation provided the most concrete manifestation of a philosophical matrix. Individual decrees and legal codes had immediate and long-range political objectives set within a philosophical matrix. Codes in particular served ritualistic and symbolic functions useful in the constant struggle to preserve royal authority.[6] Underpinning the entire structure was a well-developed body of political theory. Theorists determined how the Crown posed the ideal reflected in law. Viewed in isolation, however, the notions of philosopher-theorists appear to be an intellectual maze. Many medieval thinkers attempted to accommodate contradictory ideas within a universal synthesis; thus an examination of ideas without reference to action makes it impossible to separate operational from inconsistent or tangential notions. The law, administrative regulations, the actual behavior of officials and those they governed, as well as the work of theorists, must be integrated in order to reconstruct the philosophical matrix. In short, it is important to pay attention to what is both said and done. Other considerations also influenced developments. Yet, geography, demographic resources, and the level of technology resulted in adjustments that modified the structure more than the supporting ideas.

The introduction of European political theory into the New World required intellectual preparation and an eventual perceptual remolding of reality. In order to justify as well as to facilitate the application of theoretical notions developed in a totally different historical context, the entire history of the Americas had to be recast and rewritten. Indian political history had to be forced into a European frame of reference. The elaboration of an acceptable American past required extensive debate. Such debate took the form of intellectual contests that sought to establish the legitimacy of European intervention in the Western Hemisphere. Even Spanish settlers found it necessary to justify the desired order. Thus the municipal council (*ayuntamiento*) of the City of Mexico commissioned Francisco Cervantes de Salazar to write a history of the conquest that supported their domination of the aboriginal inhabitants.[7] In a similar fashion, Viceroy Francisco de Toledo's interpretation of Inca history met European needs. Toledo gathered his *Informaciones* with Castilian political principles in mind. Questions concerning tyranny and original consent of the governed leave little doubt about his intentions.[8] Subsequently, Viceroy Toledo sponsored Pedro Sarmiento de Gamboa's *Historia de los Incas* to counter the *Historia del Peru* of Diego Fernández which asserted that the Inca leaders functioned as natural lords, having been elected originally by their chieftains.[9]

Juan Matienzo, a judge of the Audiencia of Charcas, wrote *Gobierno del Peru* (ca. 1560-1573) in yet another attempt to justify Spain's presence in the New World on the basis of a tyrannical Inca regime. The gifted mestizo writer and humanist, Inca Garcilaso de la Vega (1539-1616), a descendant of both Inca and Castilian nobility, took a more balanced approach that reflected an understandable degree of cultural and ethnic ambivalence. Nevertheless, he considered the Spanish conquest beneficial.[10]

Regardless of one's position or racial background, the nature of the Indian political experience had to be cast in European terms. Astute Indians soon learned how to manipulate the philosophical matrix. Huaman Poma, son of a pre-conquest Inca official, composed his massive *Nueva Crónica y Buen Gobierno* (ca. 1567–1615) within the context of the common good and obligation to provide justice. Poma compared the Inca system with that of European dukes, marquises, and counts. He directed his account to the king in an attempt to secure positions for caciques within the colonial political and administrative system. Poma noted that "by natural right" Indian leaders ought to have authority over Spaniards. In common with the works of self-interested Europeans, the *Nueva Crónica* placed political desires within an acceptable philosophical framework.[11] Indian theorists, as well as the aboriginal population in general, responded rationally to the new philosophical and material environment. By modifying their perceptions and actions to fit the new imperial situation, they themselves helped to destroy the pre-Cortesian reality.[12]

The ideas that constituted the philosophical matrix within which both the Indian and European struggled to develop a perceptual image of empire and determine how it should function were not uniquely Spanish. The Castilian monarchy drew upon the same fund of knowledge as other Western European states, albeit with particular aspects drawn from the peninsula's own historical experience. Spanish activities in Italy and elsewhere assured exposure to a wide range of political theories. Some two-thirds of sixteenth-century intellectuals traveled outside of the two major kingdoms of Castile and Aragon, while one in ten had crossed the Atlantic as well as visited Flanders. A good one-third of Spanish scholars and thinkers visited or lived for a time in Italy. In the seventeenth century travel by intellectuals declined, partly as a consequence of a deteriorating economy as well as the changing geographical nature of Hapsburg domains; nevertheless, over one-third traveled abroad.[13]

Within Spain itself, the latest works of political theory could be acquired in spite of the efforts of the Inquisition. Some of the most esteemed intellectuals served as censors, thereby gaining access, albeit in a negative fashion, to controversial foreign works. When the library of Joseph Antonio de Sales went on sale in 1651, 10 percent of his 2,424 volumes appeared objectionable to the censor.[14] The imperfect nature and magnitude of the censorship process resulted in a mixed performance and lack of predictability. Books banned and burned in other parts of Europe might escape such a fate in Spain. Book fairs helped disseminate ideas throughout the Spanish world.[15] Moreover, a continuous stream of officials nourished the philosophical underpinnings of the monarchy in its American setting. The inauguration of the University of Mexico (1553) and San Marcos in Lima (1571), as well as a number of more provincial universities, and an impressive network of colleges (secondary schools) assured the internal elaboration of ideas. Yet, although American scholars made advances in linguistics and cultural anthropology, their philosophical writing tended to be traditional expositions. Thus the *Lógica mexicana* of Antonio Rubio Rodensis (1576–1601), a resident of New Spain, served as a text at the Spanish University of Alcalá.[16] New World intellectuals contributed to the dissemination and reinforcement of the Ibero-American philosophy rather than suggesting new departures.[17]

In the eighteenth century, the philosophical foundation of Castile and its American empire continued to represent a variation of Western European thought. Yet the ideas that underpinned the sixteenth- and seventeenth-century colonial regime, while modified in the eighteenth century, continued to exert a powerful influence. As O. Carlos Stoetzer observed, late Spanish scholasticism demonstrated the unique ability to absorb without itself being absorbed.[18] Thus the eighteenth century cannot be understood apart from the Hapsburg period, but must be viewed as a potent overlay of an established philosophical matrix.

Confronted with the difficulty of demonstrating the influence of ideas, one is tempted to conceptualize human interaction as a process that moves without conscious reference to ideas—governed perhaps by an iron law of political survival or economics that may be uncovered through mental activity, yet itself unaffected by ideas. It is not clear, however, why actions and ideas must be pulled apart. A fusion of the two is closer to reality. To discuss aspects of the imperial regime without reference to their philosophical formulations is not fruitful. As J. B. Bury admonished, "it is impossible to imagine the slightest theoretical importance in a collection of facts, or in a sequence of facts, unless they mean something in terms of reason, unless we can hope to determine their vital connection in the whole system of reality."[19] Yet ideas must be placed in context. They are important only when they have an effect in some fashion.[20] Ideas must have a reflection in the society that holds them to be important, or they become dormant and disappear into the realm of intellectual curiosities.

This study links ideas to actions within the political context of the Spanish-American empire. The constant manipulation of philosophical principles at all levels resulted in a highly flexible and responsive state able to make timely adjustments and sociopolitical compromises. Political flexibility faltered after the introduction of an ideological factor in the eighteenth century but began to reassert itself even before the end of that century. The initial chapter of this book reconstructs the general philosophical formulations of the Hapsburg monarchy. The following chapter notes the concrete manifestations of ideas as reflected in the structure, attitude, and actions of officials and society. Chapter three demonstrates the manipulation of the philosophical matrix by groups seeking a particular objective, and the conditioned response of the monarchy. Chapters four, five, and six discuss the elaboration of an ideology in the eighteenth century—the selection and construction of a pattern of ideas aimed at achieving material goals.[21]

The struggle to comprehend the past has important implications for the study of the present. Latin America's colonial heritage is referred to frequently as a factor in maintaining a distinct governing style, ability or inability to accept certain forms of government, socioeconomic and political relations, and general attitudes.[22] Consequently, without a workable perception of historical reality, those concerned with contemporary events may ascribe too little or too much to the colonial past, and on the basis of a false reading neglect to examine other possibilities. It is worth pondering G. K. Chesterton's lament in his study of Chaucer: "Why do I sometimes seem to be writing about modern politics instead of about medieval history? I am left with an overwhelming conviction that it is because we miss the point of medieval history that we make a mess of modern politics."[23]

I

The Monarchy As an Intellectual Construct

THE PHILOSOPHICAL MATRIX OF SPAIN and its empire may be divided into three categories: the nature of a monarch's moral and political subordination to divine authority; a ruler's relationship with his subjects; and last, the extent to which legislated law, and proprietary rights, conveyed actual authority. Only after the philosophical matrix has been established is it possible to suggest the extent to which the institutional practice reflected ideas.

The King As Divine Agent

By definition, a Christian monarchy maintained a divine relationship based on a religious perception of the monarch's role. The notion of a hierarchy capped by a divine, responsive, and compassionate ruler reflected a Christian view of authority.

A clear sense of hierarchy is evident in the *Fuero Real* (1255), which noted that God organized his court with himself at its head, served by archangels and angels, and then extended that order into the temporal realm—a structure that implied the political unity of all believers.[1] The concept of an all-encompassing ecclesia (assembly of the faithful) incorporated the platonic ideal of a society composed of organically layered ranks under a wise ruler, as well as the stoic notion of a universal commonwealth of the right-minded, right-living. In sociopolitical terms, it suggested a society composed of many parts, each with its own role or calling that contributed to the good of the whole.[2] Preservation of the ecclesia, as an expression or an indivisible corporate unity, became a

1

primary purpose of government. Nevertheless, subjects had to be permitted to fulfill their individual calling in order to assure the functioning of an orderly and harmonious community.[3] Consequently, political arguments revolved around the proper distribution of authority.

Secular rulers emphasized the spiritual basis of their government and its divine legitimacy, while prelates provided clerical validation.[4] Kings sought to weaken the role of custom in favor of an acceptance of the idea that the ruler's legislation translated divine justice into legal *dicta*.[5] A government thus had a directive as well as spiritual goal. Spain's Visigoth rulers skillfully manipulated religion to establish a comfortable distance between themselves and the drawbacks of the Teutonic elective kingship. They recognized the political role of spiritual beliefs and procedures, as distinct from the question of the authority of the clergy itself. An appreciation of the usefulness of the manipulation of religion survived the Moorish conquest intact.[6]

Subsequently, the Aristotelian emphasis on the common good became part of the religio-political schema. In the twelfth century, the Caliphate of Córdoba served as the Arabic intermediary through which Aristotle's works filtered into Europe.[7] Saint Thomas Aquinas accepted and adapted Aristotelian political and moral thought to meet the needs of the time.[8] While Aristotle envisioned the political community as complete and an end in itself, Christian beliefs required recognition of the spiritual continuation of life. Consequently, the community represented a guiding force, not an end. The monarch's intervention could be justified only on the grounds of the common good, moral as well as physical, and benevolent intent (*beneficium*). Both the hierocratic structure with its divine source and the Aristotelian radicalism elevated benevolence to an operational principle of government.

It is not surprising that the first formal attempt to achieve royal legal superiority reflected hierocratic benevolence. Designed as a uniform code for both Visigoth and Hispano-Roman subjects, the *Fuero Juzgo* theoretically remained in force from the seventh century to 1254 or 1255. The Fuero Juzgo recognized God as the remote first cause "who can do all things," followed immediately by the king.[9] Ideally, the king possessed the two most important virtues required of a ruler—justice and truth. A monarch, responding to spiritual law, provided an orderly and just structure regulated by judicial procedures. The model ruler sat in judgment mirroring the celestial function. As a regulator, justice not force, served as the principal instrument. Subsequent codes continued to emphasize the natural benevolent action of the government toward its subjects. The notion, although progressively weaker, remained a feature of all Spanish codes into the nineteenth century.

A ruler's position within a divine hierocratic structure made political relations with the priesthood a matter of concern. Because Christian principles constituted an important element of legitimacy, religion could not be left unregulated in clerical hands. Iberian kings realized that there could be only one interpreter of the divine will in political matters. The monarchy and the Church struggled over theory, not the de facto superior position of the king that had already been established at least as far back as Fernando III (1217-1252). San Fernando, who unified the kingdoms of Castile and León, roamed unchallenged through the Church's coffers. Subsequently, Pope Clement IV assured Alfonso X (El Sabio) of his acceptance of royal domination of the Church, a concession after the fact.[10] Although Iberian monarchs achieved material authority over the clergy, the other task, the intellectual modification of clerical authority in order to further the monarchy's political objectives, remained.

Initially, in the struggle for philosophical supremacy, secular rulers functioned at a disadvantage. A kingdom theoretically represented only a political and territorial division within the universal Church founded by Christ himself. Christianity subordinated all temporal affairs to overarching religious objectives; consequently, the pope, as God's vicar, occupied the supreme office on earth. Thus, in St. Augustine's *City of God*, religious responsibilities take precedence over secular concerns. Many theorists insisted that a pope, rather than a king, exercised supreme temporal authority. A succession of popes attempted to sustain such a theory through canon law.[11]

The philosophical struggle to establish an independent secular sovereignty able to resist papal political challenges faced major intellectual obstacles.[12] The Christocentric nature of political philosophy compelled secular proponents to employ the same arguments presented by the Church, although reinterpreted in their favor.[13] The most monarchs could hope for was a favorable redefinition of roles that freed them from papal supervision. Thomas Aquinas offered support with his assertion that each monarch functioned as a vicar of God in his own kingdom as "king by the grace of God," a position that made it possible to argue that a secular Christian ruler could function without direct papal direction. Moreover, Aquinas's acceptance of the idea of a natural political society, which responded to the laws of nature, implied no need for papal direction. A political community, as a natural development, differed from the Church, which represented a supranatural creation. By defining each differently, Aquinas provided the opening necessary to establish separate and distinct functions.[14]

In similar fashion, Dante, personally involved in the struggle against papal ambitions in Italy, insisted that man had two ultimate goals—spiritual salvation facilitated by membership in the Church, and temporal happiness achieved under the guidance of a just ruler. Such a concept acknowledged the importance of each but clearly assigned separate functions to the Church on one hand, and the ruler on the other. Dante's theory subordinated papal authority to the emperor.[15] Marsiglio of Padua (ca. 1275-1342), motivated by the same political considerations, went further and attacked the Church's entire organizational concept. Rather than being a jurisdictional body, Marsiglio claimed, the Church constituted a congregation of the faithful without coercive powers. Actual regulation of society thus fell to a "faithful (but secular) human legislator."[16] Citizens, whether Christian or pagan, functioned as a political community without the need of clerical intervention. Within the community, both lay and cleric functioned on the same footing as citizens. The Franciscan scholar William of Ockham (ca. 1285-1347), while more moderate than Marsiglio, argued that the pope, as head of the Church, did not possess absolute authority but only the power to benefit the faithful. Ockham suggested that the pope in effect exercised the constitutional power extended, as well as restricted, by Christ. As a consequence, the pontiff inherited ministering powers to be used to save souls, not to become involved in political affairs.[17] John of Paris had already reached the same conclusion. He argued that Christ had ruled the world by faith alone, therefore so should his vicar.[18]

Attempts to separate spiritual and political authority had to avoid weakening secular rulers by depriving them of divine validation, while at the same time restricting the clergy to otherworldly concerns. Don Juan Manuel (1282-1347), nephew of Alfonso the Wise (El Sabio), suggested a fusion of spiritual and temporal pursuits in the person of a secular ruler. Don Juan, while conceding the exalted nature of the spiritual life as well as the expectations of damnation of those more worldly, nevertheless ventured the opinion that a person able to respond to both could achieve sanctity. Contained with his exposition, entitled *Libro de los Estados*, was the notion of the worthiness of secular political activities.[19]

On the eve of the Protestant Reformation, the papacy, under pressure from secular rulers intent on securing formal political and economic control over the Church in their own kingdoms, conceded. In a series of concordats, monarchs acquired de jure political superiority, and succeeded in establishing a sense of clerical dependency on secular authority.[20] The transformation of the universal Church into a series of national churches in countries that remained faithful to the old religion, as well as in Protestant states, resulted in what Quentin Skinner identified as a "distinctively modern concept of political obligation."[21] Secular authorities legitimately claimed to be the only jurisdictional authority within their kingdoms, and as such, the rightful and sole recipients of the people's political loyalty. The Spanish Crown won the philosophical contest for political supremacy and fashioned Rome's remaining claims to temporal authority into an instrument of the monarchy in the New World empire.[22]

In Spain, scholasticism provided the philosophical tools that enabled the Castilian Crown to uphold the Church's authority in order to manipulate it politically. With the exception of Cardinal Robert Bellarmine, the scholastics supported papal authority over temporal affairs, but only in certain situations.[23] Francisco de Vitoria (1485-1546) maintained that in the event of some spiritual crisis, the pope could intervene in temporal affairs. In a similar fashion, Francisco Suárez (1458-1517) asserted that a pontiff could exercise coercive force against a ruler in cases of heresy, basing his opinion of the pope's divine appointment as shepherd of the faithful.[24] Vitoria and Suárez tied papal temporal authority to exceptional circumstances, thus restricting its application without closing off the possibility, or denying its existence.

While the secular sword normally exercised the Church's temporal authority, the pope, nevertheless, retained the ability to pressure monarchs, albeit carefully and philosophically. Christians could not disregard Rome. Melchor Cano thus reminded Felipe II that in spite of the pope's personal weaknesses, he remained Vicar of Christ, and if the pope were recklessly challenged, the monarch could damage his own authority. In addition, public controversy with the pope weakened the perception of the unity of authority that constituted a significant element of the Crown's governing mystique. If properly handled, however, Rome supplied financial subsidies.[25] Popes as well as kings understood the political aspects of religion.[26] Consequently, astute papal diplomats brought philosophical arguments into play when pressed overly aggressively by the Castilian monarchy.

In the late fifteenth and early sixteenth century the works of Desiderius Erasmus (1464-1536) introduced a new intellectual current in Spain. With the establishment of the University of Alcalá de Henares (1498), humanism developed a Castilian institutional base.[27] Erasmian thought penetrated every aspect of intellectual life, including political theory. Explorers, conquerors, and missionaries carried his work into the New World setting. Pedro de Mendoza, the first adelantado of the Río de la Plata, reputedly brought a work by Erasmus along on his ill-fated expedition (1536). More than likely, he carried a copy of the *Manual del Soldado Cristiano*, first published in Spanish in 1526.[28] Erasmus drew together the various strands of humanistic thought and presented them in a cogent fashion. His friendship with many of Europe's most powerful rulers testified both to his influence and to the fact that monarchs found little to object to in his didactic writings.[29]

Although Erasmus touched on his conception of the ideal prince in a number of studies, his *Institutio Principi Christiani* (The Education of a Christian Prince), dedicated to Carlos V in 1516 and reworked two years later for Fernando of Aragón, is the most important. In the Erasmian view, a kingdom should be governed like a family with the monarch as paterfamilias.[30] Just as God required no recompense for His beneficent gifts, so should the king undertake works of kindness without thought of compensation or glory.[31] Erasmus compared God and the "good prince," noting that the ruler represented the "tangible and living image of the deity."[32] Such notions, while they flattered and exalted monarchs, emphasized the emotional and mystical aspects of a ruler's position—an approach that obscured and devalued the concept of natural law as well as the monarch's ability to interpret the divine will. Erasmus reflected the concern of sixteenth-century humanists that individualism threatened the community and warned that the ideal monarch should not gauge the state of the kingdom in material terms. Rather, a king must assure that the people conduct themselves in an honorable and disciplined fashion, disdaining greed and living together in harmony.[33] True happiness could only be spiritual, while the prince's esteem rested on his "kindness and beneficence." Erasmus's monarch served as an understanding guardian, and even when faced with rebellious subjects, acted with patience and restraint—as a father, not a master. Erasmus warned against political innovation, observing that the confusion that attended change itself becomes a problem. Only when a situation became unbearable should action be taken, and then slowly and with great caution.[34] He admonished princes to remember that "dominion, imperial authority, majesty, power, are all pagan terms not Christian," and that the rule of a Christian state required "administration, kindness, and protection."[35]

In spite of Erasmus's influence, Thomism and Suarezism responded more to pragmatic needs than did humanism. Scholasticism objected to the humanists' slighting of natural law and rejected Machiavelli's dismissal of natural law as the moral basis of political organization. For the same reasons, scholastic theorists refuted the Lutheran conception of the political community.[36] The notion that human beings, hopelessly corrupt and unworthy, could not even attempt to understand the will of God, rejected the concept of natural law as well as the authority of the monarch as an interpretive reflection of divine will.

Reacting to this perceived threat, Domingo de Soto stated that "every human law must derive from the laws of nature."[37] The apparent denial of the role of reason in Protestant thought prompted Melchor Cano (d. 1560) to charge that, besides being folly, it constituted an act of impiety because God is truth.[38] Moreover, the Lutheran insistence that only a godly ruler could make laws made godliness a condition of kingship, and implied the power of the faithful inferior magistrate to judge the worthiness of political superiors.[39] A horrified Francisco de Vitoria believed that such a notion destroyed the orderly hierarchy of authority as well as the organic concept of the monarchy—in essence, "the feet" could say to the "head", you are not necessary to us."[40] Although human beings were created free, the necessity, as well as the desire, to lessen uncertainty and injustice prompted them to consent to the establishment of a commonwealth. Suárez observed that the people, by agreeing to form a government, created an "authority whose duty it is to promote the common good."[41] Vitoria, uncomfortable with the notion of self interest alone, added that as the need for political organization had been implanted by God, the monarchy could not be viewed as a purely human invention. Moreover, whereas consent played an important role in its actual establishment, it did not itself convey legitimacy. The legitimate exercise of authority depended on adherence to natural law.

Scholastic thought provided secular authority with the philosophical means to defend its supremacy without dispensing with the politically unifying functions of Christianity. A monarch's activities, directed toward the common good, did not require supervision because the monarch functioned in accordance with natural law. Divine motivation of a political society, however, did not involve a human competitor for the loyalty of the community. Monarchs and their advisors, impelled by political needs, accepted this perception of authority and incorporated it as an important part of the philosophical matrix.

By the sixteenth century, Crown control over the Spanish Church exceeded that of any other European kingdom, whether Protestant or Catholic. Carlos V persuaded Pope Adrian VI to grant him in perpetuity the right of presentation to Spanish bishoprics, and by the end of his reign the most lucrative benefices fell under royal control. His son and successor, Felipe II, acted with few restrictions in filling clerical posts. Clerics understood that their position depended on the king's favor, and that appeals to Rome accomplished little.[42] Hapsburg monarchs became the patrons of a politically captive religion that reinforced their ability to govern.

The King and His Subjects

The monarch's role emphasized guidance rather than authoritarian coercion. A monarchy relied more upon philosophical acceptance than upon its actual ability to command. This fundamental characteristic of the Castilian monarchy is evident in the Fuero Real (1255) that superseded the Fuero Juzgo, and in the Siete Partidas (1265). Not in a position to overwhelm local or regional fueros, the monarchy attempted to absorb them within all-encompassing enactments. This conquest of jurisdiction remained a major objective at least through the reign of Isabel. The Crown justified its enactment as a benevolent attempt to extend law to those without a legal charter.[43] While drawing upon divine legitimacy—indeed, the first phrase is "en el nombre de Dios Amen"— the Fuero Real assigned the immediate impulse to Don Alfonso who, "aware that the people have suffered, decided to grant them this fuero."[44] In a similar manner, the Siete Partidas, the most important of all medieval codes from the standpoint of political philosophy, sought to establish a dependent relationship between a benevolent monarchy and its subjects. Its author, Alfonso X (El Sabio) already had diminished the influence of the *Grandes* by staffing the royal household with appointed administrators. The *Siete Partidas* attempted to go further and established in principle a difference between private grants (*feuda*) and an official appointment that constituted an honor to be conveyed or withdrawn by the king. Alfonso hoped to gain acceptance of the notion that provincial governors (merinos, mayores, and adelantados) exercised a royal jurisdiction superior to all others.[45] In reality, competing jurisdictions could not be subordinated so easily. Nevertheless, the *Siete Partidas* helped formulate a perception of royal authority that was manipulated by subsequent monarchs to strengthen their position.[46]

The implied benevolence of a paternalistic monarchy evident in the *Siete Partidas* defined the law's objectives as: (1) to inspire confidence, (2) to regulate, (3) to command, (4) to combine (unify), (5) to reward, (6) to forbid, and lastly (7) to punish.[47] Movement is from gentle guidance to a graduated harshness as a last resort.[48] The *Siete Partidas* defined the people as "the union of all men together, those of superior, middle, and inferior rank."[49] Such a definition, while recognizing a social hierarchy, placed all under the same philosophical umbrella. The king exhibited his divine benevolence in three ways:

> First by conferring benefits upon them, and doing them favors...it is eminently proper that he bestow favors upon them....Second by showing compassion upon them...he will be to them as a father who brings up his children in love, and punishes them with mercy....Third

by having pity upon them, and remitting at times the penalty which they deserve.[50]

A monarch, as had God, placed himself at the head (*cabeza*) of his court for the purpose of shielding the people from harm. As *señor natural*, by virtue of his position and responsibilities, his subjects owed him reverence, honor, and obedience, insofar as he represented the divine will as indicated by adherence to natural law.[51] The Fuero Real which states that as the head does not injure the body so must the body protect the head, suggests a sense of mutual responsibility and the positive intent of the ruler.[52] A monarch governed over the commonwealth, he did not absorb it.[53] Theorists made a distinction between civil power and authority, the right to administer the community's power. A king possessed only the latter. His obligation toward the community rather than direct consent, or accountability to the governed, served to restrain arbitrary acts, and, in theory, violation of that trust resulted in forfeiture.[54] Vitoria extended the notion of the monarch's community obligation to the New World in his assertions that overlordship must be established strictly for the benefit of the Indian, not for the profit of the European.[55] What constituted a benefit remained open to interpretation.

The residual feudalism that continued to influence Castilian political relations also restricted the free exercise of authority. The notion of a legal bond between lord and vassal implied a contract that bound both parties. A perceived contractual binding of the ruler, in particular in his dealings with the aristocracy, made it difficult for a king to revoke privileges once conceded. The breaking of an implied contract required the consent of the parties involved, a position of equality a monarch preferred to avoid.

Reluctance to concede active consent complicated the monarch's relationship with the Cortes (the representative assembly) over the issue of taxation. Royal concessions, political theory, and custom required the consent of the Cortes to new tax measures. In return, the Cortes sought to influence policy and to exercise indirect supervisory functions. When its approval was solicited, it often pressured the Crown to address particular grievances. As a result, a monarch avoided such a disagreeable process as much as possible. Royal revulsion to such bargaining blocked fiscal reforms and perpetuated an irrational tax structure. In the American empire the issue of taxes posed fewer political problems. Major sources of revenue, including the mining fifth, tribute, and the tithe required no formal consent. Theoretical royal ownership of subsoil wealth, and the Roman origins of the mining tax, made payment acceptable, subject to adjustment. In a philosophical and legal sense, the conquest justified the tribute payment, while the tithe, although controlled by political authorities and subject to serious squabbles over payments and taxable items, historically represented the duty of all Christians to support the Church.[56] These major taxes continued to be levied even after independence.[57] Other sources of revenue, including customs duties, stamped paper, and the alcabala (sales tax)—related to an increasingly complex economy and the rise of diverse interest groups—proved politically more sensitive. The alcabala, introduced in New Spain in 1571 and five years later to Guatemala and eventually throughout the empire, caused great resentment. New World inhabitants did not accept the extension of the tax into the American empire based on the Cortes of Burgos 1342 grant. Initially pegged at 2 percent, it reached 8 percent by the mid-eighteenth century. Municipal councils resisted the alcabala, on occasion violently. The introduction of the tax in Quito in 1592 resulted in a bitter popular protest, the "Revolution of the Alcabalas," required the dispatching of troops.[58] The king's American subjects required at least ambivalent acknowledgment of the notion of consent of the governed, particularly on tax matters. Consent, implied or otherwise, appeared to challenge the monarch's ability to act on his alleged superior understanding of natural law and to legislate independently.

The issue of consent was closely linked to the notion of tyrannicide. For the head to dismiss arbitrarily the functions of the parts violated the hierarchical sociopolitical order. Theoretically, an arbitrary monarch became a tyrant, forfeiting the cooperation of his subjects as well as the divine blessing. Subjects, in theory, had the right to repel tyrannical acts with force.[59] Francisco Suárez, perhaps influenced by the Ockhamists, posited the notion that just as the right to preserve one's life is basic, so is the commonwealth's right to prevent a ruler from destroying it. Suárez moved beyond traditional natural law by asserting that genuine self-protection constituted a natural right. Such a fruitful notion gained strong acceptance. More than a hundred years later, the king's rustic vassals in colonial Asunción (Paraguay), seeking to justify the expulsion of the Jesuits from the city (1649), explained to the Audiencia of Charcas that they had exercised their "natural right" to defend themselves against those whose sought to destroy them.[60]

Suárez elaborated a deliberative procedure by which the people might remove a king, requiring action by an appropriate representative body after wide and exhaustive consultation.[61] To avoid frivolous resistance, overwhelming evidence that a ruler had ceased to pursue the common welfare was required before tyrannicide became a possibility— obviously an abnormal and rare occurrence. Juan de Mariana (1536-1624), in a blunter fashion, asserted that the king received power from the people in order to benefit the community. If a ruler abused his trust, it could be reclaimed. Absolutism in Mariana's view appeared as a form of flattery or fallacy. A wayward king, however, should be reasoned with before taking the ultimate step. If the king took up arms against the people, then he became an enemy of the country and could be killed lawfully by anyone. Mariana, like Suárez, cautioned against lightly jeopardizing order.[62] Over a century later, Fernando de Mompó y Zayas, attempting to provide the Paraguayan *comuneros* with an ideological basis for their revolt against royal authority (1730), realized the fears of Suárez and Mariana that their notions might be employed casually. Mompó argued that God vested political authority in the *común*, whose power transcended that of the king. Legitimacy thus depended upon the conscious and deliberate acceptance by the people of both governors and the laws. Acting on these ideas, Mompó and his followers established a Junta Gobernativa (governing committee) elected by the rebellious comuneros. Royal officials understandably viewed the junta's creation as an act of treason.[63]

The question of order, made more immediate by the religious struggles of the sixteenth century, tended to make tyrannicide less acceptable even in theory. In times of political crises, to discuss it appeared almost to facilitate it. The revolt of the Huguenots in France pushed moderates into a defense of absolutism, even the tyrannical exercise of sovereignty, as the lesser evil. Social and political disintegration overshadowed more abstract and theoretical problems. Michel de Montaigne and Jean Bodin, responding to such fears, virtually ruled out tyrannicide for all practical purposes.[64] In the Spanish Empire, the revolt of the Netherlands brought the dangers of Huguenot theories into sharp focus. The rebels turned to the theories of Theodore Beza, Philippe du Plessis Mornay, and other Huguenots to defend their actions.[65]

In Spain, the concept of tyrannicide became such a remote theoretical possibility that it functioned more as a cultural restriction than as an actual kingly penalty. Moreover, to declare a monarch a tyrant, or subjects rebels, forced a confrontation that could be resolved only by force—a disruptive process not to be lightly contemplated. By making the notion of the ruler's true and beneficial intent a central consideration, however, both the government and its subjects achieved a useful degree of flexibility without the need to threaten the monarchy itself. It permitted the government to reverse itself without political damage. Nevertheless, lingering concern for a doctrine perceived to be pernicious carried through into the eighteenth century. Enlightened ministers viewed the doctrine of tyrannicide as an active threat to authority.[66] Recognition of the role of scholars in the elaboration, as well as refutation of such a politically unacceptable theory, is evident in university regulations. For example, the constitution of the University of Caracas approved by Felipe V in 1727 required the faculty to swear to "abjure and enveigh" against the doctrines of tyrannicide and regicide.[67] Ironically, in the early nineteenth century, General Pablo Morillo, engaged in bloody repression in New Granada, boasted to Fernando VII that he had cleansed the viceroyalty of intellectuals "who always are the promoters of rebellion."[68]

The administration of justice incorporated and demonstrated the benevolent virtues of a king, providing a direct link between the monarch and his subjects. The preservation of order represented a tangible social benefit and demonstrated the monarch's ability to impose sanctions. It reinforced Crown sovereignty by extracting punishment as well as providing an opportunity to show compassion. Moreover, under certain conditions, pardons served political interests by publicly displaying the monarch's compassionate benevolence as well as his power to alter legal status. The *Siete Partidas*, reflecting the political importance of the authority to pardon, devoted a separate section to the subject, noting that pity was a quality that those who "sit in judgment and govern countries should especially possess."[69] Thus, while a monarch executed justice firmly, he must also pardon. Moved to compassion for the suffering of the condemned, or aware of some past service rendered, the king demonstrated mercy or performed an act of pure grace, as a "gift."[70]

Judges, according to the *Siete Partidas*, must reflect the royal attitude and take into account mitigating circumstances—in effect, establish some reason for moderation. Social status, economic factors, and age had to be considered. If possible, the young or very old were not to be held responsible. Offenders guilty of a crime against a party to whom they had some obligation deserved severe punishment. As a reflection of the hierarchical political structure, failure to demonstrate loyalty and gratitude became part of the crime, as did the manner and place of commission. If committed in a church, royal palace, judicial chambers, or the house of a friend, the crime must be viewed without compassion. In a similar fashion, crimes committed under cover of darkness called for more serious attention than those perpetrated in broad daylight—to kill openly was one thing, to murder treacherous and perfidiously another.

The compassionate impulse that withheld full punishment placed both the guilty and those who stood in judgment within a religio-political context. Repentance and forgiveness avoided the potentially damaging perception of an uncompromising battle between criminal elements and society. It implied that guidance constituted the remedy. Inherent in this approach was a sense of disappointment that the guilty had not conformed to the norms established by society as a reflection of the heavenly kingdom.[71]

The King and the Law

The relationship between the legislator and his own legal creation posed a difficult political question. Visigoth theorists subscribed to the notion that the law existed as an expression of justice but did not itself create justice. As violations of justice became evident, a ruler created new laws; justice itself remained eternal and external. Once created, legislation assumed eternal validity, and while it could be superseded by other expressions of justice, it could not be discarded. In order to avoid becoming mired in past legislation, some flexibility had to be found. The difficulty of working out a philosophically acceptable method to justify flexibility led to reliance on technical solutions. Visigoth monarchs conceded that they were subject to the law because God's will, expressed in legislation, bound all. However, as a divinely sanctioned ruler, the king's actions, including ignoring the law, could be challenged only by God.[72] The contradictions engendered by this perception of royal power remained a political problem long after the collapse of the Visigoth kingdom. Although a monarch did not want to be hampered by past enactments, he could not, at the same time, risk being perceived as arbitrary or unpredictable. The thin, but important, distinction between flexibility and violation of the spirit of justice could not be made easily. The *Siete Partidas* stated that a monarch who violated his how king-made laws invalidated them for everyone.[73] Both the Fuero Juzgo and the Fuero Real declared that king-made law honored and taught God's intentions and, therefore, had to be respected both by the people and the king.[74] This ideal perception of the law's purpose carried through into the nineteenth century, being repeated in various codes and compilations, including the *Novísima Recopilación* of 1805.[75] To violate enactments once proclaimed implied an attack on the faith—as well as on the medieval notion that only through the law could a Christian political body survive and reach the desired goal.[76]

Sanctification of the law, and the consequent belief in the legal process, made it preferable to allow enactments to lapse rather than risk a reaction by officially abrogating them. For revocation of valid legislation, or in cases where a new law outrageously clashed with the previous enactments, consent of the Cortes theoretically had to be sought, as specified in the Ordinance of 1387.[77] The tendency to leave enactments on the books made for a mire of conflicting statutes, a situation somewhat alleviated by attempts to establish orders of precedence. Nevertheless, a diligent and skillful lawyer could confuse the issue until a case arrived at the highest level—the high court (Audiencia) or the king himself. At that point, justice clarified existing law and might call for yet another legislated reflection of divine justice.

The means by which the king could circumvent his own legislated restrictions without destroying their general validity or applicability within society had to be provided for in some fashion. As a result, political theorists suggested degrees of legal subordination ranging from the absolute to the moral, but not actual, requirement to obey. Erasmus, who considered the ruler within the law, failed to allow the flexibility needed to manipulate a complex society. The sixteenth-century Thomists, however, provided the philosophical means to justify political flexibility without relieving a monarch of all restriction. The Thomists reiterated Aquinas's position that the primitive community, by transferring its power to a ruler, abrogated it as well. Following the same logic, Domingo de Soto deduced that a ruler, as head of the body of the commonwealth, must necessarily be greater than all its members. Similarly, Francisco Suárez asserted that a monarch possessed absolute authority, following Aquinas's notion that a prince had no superiors. While they hoped that a ruler would feel morally bound to obey his own laws, he could not, in their view, be held accountable to legislated law. Such thought strengthened the absolutist monarchy and provided the means to maneuver around the philosophical and legal limitations imposed on the king by the *Siete Partidas* and other legal codes. Moral obligation provided the restraining influence.[78] Consequently, Juan de Mariana's *Del Rey y de la Institución Real*, dedicated to Felipe III, conceded that all laws did not apply to the king. He expressed, however, the hope that a ruler would consider himself bound by law and conscience.[79]

Acceptance of the king's superior authority did not settle the question of the actual ownership of the kingdom itself. While Roman law made a distinction between office and personal patrimony, as did Visigoth law, a precise line could not be drawn. The question remained a political problem until the depersonalization of the state in the nineteenth century. Yet, the need to secure private land holdings required general acceptance of Crown proprietary rights in order to legitimize the transfer of property acquired as a consequence of Christian reconquest, and the conquest of America. Confirmation of land titles implied the royal right to convey in the first place. Vesting subsoil rights in the monarch also proved useful in that it permitted the government to override surface proprietary rights to license the working of mines. Thus the *Siete Partidas*, and subsequently the *Ordenamiento de Alcalá*, clearly separated surface and subsoil rights, vesting the latter's ownership in the monarch. Felipe II exercised control of mineral deposits be declaring that any person could work mines, with or without permission of the surface owner, provided he paid the royal fifth. Felipe, like his father Carlos V, encouraged the development of American mines by Indian or Spanish developers. Such zealous encouragement and liberal concessions prompted theorists to speculate whether the monarch in fact had effectively alienated mineral rights. In general, however, most accepted the notion that ultimate ownership lay with the Crown.[80] The security of private property nevertheless made it desirable to avoid the amalgamation of political authority with universal property rights, while preserving the usefulness of the Crown's proprietary ability to legitimize private holdings.

The absence of set limits made encroachment by the monarchy a possibility and encouraged a king to treat the nation's resources as his own. Jean Gerson advanced a theoretical separation between a ruler's proprietary rights and those of his subjects. While intent on reinforcing the notion that the pope exercised only constitutional powers subject to authority of the General Council of the Church, he followed his ideas into the secular sphere and concluded that the government's authority ultimately rested with its citizens. Defining a right as the ability to dispose of freely, Gerson asserted that a monarch did not have the power to dispose of the commonwealth, nor the property of its members.[81] Gerson's theories enjoyed renewed interest in the sixteenth century. Thus Francisco Suárez asserted that the ability to dispose formed the basis of the notion of rights, and gave an owner the right to his possessions.[82]

To sustain the subtle distinction between a ruler's paramount political jurisdiction and proprietary rights (the ability to dispose) constituted a problem. Inevitably, authorities blurred the separation when convenient. Such a tendency prompted Juan de Mariana to insist vehemently that kings did not exercise dominion over private property. Drawing upon Roman law, he asserted that the king could not size his subject's possessions, not appropriate part of them as a tax without consent. In his treatise, *De monetae mutatione*, he attacked the monarch for debasing the currency, thus imposing a hidden tax, and circumventing the consent of the governed. Mariana declared that a ruler who deceived the people in such a fashion acted like a tyrant.[83] Such criticism resulted in his arrest for *lèse majesté*. In a more diplomatic fashion, Jean Bodin attempted to devise a limit on actual royal proprietary rights, while preserving the useful aspects of Crown authority over property. Bodin asserted that even an absolute monarch exercised only the power to use, not actual ownership.[84] He suggested the existence of a type of political usufruct that coexisted with private property rights. Bodin thus separated the advantages arising from property into material and political benefits.

Royal jurisdiction (*realengo*) thus constituted a type of property, although vested in the Crown itself, not the reigning monarch. It formed part of the royal patrimony. In fact, realengo competed with long-established privileges as well as with local and regional elites—a fact that made jurisdiction, except at the abstract level, difficult to sustain. Moreover, in Spain a considerable number of towns operated under seigneurial control. Melchor de Macanaz reported that in Valencia the king controlled only 73 population centers while another 300 remained in seigneurial hands. Even at the end of the eighteenth century, the Crown theoretically controlled less than half of the country's towns and cities, although virtually all major centers remained under royal jurisdiction (*realengo*).[85] In centers under Crown jurisdiction, the king theoretically had the power to appoint officials and collect revenues. In fact, actual power fell to local elites. The reality of local power contributed to the willingness to sell towns, transferring them to seigneurial, or independent, control. Even in the "sale of vassals," the Crown retained jurisdiction in the event of conflict between the townspeople and the seigneur.[86] In essence, the Crown sold the right to administer while preserving its overriding jurisdiction. Such an approach acknowledged the lingering aspect of the feudal tradition in Spain, and also removed the Crown from responsibility in the first instance. Mutual manipulation of the notion of royal proprietary rights by the monarchy and its subjects reinforced the perception that property ultimately belonged to the realm in a political rather than personal sense. This strengthened the notion of a distinct entity—the nation-state.

In the New World, Queen Isabel and her consort, Fernando of Aragón, asserted rights based on proprietary claims. By doing so, they declared their full possession of the Indies as well as the theoretical right to dispose. The Crown, in the Western Hemisphere, moved into a jurisdictional vacuum, although willing to recognize the subordinate authority of Indian caciques. *Solariego* and *abadengo*, lordship of noble and ecclesiastical seigneurs, did not exist in the New World. The monarch did not have to contend with competing jurisdictions except for those introduced by the Crown itself. Subsequent concessions made to principal conquistadores constituted only a restricted solariego that conveyed a diluted *señorío* subject to progressive encroachment by the Crown. Some clerics exercised de facto abadengo under the guise of missionary activities, but, except in marginal areas, once the organizational period passed so did their assumed authority. Nevertheless, realengo (royal jurisdiction) in America, although infused with a more concrete sense of property rights than in Spain, also functioned most effectively as a species of political usufruct.

Philosophical and papal restrictions, quite apart from the physical impossibility of direct control of the land by the monarch in a vast empire, provided for political rather than actual proprietorship. The Alexandrine Bull of 1493 (*Inter caetera divinae*) restricted the right to dispose while simultaneously conveying lordship with "full free and all embracing power, authority, and dominion." The pope furthermore donated, granted, and assigned, "to you [Isabel and Fernando] and your heirs and successors, the kings of Castile and León."[87] The wording appears to circumscribe the ability to transfer freely to any but a Castilian monarch. Subsequently, the legal disposal of such rights in favor of the Castilian monarchy itself created a hybrid species of realengo not based upon ancient custom or historical jurisdictions but derived from proprietary rights. Emperor Carlos V, in 1519, transferred personal proprietorship to the Crown as an institution incorporating the Indies into the monarchy, and prohibiting future alienation.[88] Theoretically, the New World became part of the royal patrimony attached to the Crown in a proprietary manner. The extent to which material proprietary power could be manipulated freely by an institution supposedly bound by higher, and overriding, divine obligations appears to be a political contradiction. Moreover, restrictions on alienation violated Gerson's criteria, which defined property rights in terms of the ability to dispose.

Just what royal prerogatives could be derived from proprietorship remained unclear. Indeed, the organization of the new conquest into kingdoms implied that they had the rights that come with that political designation. Such entitlements could not be brushed aside. Nevertheless, the differences between Old and New World could not be ignored. When peninsula kingdoms came under royal authority, they entered such an arrangement with their own customs, laws, and government. In contrast, the creation of America through conquest implied a different relationship at the moment it entered the political structure. Consequently, the laws and customs of Castile, as the conquering power, had a currency they could not properly demand in Aragón, or the other separate European kingdoms; yet, this did not imply the domination of Castile over the Indies.[89] The establishment of a separate Council of the Indies (1524) designated as supreme thus excluded the authority of the Council of Castile. Such an arrangement constituted more than mere administrative, or organizational, adjustments between units of the monarchy. Along with form came philosophical substance. Reacting against this reality, jurist Juan de Solórzano y Pereyra attempted to assert the subordination of New World kingdoms to Castile; however, the intellectual alienation made such efforts futile.[90]

In the American kingdoms, the monarchy exercised jurisdictional *realengo* as well as *realengo de tierra* (royal authority over land), which enabled it to grant land and convey titles. As Jerónimo Castillo de Bobadilla diplomatically, yet unmistakably, put the issue in reference to the reconquest of Spain, the monarch, out of customary magnanimity and liberality, recognized the great service of those who had regained the land by dividing it among them and raising them to noble status, so that they became "the bone and sinew of the state without whom it would be a boneless, nerveless, mass of pulp and flesh."[91] The conquest of the New World required recognition and reward for identical reasons.[92] Individual claims on the monarchy, established during the armed struggle for empire, as well as the philosophical requirement to attend to the common good and well-being of its subjects, clashed with the inherent right of property—the power to retain. Although the Crown might apply certain restrictions, including monetary payments, it had to comply with the demands of its subjects.[93] Nevertheless, the internal alienation of land did not include proprietary sovereignty, which remained with the king. Colonial subjects depended on the monarch's legitimate right to bestow land titles; thus they recognized a sovereign proprietorship over American land. In the end, the American experience, given the vast amount of land converted into private property, significantly advanced the philosophical and psychological separation between the property rights of the monarchy and those exercised within the political entity itself by its subjects.

In summary, it is evident that a useful ambivalence characterized the philosophical matrix. The extent of a ruler's political subordination or relationship with divine authority, the pope, natural law, royal legislation, and the people depended on an interpretation that often bordered on manipulation. Learned disputations served political purposes. Nevertheless, philosophical notions restricted arbitrary acts and modified, as well as determined, the extent to which an objective could be attained. Negotiations within the framework of the common good and the ruler's benevolent intent provided a broad and fluid political arena. The process offered assurance of predictability while permitting flexibility.

The notion of a constant and external justice made law a device as well as a demonstration of the king's obligation to provide for the orderly Christian community. The monarch, as the temporal interpreter of the divine will, remained above his own legislated creation, but his position as a divine agent provided sufficient guarantees that he would not disregard the laws in a casual fashion. The concept of tyrannicide, while carefully encapsulated, served as a philosophical restraint. The acceptance of a proprietary political usufruct in the New World that overrode the property rights of others, while not extinguishing them, avoided conflict over actual land ownership. Less positively, the ambivalence about the extent to which proprietary rights conveyed political power in the American empire encouraged officials to ignore technical or theoretical restriction when convenient and politically possible. Nevertheless, when officials attempted to use proprietary rights in a simple fashion, asserting that the Crown could act without restriction in the New World, they encountered strong philosophical barriers.

In reality, the transfer of the Indies to the Castilian Crown produced a fusion of European political theory with a new proprietary element of uncertain force. As a consequence, the basis of law in the New World differed, but not completely, from that in Spain. The notion of proprietorship in the empire and its implied lowering of the source of authority from the heavenly kingdom to a temporal level, however, introduced an element of arbitrary authority in the New World not present in the Old.[94]

2

The Structural Reflection

THE PATTERN OF IDEAS SHARED by the Hapsburg monarchy and its subjects had a formative as well as regulative influence. Philosophical notions engendered social and political expectations. The king's subjects expected a type of response and organization that reflected the accepted basis of authority. The monarchy legitimately exercised jurisdiction in accord with such expectations. As a regulating force, the monarchy readily acknowledged interest groups and often endowed them with self-policing powers and responsibilities now associated with the modern state.

The notion that the ruler had a guiding and protective role served as the major operational principle. As an agent of a celestial force, the Crown reflected divine intent. Moreover, as the recipient of power originally held by the people, the king accepted the duty to govern in the community's interests. The monarch functioned in a role philosophically bracketed between the people below and the divine above. His subjects (flock) expected their ruler to exercise a benevolent paternalism and attend to their well-being. As a result, a monarch could not deviate easily from the pursuit of the common good. At the same time, he relied upon the general assumption that royal acts were intended to be beneficial, even if this intent was not immediately evident to the governed. Positive assumption reinforced the ability to govern. When a miscalculation occurred that provoked active or violent opposition, the king remained shielded behind the assumption of benevolence while his ministers accepted responsibility for not following the monarch's true intent. Thus angry mobs shouted, "Muera al mal gobiero, viva el rey" (Death to the bad government, long live the king).[1]

The fact that the councillors became expendable in a political crises acted to restrain their activities by placing a degree of personal responsibility on each advisor. Theoretically, a councillor once convinced of the misguided nature of royal policy had an obligation to advise the king, a notion that permeated all levels of society. For example, when various clerics denounced the excesses of Chilean Governor Lazo de Vega in 1632, they asserted that they did so out of an obligation to God and "their zeal for the common good, divine as well as royal service."[2]

A governing structure capped by an assumed to be benevolent ruler could survive a tremendous amount of disorder without risking a direct attack on the nature of the regime itself. Accountability to the common good theoretically subordinated the use of power to principle. As Fray Martín Ignacio de Loyola, bishop of La Plata, reminded the Cabildo of Buenos Aires in 1606, the law must not be enforced rigidly, but judiciously and prudently interpreted with the ultimate aim in mind. If implementation conflicted with the true royal objective, the law should be respected but not executed for "such is the teaching of true theology."[3] The administrative device by which officials suspended royal orders represented the important notions in action. A legal formula, *obedezco pero no cumplo* (I obey, but do not execute), permitted affirmation of the Crown's jurisdiction without the obligation to implement orders. An officially sanctioned procedure that was described as follows: "Ministers and judges should obey, but not comply with our decrees and orders in which the vices of obreption and subreption have intervened, and at the first opportunity should inform us as to the reasons why they did not execute it."[4] Newly legislated law in the Indies consequently had a tentative quality that invited correction.[5]

The emphasis on loyalty, as distinct from obedience, made ceremonial reaffirmation important. Coronations, royal marriages, and births required a municipal council to convene and listen to a public reading by a senior official who then passed the document down by rank. Each official kissed the communication, held it above his head, and swore allegiance. In a similar fashion, the royal seal held by the Audiencia merited reverence as the symbol of justice and legitimacy. A broader public demonstration occurred each year on the day devoted to a city's patron saint. The standard bearer, the *alferéz real*, received the royal banner from municipal worthies who enjoined fidelity to the monarch. After taking an appropriate oath, the smartly dressed alferéz, mounted on a caparisoned horse, led a procession to the cathedral. The annual act of fidelity constituted a symbolic act, not a promise of obedience. Acts of allegiance implied that political struggles would occur within the established structure.[6]

Reception of royal agents from corregidores to bishops and viceroys amid pomp and ceremony similarly indicated respect. A viceroy's arrival provided an opportunity to proclaim loyalty and accept publicly the jurisdiction of the king's personal representative. It also served to give the monarch's agent an immediate, often vivid impression of the influence, status, and economic, thus political, power of the colonial elite. The official *recibimiento* marked a new political term and the possible emergence of a different balance. The politically astute struggled to make an impression, proclaim their loyalty, and prepare to manipulate the situation to their advantage. Lavish displays and gifts made the point, in spite of Crown efforts to legislate maximum expenditures.[7] When the Conde de Castellar officially entered Lima in 1674, silver showered before his horse as he passed through an arch paved with precious metal. Incoming viceroys customarily received a gift of a carefully selected horse and finely worked, bejeweled saddle to mark the occasion.[8] Gifts and their acceptance established a sense of mutual obligation.

The institutions that the colonial inhabitants manipulated carried with them important philosophical implications. Transplanted organizations implied recognition and acceptance of the philosophical base upon which they rested—modified only by the proprietary rights held by the Crown, and necessary accommodations to the physical environment. Thus, within less than a quarter century after the discovery, European settlements in Española petitioned for recognition of the same authority and privileges vested in Castilian municipalities. Subsequently, the monarchy conceded the standing and privileges of towns on fourteen settlements, along with the right to select their own officials in conformity with customary procedures.[9] Responding to the well-understood authority of municipal bodies, particularly in a frontier situation, Fernando Cortés established the municipal council of Veracruz in order to resign his commission from the governor of Cuba and receive a mandate to conquer from his own creation.[10] The cabildo of Santiago de Chile acted in a similar fashion when it offered Pedro de Valdivia the post of governor.[11] Implied privileges and authority could be modified in the New World but not suppressed. Juan de Solórzano y Pereyra, for example, acknowledged that colonial inhabitants, in the absence of royal authority, could elect municipal magistrates according to natural law.[12] In spite of reluctance to encourage the self-contained and internal sovereignty of municipal councils, the Crown had to concede. Thus, when Pedro de la Gasca sought to gain support prior to launching an assault on the rebellious Gonzalo Pizarro (1547), he pledged to consult the various Peruvian municipal councils and, with their agreement, take appropriate action.[13]

In marginal areas economically unable to support the expense of royal administration, municipal councils exercised a wide array of authority, often assuming many of the powers originally conceded the Crown-authorized *adelantado* (explorer, developer). For example, in sixteenth-century Río de la Plata, Carlos V, in a *cédula* (decree) dated September 12, 1537, extended authority to the survivors of the Pedro do Mendoza expedition to elect freely, in the king's name, a provincial governor in the event the adelantado had not named a successor, or that individual had died. In practice, the municipal council, as the primary political level, incorporated this authority and used it over the next two centuries to elect new governors and topple unpopular regimes—even governors appointed directly by the king or viceroy of Peru. Finally, in the bitter aftermath of the comunero revolt (1721-1735), Bruno Mauricio de Zavala declared the cédula null and void, noting that it had not been incorporated into the 1680 compilation of laws. Moreover, in view of the region's turbulent history, he warned that any effort to employ the cédula of 1537 would be considered treason. Paraguayan historians view the cédula as a keystone of national autonomy, and at least one has referred to it as a colonial Magna Carta.[14]

In economically and politically important regions, Crown institutions provided a more formal as well as complex political arena, yet municipal councils retained their privileges and perceived place within the political structure. Thus the municipal council of the City of Mexico, responding to the Iberian legacy, requested the privilege of voting first in any gathering of municipalities. Emperor Carlos V granted the request and held open the possibility that New Spain's municipalities might meet as the Cortes (parliament) cities of Spain. The decree (1530) granting the privilege warned, however, that the king did not intend for them to meet as a group except under Crown supervision and control. Major colonial cities also attempted to retain authority over the administration of justice rather than accept the jurisdiction of a royal appointee, the corregidor or alcalde mayor. These officials represented the Crown on the municipal council and served as its president. In Spain corregidores effectively brought cities under a degree of royal supervision. In the New World, Mexico City and Lima in particular sought to retain control over this attribute of municipal sovereignty. Mexico City, Puebla, and Antequera (Oaxaca) in New Spain all briefly enjoyed the privilege; however, only Lima successfully held on to the symbolically important concession throughout the colonial era.[15]

While municipal governments rarely attained concrete concessions, they could be relied upon to express their claim to the authority and respect that arose from the original community that antedated the royal establishment. Maintenance of permanent agents in Spain by major New World municipalities, as well as the dispatching of special delegations, further reinforced the implied representative nature of municipal councils.[16] An ambivalent Crown sought to weaken the political impact of original consent. A decree of 1623 ordered that agents be elected by the councilmen and not by the assembled citizens (*cabildo abierto*).[17] In practice, municipal authorities, faced with the expense of supporting an agent, often preferred to take the issue to the citizens in order to elect a representative and provide the necessary financial contribution. Regardless of how they were selected, general recognition that municipal bodies incorporated certain political functions compelled royal officials to take them seriously and deal with their representatives. Thus, following well-established precedent, Francisco de Toledo, on his arrival at Trujillo in advance of assuming the viceregal office in Peru, reassured apprehensive settlers by taking a solemn oath to respect and protect the privileges and liberties previously granted the city.[18] An important part of the *recibimiento* (reception) of the new viceroy involved a public oath to honor and protect all the "fueros, franquezas, libertades, preeminencias y mercedes," made by kings or previous viceroys in his name to the municipality of the viceregal capital. Only in the latter decades of the eighteenth century did the Crown take steps to avoid such a public and unmistakable recognition of municipal rights.[19] When the representative of the municipality of Lima arrived at court in 1692, he entered the royal presence with an escort of high officials and nobles after being ceremonially urged to "enter City of Lima, His Majesty awaits you"—a heady individual experience as well as acknowledgment of the place of cities within the structure. [20]

At a higher level, the creation of various kingdoms in the empire implied the acceptance of the philosophical supports that surrounded the notion of a kingdom. Consequently, Francisco Falcón argued before the members of the 1567 ecclesiastic council in Lima that because each kingdom existed apart, the Crown could not transfer revenue until the Kingdom of Peru's own urgent requirements had been satisfied. Falcón suggested the existence of an unjust, illegal, and parasitic relationship that violated the perception of each kingdom as its own social and political entity. He asserted that the monarch ruled separately over them and owed each political unit responsibility for the common good and well-being of its inhabitants.[21] A financially pressed monarchy rejected Falcón's contention. While Francisco Falcón resorted to the philosophy that accompanied the concept of a kingdom, the Crown countered with proprietary claims.

A revenue question again brought the issue of common good forward, this time by the Council of the Indies. Felipe II's plan to sell Peruvian *encomenderos* (assigned beneficiaries of Indian tribute), permanent titles, to include civil and criminal jurisdiction, prompted the council to assert that, because it benefited so few to the exclusion of so many equally worthy individuals, a cortes should be called so that Peruvian representatives could consider the issue of whether the common good would be served.[22] Given the turbulent history of sixteenth-century Peru, neither the king nor the council would have dared to authorize a Peruvian cortes, yet the argument had to be given serious consideration.

A seventeenth-century reminder of just how inconvenient the acceptance of Iberian political notions in the New World could be occurred with the attempt to impose new tax measures in support of the proposed Union of Arms. Envisioned as a common military effort, it required raising substantial funds. In Spain, as customary with a new tax, the proposal went before the various cortes; in New Spain, however, the viceroy laid the matter separately before the major municipalities. They petitioned for a convening of an assembly of municipal delegates along the lines of a cortes, and even attempted to gain concessions from the Crown in return for supporting the new tax.[23] A scandalized and angry viceroy rejected attempts to exert Old World privileges in the Indies in violation of political authority based on proprietary rights. A combination of shrewd manipulation, and threats, enabled Viceroy Cerralvo to obtain the agreement of the city councils of Mexico City and Puebla. Lesser councils dared not refuse the determined viceroy.[24]

The relative ease with which the viceroy obtained consent should not obscure the philosophical importance of the need to do so. Nor did this defeat end the efforts of Mexico City's council to negotiate concessions in return for financial cooperation. A special delegation (1635-1639) lobbied for favors in return for raising new taxes needed to finance military expenditures. The proposed naval force alone required a substantial subsidy; thus the cooperation of Mexico City's municipal council became vital. Councilmen consequently drew up a long list of demands that included reserving half the seats of the Audiencias of Mexico, Guadalajara, Guatemala, and Manila for Americans, as well as recognizing Mexico City's council as the third level of authority after the viceroy and the Audiencia.[25] In the end, the Crown made few concessions, but the point had been made once again.

In Peru the political process required to impose new revenue measures in support of the Union of Arms required nine years of maneuvering. Viceroy Chinchón expressed the opinion that the project required a delicate touch because the Peruvians appeared to be more unruly and vexatious than the Mexicans. Officials considered his prolonged and only partially successful attempt to raise taxes as Chinchón's major career contribution.[26] The viceroy's difficulties demonstrated not only the limitations of proprietary rights but also the extent to which both American subjects and the Crown manipulated the philosophical matrix. Chinchón laid it out clearly at the outset in a letter (March 31, 1633) in which he observed that even though the Indies did not meet in cortes, or have a nobility entitled to corporate privileges (*brazos*) or other estates (*estamentos*) or parliaments, and the king's authority was free and absolute, it was advisable to gain the acceptance of his American vassals.[27]

The procedure suggested by Viceroy Chinchón amounted to a political strategy. First local officials with political and social status had to be convinced, then prominent individuals and merchants. Only when substantial cooperation had been gained was the matter to be laid before the municipal councils. Chinchón proposed a series of favors to strengthen his hand. In effect, the viceroy advocated almost the same process used in Spain, where the Cortes bargained in exchange for approving new revenue measures; however, in Peru concessions would be offered in advance and without bargaining. The proposed favors themselves indicated an understanding by royal officials of the implied rights of the Kingdom of Peru. Among other favors, he proposed that four *procuradores* (representatives) be sent to the Cortes of Castile when it recognized the ascension of the monarch, that one or two positions on the Council of the Indies be reserved for Peruvians, and that a certain number of offices, both clerical and secular, be held for them. Officials rejected the proposals on technical grounds and also because they appeared to limit the king's authority to act as he pleased in filling positions.[28] Chinchón observed that his perceived obligation required him to confer with at least one councilman and a prominent encomendero from each major municipality before imposing the new revenue measures. With favors (i.e., concessions) in hand, he could avoid the bargaining process that implied consent. In the end, the viceroy devised tax increases that could be implemented by executive action rather than new measures. Although Chinchón claimed that his contacts with municipal officials represented merely an act of *ex gratia* consultation, it is evident he recognized political reality.[29]

Both the Mexican and Peruvian examples indicated the extent to which officials accepted political units entitled to function apart from Crown sufferance, as in Europe. It also became obvious that the municipal councils constituted the most troublesome institutional depository of European political ideas. Paradoxically, while the councils seldom won concrete demands, they forced the Crown to conform to the dictates of the philosophical matrix. Consequently, uncomfortable royal officials both in Spain and the Indies did their best to restrain municipal lobbying. Officials employed various means to discourage the sending of delegations to Spain in spite of the cédula of 1539, which prohibited any obstruction. In a 1659 decree, subsequently restated in 1692, the Crown ordered that, in case of an emergency, the viceroy had to give his permission, whereas normal requests to send representatives had to be cleared by the Council of the Indies.[30] In practice, lobbying by a municipal delegation, or an agent resident in Spain, could not be controlled. Moreover, appeals to the monarch, either through representative or written petition, constituted a useful political device that conformed to the socio-political process inherent in the philosophical matrix. Nevertheless, officials demonstrated their annoyance with the willingness of American cabildos to exploit any political advantage arising out of Crown necessity.

Although royal officials in the American empire evoked proprietary authority when politically convenient, natural law, the core of the philosophical matrix, played the major role. It integrated the European and Indian community politically and made it possible to acknowledge that non-Christian states and laws possessed validity. Recognition of a political system tailored to the needs of particular subgroups or regions did not imply equality, and could have a negative effect. While incorporating them within the political structure, such a system also separated the king's subjects into subgroups with different political and judicial relationships to the Crown.[31] Although it initially recognized the various existing elements, the Crown soon moved to reconstitute them. The recognition of a separate Indian juridico-political body in the American empire—the *República de los Indios* counterposed to the *República de los Españoles*—established a uniform relationship between the monarchy and a disparate native community. Theoretically, Indian customs and legal practices received the support of the successor state to the extent that the Castilian monarchy stood ready to enforce them.[32] The Crown viewed Indian legal and customary law as a type of *fuero* following the Spanish experience.[33] Yet, by choosing not to treat individual Indian groups as separate political units, each with its own laws and legal philosophies, the Crown imposed an artificial uniformity. As a consequence, a weakened native legal tradition could not withstand the demands of, or strongly influence, colonial society. Minor legal customs survived at the local level among distinct groups but could not be employed effectively in the broader society, or to protect the group against external pressures. The Indian population found it necessary and advantageous to adapt to the new system. In addition, a decision to hold the Indian to a lower standard of responsibility as "gente sin razon" (people without understanding), coupled with recognition of a separate Indian Republic, established a legal dependency on the Crown.[34]

The paternalism evident in the *Siete Partidas* toward those identified as weak encouraged an informal arbitration of Indian disputes. Thus the Crown in 1530 ordered that in cases involving abusive words or physical violence not employing weapons, local officials need not draw up formal charges, but merely intervene to reestablish tranquillity.[35] The New Laws of 1542 instructed judges to shield Indians from the machinations of malicious lawyers, and attempt to settle disputes according to aboriginal usage and custom. The warning not to permit native lawsuits to become common reflected growing concern with Indian readiness to resort to Spanish judicial procedures.[36] In a similar fashion and for the same reason, the Crown ordered (1580) the Audiencia of La Plata to respect aboriginal law.[37] In fact, Indians shrewdly manipulated Crown paternalism when convenient and applied other forms of pressure as well, including judicial action. Although not successful on all occasions, they rapidly adapted to the fluid political arena and the utility of Castilian law. In order to handle the volume of suits brought by Indians, the Crown in 1551 ordered the Audiencia of Mexico to reserve at least two days a week to hear them. The fees and related expenses associated with litigation supported a horde of lawyers and notaries, and provided abundant fees for public officials. Often frivolous cases were pursued and others prolonged at the plaintiff's expense. As a result, the judicial system labored with increasing difficulty. In 1591, in an attempt to gain control over the alarming growth in litigation, the Crown established the General Indian Court of New Spain. Freed of the burden of fees and represented by salaried defenders, the court's Indian clients could be protected as well as directly regulated by the viceroy. As a court of first instance; the Indian Court relieved some of the Audiencia's work load.[38] Although the expense and time involved aggravated judges and concerned the Crown, legal procedures encouraged a politically useful dependency within a controlled arena.

In addition to establishing civil groups, each with a distinct relationship to the Crown and the law, the monarchy modified and controlled the American Church. The successful drive to establish systematic clerical dependency took its full institutional form in the New World. Queen Isabel fell heir to various pontifical concessions, as well as de facto regulations and customs that provided control over the Spanish Church. The cumbersome mixture of devices placed fragmented and particular, rather than universal, control in royal hands.[39] The campaign against the last Moorish stronghold provided the pretext to strengthen and simplify Crown control of the clergy. Noting the disgraceful state of the clergy, Isabel requested authority over missionaries. The Bull of Granada (1486) conceded the right of clerical selection (presentation) and charged the Crown with undertaking the task of converting and maintaining the new subjects in the faith. All the elements that subsequently would be expanded upon to form the basis of the *Real Patronato de Indias* may be found in the Granadine concessions.[40] The Bull of Granada demonstrates the extent to which the papacy had become dependent on secular rulers. Rather than the Church acting to strengthen kings, the document suggests that the opposite was true, as evidenced in the phrase, "thus fortified by the protection of the same kings as patrons, and by their help and favor."[41]

The New World discovered shortly after such major concessions provided an ideal environment within which to further subordinate the Church. In the American empire, monarchs directed the Church as an instrument of conquest and consolidation.[42] The flowering of the royal patronage in the Indies represented a logical culmination of the political struggle joined centuries earlier. Pope Alexander VI's bulls of 1493 and 1501, coupled with the conveying of full patronage by Julius II, completed the structure of royal control over the clerical enterprise in the New World. Subsequent pronouncements merely confirmed what had already been granted. Theoretically, the Church asserted its temporal authority to override the rights of pagan societies so that missionaries could freely preach, as well as judge rulers according to the laws of the New Testament and the Church, and then conveyed such rights to the monarchy along with the obligation to carry them out. The Crown eagerly accepted both the theory and the charge to undertake the task because it justified displacing Indian rulers. Moreover, it implied a benevolent intent behind the seizure of political power in the New World.

The religious charge accepted by the monarchy bound together proprietary rights and divine derivative authority. The missionary obligation conveyed by the pope provided the basis upon which the Crown defended proprietary claims and reaffirmed its duty to attend to the common good. The Crown hastened to explain the philosophical basis of royal authority to the Indians. As early as 1509, Alonso de Ojeda read a formal explanation to the aboriginal population of Cartagena.[43] The primitive draft subsequently evolved into a more polished document known as the *requerimiento*. Intended to be read to newly contacted Indian groups, the document presented the theoretical basis of authority. It explained the Christian perception of human events, starting with

Adam and Eve and the subsequent dispersal, and emphasized Saint Peter's appointment as lord and superior and the pope's inherited powers. Such continuity allegedly established the legality of the papal donation of the New World. The requerimiento even offered to permit the inspection of supporting documentation.[44] While many conquistadores, as well as one of the document's author, Juan Ginés de Sepúlveda, appreciated the amusing aspects of reading such an instrument to hostile Indians, its purpose remained. Once the document was read, an official secured the necessary signatures and dispatched them to Spain as part of the formal record.

One might question the notion, as did Francisco de Vitoria, that the pope's missionary authority served to convey sovereignty but not the need to establish some legal basis for royal authority in the hemisphere. In at least one case, an Indian cacique disputed the political logic of the requerimiento and challenged the pope's ability to convey dominion over others—in effect, engaging in a debate that intellectually joined him with European opponents of papal temporal power.[45] As Liss noted in the case of Mexico, the aboriginal population, long familiar with Aztec imperial demands, understood the requerimiento's political implications.[46] Bartolomé de las Casas, while insisting he did not know whether to laugh or cry over the document, also understood its purpose. As a consequence, when he convinced the Crown to end its use, he recommended the substitution of a letter that promised mutual respect and advantage in return for acknowledgment of royal authority. Spiritual well-being, and the common good stemming from a beneficent monarch, constituted the implied promise of both the requerimiento and its letter substitute. In the New World setting, the requerimiento demonstrated the Crown's ability to employ the remaining philosophical shreds of papal temporal authority for its own political needs. Recognition of the authority of the Castilian monarch made hostilities an act of treason subject to harsh penalties.[47] The requerimiento provided the means by which the monarchy transformed a spiritual notion into secular jurisdiction.

Civil administrative supervision demonstrated clerical dependency and subordination in a concrete fashion. Whereas the monarch as patron possessed wide authority, viceroys, Audiencia judges, and provincial officials functioned as vice-patrons and defended royal privileges. Felipe II codified practice in his decree of July 10, 1574, and made it clear to all clerics that the monarch exercised an all-encompassing patronage directly or through designated representatives. In the American empire, even the parish priest felt the royal hand. The highest ranking official in a particular province selected a priest from a list supplied by the archbishop. Violations of the royal patronage became a civil matter.[48] Audiencias exercised control over the clergy through the *recurso de fuerza*. Judges heard appeals from ecclesiastical courts and intervened if they decided the clerical authorities had overstepped their authority, failed to follow procedures, or blocked legal appeals.[49] Even decisions of ecclesiastical tribunals or clerics, including the archbishop, could be suspended pending review. The Audiencia could raise sanctions and take steps to prevent future abuses. Nevertheless, the Crown instructed its agents to avoid publicity and proceed with discretion in order to preserve a unified facade. If the proper balance could not be established quietly, the Audiencia could remove and exile clerics and even obstinate prelates.[50] Normally, however, the Audiencia's authority to intervene served as a restraining force without the need to become involved actively. Only the Inquisition remained outside the high court's regulatory authority, being subordinated directly to the Supreme Council of the Inquisition in Spain. Yet, even that institution could not challenge or provoke political authorities without risk. Viceroy Toledo, for example, deprived the commissioner of the Inquisition in Cuzco of his position and fined and sentenced him to a year's seclusion, to be followed by expulsion from the Indies.[51]

Civil officials, in a similar fashion, controlled the use of ecclesiastical censure, including interdict and excommunication. As a result, both these theoretically grave censures were reduced to political ploys, the threat of which gave a prelate some influence, while actual implementation provoked an official response—either hostile if it interfered with government objectives, or judgmental in that the Audiencia determined if such actions were warranted.[52] Any investigation of clerical sanctions automatically suspended implementation. Nevertheless, in certain instances, a contentious prelate could take advantage of weak secular authorities, or in the event they appeared divided and discredited, skillfully employ clerical censure. Archbishop Pérez de la Serna, supported by a clerical faction, employed excommunication as well as *cessatio a divines* (general withdrawal of all services) to manipulate public opinion and eventually force the Viceroy of Mexico, the Marquis de Gelves (1621-1624), from office.[53] Under normal conditions, the political balance favored the viceroy and the Audiencia. In all cases, the Crown sought to employ its regulatory authority without diminishing the Church's status either in a spiritual or political sense.[54] Until the eighteenth century, a politically directed Christianity proved too valuable to be dispensed with in a casual fashion.

The monarch also exercised personal patronage over the Crown's secular servants. The fact that natural law served as the basis of legitimate authority, rather than consent of the governed, theoretically permitted the king to make independent decisions, including appointment to high office. A prudent monarch nevertheless conceded consultative powers to others in order to develop wider support and to deal with the mechanics of the selection process itself.[55] In 1588 Felipe II appointed the *Real Cámara de Castilla* to handle royal patronage and assure competence. The Cámara exercised its duties until the eighteenth century when the ministry of Grace and Justice assumed its responsibilities. Only the Inquisition, the Council of Military Orders, certain positions on the Council of Finance, military offices under the Council of War, and American appointments remained outside the Cámara's jurisdiction, while the Council of the Indies served to screen New World appointments.

Nomination became a bureaucratic function, whereas appointment remained a distinct and separate royal act. Yet the king could and did ignore candidates presented until nineteenth-century reforms restricted royal authority. Nevertheless, selection bodies set standards that made it embarrassing for a monarch to appoint patently unqualified individuals. Consequently, when Felipe III appointed a candidate without the necessary academic requirements to the Audiencia of Seville in 1611, he had to fend off protests. The Cámara observed that marriage to an influential woman at court, the "marriage road" to a bureaucratic career, discouraged others from obtaining the proper training.[56] In spite of such protests, the king often selected his own advisers and agents on personal or arbitrary criteria.

The perception that actual appointment remained a royal act, whether recommended by others or not, tied each official to the head. Drawn into an emotional as well as political relationship, officials believed that the king had an obligation to them, even though they might not be worthy of such consideration. The monarch responded by rewarding them with other appointments, honors, and favors. Felipe II, in the process of accepting Mateo Vázquez de Leca as his personal secretary, forged such a bond by stating, "I trust you and I will bear in mind and care for you...as is only right."[57] In the American empire, the Crown expected viceroys to recommend individuals for recognition, favors, or honors.[58] The potent combination of personal recognition and benevolent favor bound the person so honored to the king. The connection between honors and recognized personal loyalty to the monarch made them coveted assets. Although vanity played a role, the resultant prestige could be employed to further individual political and socioeconomic objectives. Honors, even those that appear empty, separated and distinguished an individual from the crowd.[59] The importance of recognition encouraged obsequious requests for rewards (*mercedes*) from the lowest to the highest social level. Typically, requests included glowing accounts of past activities. Viceroy Toledo, at the close of his career, petitioned the king for a monetary reward, membership in the Council of the Indies, and the position and status of a knight commander in the order of Alcántara.[60] Requests from less exalted individuals without social or political pretensions usually concerned a pension for an impoverished heir or an ill, aged, or disabled person or widow. Economic survival made the prestige of a royal pension a secondary consideration to those in such circumstances. The fact that the king often responded to petitions from the lowly enhanced the public perception of a benevolent, compassionate ruler.

The sense of mutual obligation arising from royal favor weakened, but did not disappear, with the vending of positions by the financially desperate monarchy. Minor offices posed few problems, but the systematic sale of high treasury posts in the Indies that began in 1633 appeared both unwise and dangerous. The Council of the Indies, while recognizing the monarch's right to sell offices, opposed the policy. Inept and inefficient tax collection, as well as the possibility of collusion with family and friends, would have a direct impact on revenues. Beyond functional objections, the Council of the Indies understood the emotional, and thus political, difference between an office bestowed by a monarch in all his benevolence and one that had been purchased. Those who bought a position theoretically had the same obligation to the king as purely favored appointees, but the sense of a personal tie could not be the same. The Conde de Peñaranda, President of the Council of the Indies, thus warned the newly appointed Viceroy of Peru, the Conde de Lemos (1667), that those individuals who had purchased treasury posts might not respect his position and might undermine the imperial system.[61] Subsequent expansion of the sale of public office to include corregidores and alcaldes mayores as well as Audiencia judgeships posed similar difficulties.

Political paternalism encouraged the development of secondary patronage. The old-boy network of the *colegios mayores* became notorious. Pablo de Talavera, Bishop of Puebla (New Spain), allegedly received the appointment because of the efforts of an alumnus, Sebastian Ramírez, Bishop of Cuenca. Toribio Alfonso Mogravejo, Archbishop of Lima, advised his old college in 1589 of the favors he had bestowed on several recent graduates, and then, after requesting they keep him informed of any other service he could provide, acknowledged the scholarship conceded one of his relatives.[62] In a fluid political arena, advancement—even social or economic survival—depended upon carefully cultivated alliances, exchange of favors, and the placing of family members in useful positions. The ability to muster support could make a difference in one's career possibilities. A minor example of the mobilization of influence, as well as a model solicitation, is provided by a letter (1544) written by the Bishop of Mexico, Juan de Zumárraga, to the Council of Indies seeking favor for the son of a Mexico City physician. The bishop placed his own prestige and influence in play, noted the social contribution and great merits of the father, and finally pointed to the skill and virtue of the son.[63]

Whereas an unknown required a patron, the powerful needed supporters. Given the right circumstances, the mighty could be as eager to extend favors as the recipients to accept them. The Crown warned viceroys and other officials, without much success, to limit such a tendency.[64] Astute individuals strove to maintain contacts and enhance their own influence through the exchange of favors.

The implied favor inherent in an appointment, and the mutual obligations it engendered, also had a less than admirable reflection. Public office functioned as a personal asset from which the incumbent expected some advantage, whether in fees, influence, status, or salary. No perceived conflict existed between an individual's interests and Crown service. The king and those favored individuals understood the varied rewards of office. The expectation that an officeholder would pursue his own interests as well as those of the monarchy encouraged the manipulation of such assets as status and political authority. Indeed, in modern terms, direct material support appears parsimonious. Viceregal remuneration, for example, usually included expenses. As a result, the 20,000 ducats awarded the viceroy of New Spain and the 30,000 assigned to the Peruvian office hardly sufficed. Typically, a viceroy arrived with some seventy retainers, and perhaps twenty black slaves. In addition, his wife could be expected to bring a staff numbering in excess of twenty. To support the combined personal staff required vast amounts of money. Similarly, funding of less exalted offices was not generous, and differed dramatically from one region to another. Corregidores in sixteenth-century Central America received the inadequate sum of 150 pesos a year or less. More important centers provided better remuneration, although hardly extravagant. The corregidor of Tunja (New Granada) in 1627, Martín de Sierralta, received 1,000 pesos. By 1711 the post carried a salary of 1,800 pesos annually. Officials throughout the empire could not rely upon the treasury to provide much more than a subsidy. As a result, in the words of Juan Matienzo, they proceeded to "eat what the land offers."[65]

The Crown expected its agents to attend to their responsibilities regardless of inadequate or delayed compensation. Ambition and necessity impelled individual officials to become entrepreneurs. Antonio de Mendoza, Mexico's first viceroy, invested in commerce, textile manufacturing, and agricultural pursuits. His substantial income from investments complemented his salary. Society accepted the use of positions for private gain provided it did not become so excessive as to damage the economic survival of others. Nevertheless, given geographical isolation, and the difficulty of supervising virtually autonomous Crown agents, the line between private entrepreneurship and exploitive greed could easily be crossed. The involvement of colonial corregidores and alcaldes mayores in the *repartimiento de comercio* is well known. Functioning as business agents for merchant houses, or on their own account, corregidores used their position to direct local production and stimulate consumption. Juan Manuel de Anaya, corregidor of Lucanas (Peru), "borrowed" money from community funds, misappropriated assets for speculative purpose, and engaged in a wide variety of profitable exploitive endeavors with merchant-partners and on his own. Fifteen years later, the Crown still struggled to unravel his accounts. Such unrestrained activity had a negative impact on the local economy. In the case of Rodrigo de Flores y Aldana, governor of Yucatán (1664, 1667-1669), his greed impoverished the population and may have increased the cost of imported goods over 50 percent.[66]

Even when the monarchy made a conscious effort to insulate officials, in particular Audiencia judges, from social and business contact with the community, the tendency to pursue their own interests could not be overcome. Pedro Farfán, a judge of the Audiencia of Mexico, avidly amassed a fortune in land and other assets. As judge of *bienes de difuntos* in 1578 and 1583, he borrowed money that should have been delivered to heirs, and appointed administrators of estates with an eye to his own advantage. His willingness to employ official intimidation became notorious. Farfán finally overstepped the limits, but even then his suspension came only after a judicial career of some nineteen years.[67] In Guatemala, Alonso Maldonado, president of the Audiencia (1544-1548), entered into partnership with a sheepherder and used his position to further the business. His alleged assets included some 5,000 pesos from a Mexican encomienda, 4,000 ducats annually from Spanish investments, and other holdings worth 200,000 pesos. Whatever the exact figure, Maldonado became a wealthy man.[68] A later example is provided by Dr. Antonio de Morga, president of the Audiencia of the Kingdom of Quito, who became a silent partner in a successful textile business and ran a gambling operation supervised by his wife.[69] Morga allowed his own interest to become too public and eventually fell into disfavor. Juan Bermúdez de Castro, governor of Popayán (1628-1633), employed the same combination of enterprises as Morga. He exercised a virtual monopoly on the textile trade, resulting in higher prices locally, and operated a gambling establishment that brought in some 50,000 pesos.[70]

The vague line between venality and self-interest could be breached without too much danger. The *residencia*, a review of an official's conduct in office, served, among other things, as a restraining device by setting the acceptable limits of self-interest.[71] Fines, levied by residencia judges, did not imply condemnation but suggested lapses in judgment. The element of personal reward made it necessary to judge corruption not by the act, but by the degree, an attitude that encouraged abuse. Official toleration, rooted in benevolence and paternalism, often became excessive. The Christian concept of human unworthiness implied weakness, even the expectation of moral failure or misuse of favor. In response, a monarch balanced, corrected, and forgave, reflecting the divine benevolence. Such an attitude facilitated the return of individuals who at one point appeared discredited to positions of authority. Individuals needed political allies to reverse their fortunes, but the notion of unworthiness coupled with forgiveness that appears in all the major legal codes was an important factor.

Viceroy Toledo, aware of the adverse effects, complained that discredited officials returned to royal service without serious impediment. He noted, among other cases, that an individual ousted from the presidency of the Audiencia of Guatemala later became a member of the Lima court, and another banished from Quito for serious and heinous crimes returned to respectability as a judge.[72] Alonso Maldonado, in spite of charges growing out of his penchant for business, survived his residencia and went on to become president of the Audiencia of Santo Domingo.[73] The notorious Pedro Farfán, found guilty of seventy charges, including illegal accumulation of land, suffered a reversal of fortune, but not a total disaster. The Council of the Indies ordered restitution of property, levied heavy fines, suspended him from office for ten years, and recommended he never again be entrusted with colonial office. Nevertheless, he secured an appointment as judge of the Audiencia of Lima in 1594. Only death prevented Farfán from adding to his dubious record.[74]

Royal response reflected an unwillingness to condemn misconduct in a rigid or permanent fashion. Forgiveness established a bond between officials and the king. Benevolence and paternalism from above and loyalty from below overrode other considerations.[75] Nevertheless, on occasion individuals succeeded in outraging imperial authority. Briviesca de Muñatones, one of the three commissioners charged with negotiating the sale of perpetual encomienda titles, received a long prison term for his flagrantly corrupt collusion with Viceroy Conde de Nieva.[76] The viceroy himself and one of the commissioners died before they could be punished. Even in this case, the other agent, Ortega de Melgosa, who could not have avoided involvement, received lenient treatment.[77] Political misconduct worried the Crown much more than simple greed. Francisco de Manso y Zuñiga, archbishop of Mexico (1628-35), while feuding with the viceroy, the Marqués de Cerralvo, and engaging in disruptive political activities, amassed a fortune. The Crown, annoyed with the cleric's manipulations, particularly in the delicate political climate of Mexico following the driving of Viceroy Gelves from office, finally removed him and temporarily reduced him to bishop. Nevertheless, Manso, supported by the Council of the Indies, succeeded in becoming the archbishop of Burgos. Only his death in 1655 stripped him of political protection, whereupon the Crown seized his assets, including gold, silver, and pearls alleged to be worth 800,000 pesos.[78] In this case, the archbishop's politics, not his avarice, motivated posthumous revenge.

The principle of receiving favors directly from the monarch implied that only he could withdraw them. Legally, the king delegated authority (*jurisdictio*) not command (*imperium*). Authority reverted to the source, not to a bureaucratic system. The holder of a royal commission functioned as a political agent rather than as an administrative functionary. Appointments required a formal acknowledgment of the king's favor and trust. Officials took an oath before the Council of the Indies, or the regional Audiencia if already an American resident, as well as before the municipal council. This identified the original sources of authority and recorded recognition by various political levels as well. Reception by the municipal council implied its loyalty and consent as well as the Crown's tacit acceptance of the municipal function of representing the authority of the original community. The requirement that the municipal council witness the oath and examine the financial bond of officials charged with fiscal responsibilities, or those subject to the residencia, provided an opportunity for minor political negotiations. For example, the municipal council of Popoyán in 1658 refused to receive an official, using a pretext to mask the fact that several other influential individuals coveted the post. Only the intervention of the Audiencia of Santa Fe ended the three-year impasse.[79]

The combination of royal authority and status made each official an independent agent psychologically and politically. Although in theory, lower-ranking officials had responsibilities toward their superiors, the threat of removal from office could not be used to guarantee their cooperation. Only the king could remove permanently a royal appointee. A complaint might be made in the hope that an insubordinate official's commission would be revoked, or the viceroy could take action pending subsequent Crown approval; however, a judicial process became subject to countercharges. Only in the most blatant cases could such a process be risked. Although loyalty focused on the head of state rather than on the next highest level of the structure, this did not preclude faithful and competent performance, or the development of personal ties and loyalty toward superiors. Nevertheless, it placed the burden on personality and manipulative skills. In the New World, such structural factors, combined with frontier conditions, made a forceful personality all important.[80]

The notion that a commission represented a personal charge also retarded standardization of political functions. Although titles implied a recognized task, the Crown often pyramided titles, a practice that resulted in wide variances of responsibility among those who occupied the same post. Personalization also encouraged the use of secret instructions. For example, Viceroy Toledo, sent to establish royal control over a notoriously unruly Peru, parried questions about the extent of his authority by responding that Crown instruction could not be revealed. An official chose the opportune moment to announce the king's will; meanwhile, he maintained freedom of action and kept political opponents guessing. When Crown instruction was revealed, the results could be devastating. Juan de Palafox, bishop of Puebla and visitor-general of New Spain, suddenly produced royal instructions to remove Viceroy Escalona (1642) and assume his offices. Subtle insinuations that one carried secret instructions became a useful ploy and intimidated rivals.[81]

The implied personal charge of office made formally set terms unimportant. Appointees who enjoyed the king's favor frequently remained in harness until released by death. Petitions of aged or ill royal officials seeking permission to retire often seem pitifully pathetic. The simple desire to return home to die after years of service awaited the king's pleasure. Luis de Velasco, el hijo, in the course of a long and distinguished career served both as viceroy of Mexico and Peru, remaining in royal service from 1590 to his death in 1617. Velasco's recognized talents prompted the monarch to confer the title of the Marqués de Salinas on his ancient servant, and subsequently the presidency of the Council of the Indies. Compensated retirement remained the exception until the last decades of the empire. Officials at all levels continued to work up to the end. At the close of the eighteenth century, a contemporary observer, exaggerating only slightly, noted that decrepit employees struggled into work only to die at their desks.[82]

The many intangibles that determined influence and authority, including trust, favor, and esteem, made disputes inevitable. Although the Crown admonished its agents to avoid squabbles, the determination of jurisdiction posed a constant problem.[83] In reality, because of the direct connection between a monarch and his agents, the governing structure functioned as a series of horizontal layers rather than a vertical hierarchy. A positive consequence of the structure was the stability engendered by flexibility, and a vast number of political anchors. Each official possessed legitimacy received from above and could operate independently of other officials. The notion of personal accountability meant that individual failure did not discredit the entire structure. Even the overthrow of a viceroy, who theoretically represented the king in his very person, did not bring about a political collapse, although it was to be avoided if possible.[84] Each official claimed to represent the monarch's best interests regardless of what occurred elsewhere. As a consequence of the lack of precision, as well as the horizontal nature of the structure, officials dealt with a variety of issues from the significant to the trivial and petty. Officials could slip easily into a mire of inconsequential activity.

The absence of a vertical hierarchy permitted numerous channels of communication. High-ranking officials could not suppress or withhold information, as is the case in a rigid hierarchical organization.[85] Optimistically, Viceroy Francisco de Toledo, in an attempt to control information and establish a degree of discipline over his retainers, drew up a set of instructions to govern their conduct. Among the restrictions, Toledo forbade discussion of governmental affairs with others and prohibited appeals to the king over the head of the viceroy.[86] It is unlikely his instruction assured confidentiality. Attempts to control potentially embarrassing information, especially that divulged by insiders, were doomed to failure because of the emphasis on individual responsibility and obligation. Crown officers, as beneficiaries of favor and trust, had an individual moral obligation to administer their commissions so as to assure the common good regardless of the wishes of superiors. Moreover, all Crown officials had implied judicial responsibilities. Thus grievances could be addressed by a broad spectrum of responsible officials. Once confronted with an issue, the king's agents could not avoid some appropriate response. As a consequence, the judicial function received tremendous public respect. Reflecting such status, Audiencia members enjoyed preferential seating at public functions and avoided kneeling at minor religious celebrations. Merchants closed their shops when advised an *oidor* (judge) had been observed in the vicinity.[87] Reverence for the judicial function permeated all levels of society.

The king's subjects received favor within a highly personal system. Although implied benevolence offered the governed a degree of protection from arbitrary acts, they received it as a gift. Individually they might be unworthy of such favor; yet the monarch bestowed it upon them in spite of their failings. The people expected to be treated justly, but could not demand it—a sociopolitical attitude captured in the Pauline doctrine, "What I am, I am by the grace of God."[88] Benevolence as a gift nevertheless implied that it could be withheld as well as given. For a ruler to withdraw benevolence would have required a radical change in religious attitudes and beliefs as well as political concepts, an unlikely development. However, the difference between a right and a favor is significant.[89] Individuals remained passive petitioners even when the law or regulations favored their case. While this could lead to condescension and arrogance by the king's agents, such behavior was viewed as a perversion of royal intent. Diffusion of public resentment of the arbitrary behavior or attitude of Crown representatives constituted one of the functions of the residencia. The open, well-publicized invitation to all levels of society to present formal grievances against an official under review served to vent anger and to indicate the conduct considered to best represent royal intent. Symbolically, it united the Crown and the people in the quest to secure the common good.

Social expectations that the Crown would demonstrate justice and compassion also provided the means to adjust activities and respond to unique circumstances without appearing weak and ineffective. Faced with disorders, especially in cases where an entire village or community resisted constituted authority, the government could compromise and restore cooperation without driving the group into an intractable position or damaging its own credibility. Although the authorities might have little choice, weakness could be hidden behind the philosophical willingness to demonstrate benevolence and forgiveness. Thus, when Pedro de la Gasca arrived in Peru (1547) to put down the bloody revolt of Gonzalo Pizarro, he carried a supply of blank pardons. Without such flexibility it is doubtful he could have accomplished his task.[90] Martín de Carrillo y Alderete, sent to investigate the ousting of the Mexican viceroy, the Marqués de Gelves (1624), predictably advised the Crown to demonstrate leniency and issue a general pardon. He suggested the suppression of all evidence except in the case of the ringleaders. By assuming the loyalty of the majority, he could deal with the small group of dangerous conspirators in isolation.[91] In less serious instances, royal representatives who came in immediate contact with rioting or hostile mobs acted as buffers. Consequently, in the event of limited regional or local problems, the monarchy avoided accountability, although it might be called upon to exercise its jurisdiction and supply a remedy. Social violence tended to dissipate before it posed a serious threat to higher authority.[92]

Criminal activity, in a similar fashion, did not pit malefactors directly against the monarchy. A willingness to consider mitigating circumstances was a natural consequence of paternalism. Thus corporal punishment, generally flogging, served as a corrective. Serious crimes required more drastic measures that served an exemplary function. Public executions, while not frequent, occurred often enough to mark the outer limits of acceptable behavior, as did the pointed exclusion of certain crimes from those covered under general pardons. Lèse majesté, murder of a priest, counterfeiting, sodomy, and other acts that appeared to be direct attacks on the Crown or religion warranted no pity that could be interpreted as weakness, or even limited approval.[93] The punishment for high treason—drawing and quartering followed by decapitation and display on a pike—left no room for doubt. In addition, offenses involving property rights of others could not be forgiven because to do so would injure a third party.[94] In such cases, the Crown ordered a conditional release for a specified period to allow the parties to reach agreement. On occasion, debtors might be assisted by the "royal munificience" in settling their obligations.

Blanket pardons for specified eligible offenses, issued to commemorate a royal marriage, birth, or similar occasion, had a dual role. Such pardons widely and publicly demonstrated royal authority, but they also reduced the number of unresolved cases that threatened to undermine the certainty of punishment. An individual turned himself in within a set time period—in effect, acknowledging his criminal status—and became a petitioner for favor. The personalization of both punishment and pardon, coupled with the *cognitio summaria* approach that allowed officials to dispense with formal procedures, led to the ad hoc administration of justice. Thus judicial functions could be adjusted to meet local circumstances. Less positively, this encouraged a Solomonic and excessively political administration of justice.

Another device closely related to pardons permitted ex post facto legalization. A *composición* (legal determination) that required the payment of a fee could be utilized to give legal standing to an irregular situation. In the American empire, where land titles of dubious validity or obscure origin were common, composición ended uncertainty, facilitated mortgaging and property transfer, and permitted full utilization. It also reaffirmed the Crown's role as the validator of private property. Land had to be held at least ten years before the device could be used; therefore, the risk of overriding other active claims theoretically was minimal.[95] In the case of mines, the right to work deposits could be transferred if left unworked for more than four months; however, technically, such a transfer did not involve property considerations. Nevertheless, composición and the denouncement of unworked mines provided innumerable opportunities for fraud and collusion. For example, the guardian of the minor children of the deceased mining entrepreneur Manuel de la Borda complained to the Crown in 1796 that holdings in Zacatecas had been denounced illegally and conveyed to Fermin de Apezechea with the cooperation of local officials. In such cases, a prolonged and expensive court battle provided the only hope of restitution.[96]

Composición could be used to legalize any situation the government believed politically necessary. In 1619, for example, the Crown authorized the issuing of residency permits and naturalization papers in order to regularize the status of some 338 illegal foreign residents in New Spain.[97] The payment of a fee, and acceptance of royal intervention, met the minimum requirements needed for ex post facto approval. It acknowledged Crown authority and the former illegality of the situation, as well as the need to pay a penalty before receiving forgiveness. The flexibility provided by the device enabled the monarchy to incorporate elements or regularize situations which, if allowed to continue or left outside the law, would damage authority. Politically, composición accomplished in the civil sphere what a pardon did in the criminal.

Composición also provided a means of raising revenue. A royal cédula in 1591 ordered the sale of abandoned land (*tierras baldías*) and the confirmation of titles. In Peru, Viceroy García Hurtado de Mendoza named a commission in 1592 to undertake the task throughout the viceroyalty. Members of the commission examined titles and determined the necessary action—a process that lasted twelve years. Subsequently, Viceroy García Sarmiento de Sotomayor, the Conde de Salvatierra, reviewed earlier dispositions under instructions to restore Indian land fraudulently alienated. As a consequence, a special commission, the *junta de tierras y desagravios de Indios*, dealt with appeals and complaints. Between 1720 and 1782, a special tribunal, the *juzgado de remensuras, venta y composición de tierras*, dealt with the question of legal property.[98] The last major composición in Peru occurred in 1792. In marginal areas with limited competition over land, a review of titles followed by validation constituted a form of fiscal harassment. Society, nevertheless, accepted as well as relied upon the Crown's ability to validate private property, and reissue titles to abandoned land.[99]

A delicate play between sociopolitical expectations arising from the philosophical matrix, and the perceived authority of the Crown, characterized the Hapsburg political process. Fluid manipulation by the king's subjects balanced by that of the monarchy and its agents occurred within an understood framework. Compromise and accommodation cast within broad benevolent philosophical boundaries established an acceptable and useful balance. The perception of the monarch as a guide striving to identify the common good—sometimes with difficulty, but always with positive intent—protected the Crown from the consequences of miscalculation. As a regulator involved in a continuous search for the common good, no one act or balance represented a permanent position. The king functioned as the patron not only of the Church and other corporate groups but also of individual subjects. Within the political system, loyalty, favor, personality, and personal alliances counted far more than efficiency or exemplary conduct.

3

Philosophy in Practice

THE THEORETICAL CONCENTRATION OF AUTHORITY in the person of the monarch masked the influence of individuals, corporate groups, and the various councils. It implied a unity of interest that did not exist. Decrees, backed by the full majesty of the head of state, supposedly ended discussion. Behind this facade of unanimity, the structure in reality encouraged fluid maneuvering. From the top down, the government's conciliar organization provided an arena within which to mold policy. Although some councils and juntas had less prestige than others, and the types of problems they dealt with varied greatly in importance, all had a political role. Regardless of their function, they served as intermediaries between the Crown and those who desired a particular response. At all levels, the process required petitioners to demonstrate the importance of their case and the extent of their power to demand.

Shortly after the discovery, the Crown assigned primary responsibility for the American empire to a new organization. The *Casa de contratación*, established in Seville in 1503 as the first colonial administrative body, functioned as a part-time operation under the supervision of Juan Rodríguez de Fonseca, the Queen's confessor. Initially viewed as a means of preserving royal claims to a share of the trade and commerce of the new discoveries, the Casa immediately encountered moral and political problems far beyond its ability to resolve.[1] Following the fall of Tenochtitlán in 1521, and the subordination of millions of civilized Indians to Spanish authority, the limited bureaucratic structure required reorganization and expansion. In 1523 the Crown established the Council of the Indies, consisting of a president and eight councillors.[2] While circumstances forced the enlargement of the colonial bureaucracy, the designation of a group of officials as the Council of the Indies showed that the Crown recognized the desirability of providing the emerging empire with its own council similar to those of dependencies in Europe. The new organization assumed responsibility for political, ecclesiastical, and judicial affairs, whereas the Casa de contratción remained in charge of commerce and related matters. Modeled after the Council of Castile, the new council functioned separately, supreme in its designated area under the restrictions imposed by the philosophical matrix and the actual political superiority of the Council of State.[3]

At the imperial level, once an issue's importance had been established by the Council of the Indies, it went to the Council of State, which eventually dealt with all significant matters. Although slow and cumbersome, the process ensured that the final decision would not be ill considered and would likely not be an overreaction.[4] Councillor actions received scrutiny from interested parties as well as from above and had to be made with an eye toward the anticipated reaction. Advisors framed their views as a recommendation (*consulta*) subject to review and approval before the appropriate document could be drawn up. The king then accepted or modified the endorsement or recommendation of the Council of State.

In day to day operations, secretaries handled communications with councils, but had limited formal means of manipulating councillor activities. They did, however, prepare the agenda for council meetings and control access to the monarch. Inevitably, individual bureaucrats succeeded in becoming brokers between the monarch and the councils. Although council members resented and resisted the assumption of independent authority by the king's secretaries, Francisco de los Cobos, appointed royal secretary in 1516, became one of the most influential administrators and is regarded as a major architect of the Hapsburg bureaucracy.[5] A conscientious monarch, nevertheless, could not delegate formal responsibilities to such bureaucrats and had to devote long hours dealing with matters that required royal attention or the appearance of the king's personal intervention. Thus Felipe II, although he relied upon Cardinal Espinosa, president of the Council of State, until Espinosa's death in 1572, is viewed as a king-bureaucrat indiscriminately dealing with matters large and small. Subsequently, he found it necessary to employ a private secretary, Mateo Vázquez de Leca, and authorized his attendance at important subcommittee meetings.[6] Over a period of time, Vázquez de Leca acquired considerable political influence.

A more rational approach emerged after Felipe II's reign with the selection of a single prime minister, the *valido*. The development and evolution of the valido as a formal part of the government corresponded to the growing complexity of the monarchy, and society. A valido, although he enjoyed the favor and confidence of the king, was not a substitute for an incompetent or lazy ruler.[7] As a political figure he needed broad support; the king's favor alone could not guarantee effectiveness. Without a patronage system and substantial support from individuals or groups, a valido could not survive. In political interaction, the valido's ability to organize influence and pressure constituted a necessary tool.

In addition to the valido, the office of the *Despacho Universal* (the king's staff) began to assume de facto independent authority. The secretaryship of the Despacho created in 1621 usually fell to the secretary of the Council of State.[8] Royal orders could be transmitted directly through the Despacho Universal, and by 1700 its secretary functioned virtually as a vice-premier. As in the case of the valido, the secretary needed to develop support and political consensus. Diversity of authority encouraged the formation of factions, each vying for influence and ready to fashion alliances. The number of individuals involved in the political process consumed time but guaranteed that any decision implemented had reasonable support. The procedure also assured a reactive process: Officials did not anticipate or formulate problems to be addressed—they waited for them to be defined by events or circumstances. The perception of the sovereign as a judicial arbitrator between society's interest groups, rather than as an active intervenor, reinforced this tendency. The paramount objective, the preservation of political balance, required adjustments, but only as needed. The government avoided initiatives or innovations that might upset the balance and thus challenge its ability to regulate society.[9] A consensus was needed, and the structure of councils, validos, and secretaries provided a political arena within which to lobby, form alliances, and make deals.

Indian-European Relations

The reactive process is evident in the first major issue that confronted the Crown. During the first half-century of Spanish rule, Indian-European relations posed serious problems. The issue involved the degree of aboriginal servitude, the extent of political and social subordination of the population to the European settlers, as well as Crown responsibilities toward its new subjects. The questions, complex and important, involved both political and moral considerations.

Indian societies could not adjust easily to demands of the European conquerors. Spanish settlers sought to reorder the economic base of the

New World, while the aboriginal inhabitants, and their advocates, resisted the change. The conflict involved both land and labor. Communal landholding inhibited the individual accumulation of capital and, as a consequence, could not be accepted by the Europeans.[10] Equally unacceptable was the Indian perception of land and labor as a single economic unit. Spaniards viewed them as separate units, each to be exploited in a different fashion. To accept them as indivisible made the development of a free-floating labor supply available for wage hire impossible. Without labor, private landholding had limited value, and the accumulation of wealth, based on the utilization of economic resources, would be unlikely. The Europeans moved aggressively to establish both the concept of private property and its corollary, wage labor.

Indian resistance to detached labor exasperated the Spaniards, who tended to equate it with indolence. Subsequently, legislation identified idleness as an aboriginal vice to be cured by a benevolent Crown.[11] Mexican viceroy Antonio de Mendoza shared this view of native work habits and supported forced labor as a moral necessity.[12] The native population required paternalistic guidance until such time as they proved capable of assuming Western European socioeconomic responsibilities. Movement away from the Indian notion of labor as a function of communal land, or community service, and toward acceptance of the concept of private property initially involved the use of coercion. Abusive and exploitive practices accompanied the transition.

The primitive stage of Indian-European relations soon passed as the natives of the New World learned how to use the system to their advantage. Viceroy Mendoza, on relinquishing his post in 1550, complained of the Indian proclivity to litigate. Necessity made apt pupils.[13] Similarly, Viceroy Toledo of Peru found that Indians insisted upon legal and written conformation of titles every time a new corregidor assumed his post. They willingly paid notaries excessive amounts to employ European legal means to protect their interests. By the end of the sixteenth century, at least one group of Peruvian Indians annually named solicitors to handle anticipated legal battles.[14] The *ayllu* of Ervayesma in Santiago effectively litigated at least 150 years to protect landholdings east of Cuzco originally received from Inca Huayna Capac. Their opponents, including other Indians, failed to overturn their claim.[15] In a similar fashion, Metztitlán (New Spain), through astute and timely use of legal devices, defeated most attempts by individual Indians and others to convert its communal land into private property.[16]

Although they responded to challenges to property held in common, the records also indicate that the aboriginal population grasped the notion of private property. Land transferred in both directions was based on economic factors. The cacique of Piagua (Province of Popayán, for example, sold in 1677 land inherited from his father, who had purchased it originally from Andrés Cobo de Figueroa, a Spanish encomendero. In Peru *kurakas* (caciques), with the help of encomenderos anxious to preserve and strengthen working relations, obtained grants of land in the same fashion as Europeans.[17] The introduction of the concept of private property led to opportunity in some cases and disaster in others. Many Indians, after selling land for cash or other considerations, drifted into villages and colonial cities. Land once alienated required the accumulation of capital if an individual desired to return to agricultural pursuits, although on occasion a suit alleging that the land had been sold illegally or under duress resulted in restitution.[18] Private property became a divisive factor among groups previously exempt from the stress that accompanied the competitive race for material wealth. Moreover, an emerging class system acted to deprive them of leadership and made the economically fortunate dependent upon the new colonial regime to validate their acquisitions.

Full acceptance of the notion of private property by the Indian population was not an immediate concern; labor was the pressing problem. The monarchy had to move immediately to resolve the potentially dangerous issue. The establishment of a viable relationship between the indigenous inhabitants and European settlers could not be delayed. Isabel and Fernando, faced with the demands of colonists for labor and assertions that the Indian would not engage voluntarily in wage labor, had to respond. The Crown convened a group of councillors, lawyers, theologians, and canon law experts to examine the papal donation and other documentation to decide on the appropriate action. After considerable discussion, and in the presence of the Archbishop of Seville, they agreed that forced labor did not conflict with human or divide law. Fernando subsequently reiterated carefully how the decision had been reached; demonstrating the broad philosophical support behind it.[19]

As a result of these deliberations, forced but paid labor received royal approval in 1503. Indians technically remained free, although unable to withhold their labor. In this case, the Crown defended its jurisdiction by conceding to reality while theoretically imposing socially acceptable Christian obligations and restrictions on those who forceably employed aboriginal labor.[20] With some optimism, Marcos de Aguilar, interim governor of Mexico during the judicial investigation of Cortés (1527), noted that forcing the Indian to meet the European needs posed few exploitive problems, provided the Crown retained jurisdiction.[21] Yet faith in the benevolent nature of royal regulation also implied the obligation of the Crown to maintain its authority, and at least force superficial compliance. Aguilar's statement served both as an observation and a warning. The difficulty of establishing a balance between the king's American subjects and Spanish settlers, together with the problem of conflicting advice from many sources, guaranteed an uncertain and ambiguous reaction. New discoveries and a constantly changing situation kept the troublesome issue very much alive. It became obvious that officials had to devise other arrangements or acquiesce completely to the demands of European conquerors.

Opposing factions collided over the continuation and expansion of the encomienda system, which became the paramount symbol of the European settlers' desire to divide the spoils as they wished without reference to restrictive spiritual, moral, or political concerns.[22] To its detractors, the encomienda encompassed all the forms of mistreatment visited upon the aboriginal population, including cruelty, enslavement, and exploitation. Both pro- and anti-encomienda elements had to establish a philosophical basis for their position. Those who favored a forced adjustment of the Indians to European religious, cultural, and socioeconomic needs fell back on Aristotle's natural hierarchy of men, as well as on St. Augustine's judgment that pagan virtues "are only vices in disguise," and that left alone "nature is incapable of any good."[23] Thus, simple virtues could be transformed into laziness and obstinacy that required a firm corrective hand. On the other side, opponents of force drew upon a fund of ideas provided by the Jesuits, Trentian theologians, and selected Church fathers, which asserted that Christianity does not destroy natural virtues but rather "hierarchizes and harmonizes them."[24] Moreover, the belief shared by many missionary clerics that history moved toward the millennium in a series of spiritual stages led to the acceptance of the primacy of the task of conversion over worldly concerns. Pro Indian groups also drew upon the notion of a natural inner light or impulse that compelled humans toward the truth and hence toward God. As Fray Luis de Granada asserted, all people had a natural capacity to rise above nature (*sobre-naturalizarse*) as a consequence of the gift of grace.[25] This idea could also be used in a negative fashion, as when Fray de Pineda in his *Agricultura Christiana* quoted St. Paul on the positive aspect of inner light but observed that an individual must choose to follow it. Those who did not were both inferior and guilty of ignoring God's gift.[26] The New World's inhabitants followed the devil and therefore endured the conquest as a form of punishment and correction.

Ultimately, however, both the positive and negative approaches rested on the obligation to secure the common good. In the struggle over the method to be used toward this end, anti-encomienda elements sought a reversal of the already unfolding pattern of Indian-European relations. Their efforts, combined with Crown misgivings concerning the political power of the institution in the New World, defined the encomienda as a major problem. A series of clerics took up the struggle. Father Miguel de Salamanca, drawing upon his experience in the Antilles, denounced the encomienda as against all laws, both civil and canon, contrary to moral philosophy and theology, and against the will of God and His Church.[27] As an absolute evil, he warned, the encomienda threatened the total destruction of the land. His assault had little effect. Other clerics, such as Antonio de Montesinos, who shocked his parishioners by his condemnation from the pulpit in 1511 of those who held Indians in exploitive relationships, proved more successful. The Dominicans dispatched Montesinos to Spain to lay the matter before the monarch, while a Franciscan, Alonso del Espinal, represented the outraged encomenderos. Clerics made the issue a challenge to the monarch's legitimate right to rule in the New World.

Crown officials had to tolerate such criticisms, no matter how strongly they disapproved of the particular action demanded, or how distasteful the tactics employed to bring it to their attention. To discourage or ignore the debate would not only violate the philosophical matrix but would also throw the argument into unpredictable channels with possibly grave political consequences.

The Dominican cleric Matiás de Paz (ca. 1469-1519), professor of theology at the University of Valladolid and one of those appointed to examine official Indian policy, placed the moral issue within its political context in his work, *Del dominio de los reyes de España sobre los indios* (On the Dominion of the Kings of Spain over the Indians; 1512). He examined the issue of whether the king governed despotically, as well as whether the Crown could continue to exercise political authority in the New World. He concluded that conversion of the Indians justified the European presence thus subordinating all other objectives to the religious goals. Enslavement and tyranny could not be justified; however, reasonable service could be extracted in order to finance the religious effort. Paz thus posed and resolved the question in a fashion that affirmed the Crown's jurisdictional position.[28] In an identical manner, Juan López de Palacios Rubios (1450-1524), in his *De insulis oceanicis* (On the Islands of the Ocean Sea; ca. 1512), stressed the importance of the papal donation and the task of conversion.[29] Consequently, the Laws of Burgos (1512) reaffirmed the legality of the monarchy's presence and sought to establish a compromise between those who argued that the

New World's natives needed firm supervision and those who believed that they should retain their liberty. The Laws of Burgos, as amended in 1513, recognized regulated involuntary labor.[30] The restrictions and religious responsibilities imposed by the Laws of Burgos emphasized the monarch's benevolent jurisdiction.

Bartolomé de Las Casas

Mistreatment of the American population kept the issue of legitimacy alive. The receptivity of royal officials to reform schemes stemmed from this political concern. Fray Bartolemé de Las Casas, the famous proponent of Indian rights, pressed reforms on the monarchy as early as 1516.[31] Manuel Giménez Fernández, with some justice, referred to him as the "spokesman of the humanist opposition."[32] Nevertheless, the politically inexperienced Las Casas appeared to be no match for those skilled in such affairs. Consequently, Juan Rodríguez de Fonseca, Bishop of Burgos and minister of the Indies, rejected Las Casas's complaints, implying that he was a fool. Not so easily deterred, the energetic priest sent memorials to Adrian of Utrecht and the Cardinal Archbishop of Toledo, Francisco Ximénez de Cisneros, coregents pending the arrival of the future king. Utilizing a technique that characterized his more mature efforts, Las Casas sent three memorials. The first (April 1516) detailed the abuses, the second (May 1516) outlined the remedies needed, and the third (June 1516) denounced the officials charged with regulating affairs in the New World. Las Casas wrote each with a particular purpose in mind and crafted his communications to achieve the intended effect.[33] He developed a reform plan that rationalized the use of Indian labor but made it more humane. The plan advocated the establishment of *comunidades* with independently managed labor pools to avoid the evils associated with direct settler control of indigenous labor. Joint ownership and profit sharing would benefit all and reverse the population decline already evident in the islands. Indian laborers, as perceived by the priest-reformer, would serve a productive apprenticeship and eventually evolve into an independent laboring class. Concurrent with the establishment of these communities, he proposed the introduction of Spanish peasant families to work and instruct Indian laborers and their families. Equality and private profit would transform the New World's inhabitants into a productive peasantry further strengthened by intermarriage.[34]

Las Casas convinced Archbishop Cisneros that Indian affairs had been mismanaged. Consequently, Cisneros replaced Fonseca, Lope de

Conchillos, and their associates and established a commission to draw up plans along the lines advocated by Las Casas. The regent subsequently dispatched Jeronymite friars to investigate conditions in the New World and put the plan into operation. Those who bitterly opposed reforms, however, had not been idle. They persuaded the Jeronymites that radical changes were not required. In addition, antireform officials delayed the mission and prevented Las Casas from embarking with them. It was not surprising that the Jeronymites implemented only a small part of the reforms, did little to end the slave trade, and failed to declare the Indian free in violation of their instructions. An incredulous and outraged Las Casas, protesting in vain, returned to Spain bitterly aware that an apparent political victory could be reversed.[35]

Las Casas, backed by the Dominican Order and carrying the recommendations of the Dominican Provincial of Española, Fray Pedro de Córdoba, now attempted to make direct contact with the future king's Flemish advisors. Fray Reginaldo Montesinos O.P., the brother of Antonio de Montesinos, used his influence to see that Las Casas received a hearing. Fray Reginaldo may have been the individual who read the priest's proposal for peasant colonization to the Council of the Indies.[36] Las Casas established contact with Carlos's great chancellor, Jean de Sauvage, and became his principal advisor on Indian affairs. The new monarch's Flemish advisors, unfamiliar with the encomienda's long history in Spain, could be convinced that such an institution posed an immediate challenge to authority.[37] Las Casas and his influential supporters succeeded in forcing those involved with New World affairs to defend their actions. Chancellor Sauvage, shocked and alarmed, temporarily suspended the functions of those charged with colonial affairs.[38] The untimely death of Sauvage, however, resulted in yet another political reversal. Carlos I's powerful minister Chièvres placed Rodríguez de Fonseca once again in charge of the Indies. Las Casas charged that Fonseca had purchased the support of Chièvres. Fonseca counterattacked with his own confidential memorial expounding the reasons why Las Casas's charges and demands should be disregarded. The priest-reformer eventually saw a copy of the document in spite of the efforts of a hostile Francisco de Cobos, the political heir of the disgraced Lope de Conchillos.[39]

Las Casas's ability to draw up new schemes and modify old ones to take advantage of the perceived preferences of high officials made things difficult for his opponents. Moreover, acquiring information on the actual state of affairs in the Indies proved difficult in the early period. Each side sought to discredit the other as well as influence the nature of official reports. While Las Casas managed to have a hand in the instructions given Rodrigo de Figueroa, sent to make an inspection of affairs in the Indies, Fonseca blocked Las Casas from accompanying him.[40] In the battle for control of information, the priest-reformer had the advantage; as an experienced veteran he spoke with authority.[41] The persuasive priest was able to offer not only direct knowledge of the problems that he laid out before officials but also solutions. As a result, officials eventually accepted his peasant colonization of Tierra Firme. Even then, acceptance of his project represented only a partial victory because the antireform group blocked a more ambitious plan for peasant settlement. After considerable difficulty, Las Casas sailed from Spain with seventy laborers. The attempt to combine private profit with an acceptable degree of humanity failed disastrously, however, and a disillusioned Las Casas retreated into the Dominican Order in 1522.[42] More positively, his entry into the Order of Preachers marked the beginning of his transformation from a priest-colonist-reformer into a theologian-jurist-activist.

While Las Casas developed a new perspective, the power of European settlers over the Indians appeared to gain in strength and acceptance. With the subjugation and incorporation of millions of Indians following the conquest of Mexico in 1521, the encomienda emerged as a major institution.[43] Although Fernando Cortés received instructions not to assign Indians in encomienda, he ignored such orders. Nevertheless, officials insisted that the king's New World subjects had the right to personal freedom. The Council of the Indies on November 9, 1526, suggested that only in the event the Indians proved incapable of living independently and in peace could they be given in encomienda to European settlers. Three years later, the royal council declared that natives had no obligation to render personal service; only the tithe and tribute to be paid to the king could be demanded of them. Furthermore, because of the cruelty associated with the institution, all encomiendas should be extinguished.[44]

Regardless of the number of pro-Indian statements by officials, reality forced a compromise. Viceroy Mendoza, in his instructions to his successor, Luis de Velasco, pointed out that revenues depended on economic activity which in turn depended on Indian labor.[45] The monarchy settled for recognition of the principle of full personal freedom while recognizing the encomienda as a reward for the theoretical responsibilities toward the Indian population assumed by the Europeans.[46] In order to demonstrate royal control, a special board composed of officials and clerics theoretically regulated the institution. In 1536 the Crown confirmed the inheritance of encomienda grants for two generations, leading many to believe it might continue indefinitely.[47] Self-confident *encomenderos* now pressed their efforts to secure civil and criminal jurisdiction over tributary Indians.

The anti-encomienda force rallied to counterattack. Fray Las Casas, together with Bishops Zumárraga and Garcés of New Spain, drew up several petitions directed to Pope Paul III, and Dominican friar Bernardino de Minaya carried them to Europe. As a consequence, Pope Paul III not only praised decrees restricting Indian slavery but also issued bulls concerns the treatment of Indians. The papal pronouncements—*Veritas Ipsa*, which condemned Indian slavery, and *Sublimis Deus* (1537), which declared it heresy to accept the convenient notion that the Indian was irrational and thus incapable of receiving the faith—focused international attention on the issue. Rome made its views even clearer in *Pastorale Officium*, which provided for excommunication of those who held contrary opinions on the nature of the New World's inhabitants.[48] The pontiff's actions violated the conditions of the royal patronage which permitted the Crown to approve and forward papal decrees to the American colonies. Although Emperor Carlos V insisted several be revoked because of that important political detail, the monarch did not argue with their intent.[49] Rome could not be ignored because Spain's claim to sovereignty over the Indians rested in part on papal grants. Although papal concession hardly provided a guarantee against foreign covertness, they served as an initial basis for Spanish activities in the New World. Spain, especially in the period of settlement and organization, could not afford to have its spiritual mandate jeopardized or withdrawn.

Pressure to force the Crown to act on the issue of Indian mistreatment reached a high point with the return of Fray Bartolomé de las Casas to Spain in 1539. Except for a brief period (1545-1546), he remained in Spain until his death in 1566. Total denunciation and all-encompassing charges characterized his mature political style. His attacks cannot be dismissed as emotional rhetoric, however, but rather must be viewed as part of a comprehensive strategy.[50] He formulated problems in such a fashion that they could not be ignored.[51] In a calculating manner, he controlled the distribution of his written material.[52] A prolific writer, Las Casas had an awesome amount of material to draw upon. He mounted an attack with skill—on one hand calmly presenting a solution to the perceived problem, and on the other providing an unrestrained, highly emotional indictment calculated to drive officials to recognize the merits of the proposed remedy. In his treatise, *El octavo remedio* (The Eighth Remedy), Las Casas set forth judicious, rational arguments for action on the issue of exploitation.[53] He succinctly outlined the Crown's jeopardized interests and noted the steps needed to correct the situation. Accepting the idea that conversion constituted the central purpose, Las Casas insisted that the monarch had the obligation to remove all obstacles to that task. He identified the encomiendas as the most serious barrier to Christianization for "what thing could be more against our Catholic faith than to deliver Indians to Spaniards" (art. 10). Supposedly, those who held Indians placed their own economic concerns over spiritual considerations, even to the point of rejecting the presence of missionary friars. Rather than responding to the clergy's efforts to end exploitation, they excluded missionaries from direct contact with aboriginal population (art. 2). Settlers, according to Las Casas, thought nothing of breaking up the family, the very foundation of a Christian way of life. Free men should not lose their liberty when they became vassals of the emperor; yet the encomienda in effect deprived them of their freedom, and on occasion their lives, and led to the destruction of villages. Such a process violated God's law, natural law, justice, and all reason. He insisted that even if the Indian voluntarily entered an exploitive relationship, the monarch, guided by divine precepts, could not allow it (art. 9). Allegedly, fear and dread forced many to flee into the hills to die of hopelessness and bitterness, or to fall victim to wild animals. Apart from these compelling reasons, the encomienda appeared to be illegal. In Castile the Crown could not transfer an individual's wealth to another without violating both natural law and that of the land; however, the encomienda illegally disposed of Indian assets (art. 9). Las Casas noted that philosophically any law contrary to the common good, or divine rule, automatically became invalid.

Las Casas observed that the situation posed a threat to the monarchy quite apart from moral considerations. After all, a population decline affected the empire's military might. Moreover, Crown status and prestige would be hurt, with unimagined consequence, when the truth became known (art. 13). Other nations, scandalized by the mistreatment accorded the king's New World subjects, would view the monarchy and the Spanish people as abominable and hateful. Within the empire itself, the creation of *gran señores* jeopardized authority and required the monarch to watch them constantly (art. 14). Without a strong and determined political structure, capped by viceroys and Audiencias, the native population would perish unknown to the emperor—after all, the Crown remained distant and uninformed. If, however, the monarch acted on behalf of the natives, he would find them overjoyed to be his vassals (arts. 16 and 17). A benevolent policy would draw them back out of the mountains to which they had fled and would enrich the realm.

He skillfully touched on several key constitutional issues linked to the Crown's right to rule. Frequent use of the word *tyranny* carried with it the implication that by delivering the Indians into the hands of the Spaniards the Crown invalidated its right to govern. The mortality rate of Indians under the encomienda system, the destruction of their family life and villages, provided the ultimate proof of the damaging effects of royal policy. Las Casas implied that tyrannicide might well be justified in such a case. He noted that the failure of individual Europeans to Christianize the Indians did not excuse the Crown of the responsibilities that accompanied the papal concessions. He adroitly suggested the international political danger of the monarchy's apparent unwillingness to protect its New World subjects physically. To Las Casas the encomienda, the enslavement of hapless natives, and unjust wars were symptomatic of political and moral weakness that undermined legitimacy.

The process of forcing a decision from a reactive government required much more than rational arguments. A climate of outrage had to be created that would make it impossible to sidestep the issue. To that end, Las Casas issued his *Brevisima relación de la destrucción de las Indias* (Very Brief Account of the Destruction of the Indies), a wild, but purposeful exaggeration that elaborated on the cruel and exploitive treatment accorded the Indian population. It represented the written version of his verbal argument made personally to Emperor Carlos V and his advisors. Las Casas focused on the tragic impact of European contact on the native populations. Actual abuse and exploitation, in both an economic and cultural sense, coupled with physical distress and disease, became in his account massive, sadistic cruelty visited upon a hapless, innocent population in a random and totally arbitrary fashion. Spanish captains became not only the scourge of the Indians but also "enemies of the human race."[54] Their use of traditional porters (*tamenes*) in a society without beasts of burden became an example of European heartlessness. Repeatedly hammering the issue, Las Casas asserted that Spaniards overloaded their porters and then beat and even killed them when they faltered.[55] The *Brevisima relación* portrayed an unjust conquest followed by a cruel and immoral use of labor. Allegedly, commanders intimidated their captives by decapitating thirty or forty of them.[56] To demonstrate their disdain for human life, Las Casas claimed, Spaniards fed human meat to their dogs, even maintaining butcher shops that displayed Indian cadavers for the convenience of Europeans who purchased "a quarter of that rascal to feed my dogs."[57] Excesses of cruelty and exploitation in a frontier society became the rule, but the real victims, Las Casas noted, were Christianity and the Crown's legitimate sovereignty. Frequent use of the loaded terms *tyrant* and *tyrant-governor* made the point that the colonial regime appeared to be both morally and politically illegitimate. Las Casas concluded with the hope that "our Emperor Carlos V will harken to and comprehend the evils and betrayals against the will of God and his majesty."[58]

Alonso de Santa Cruz, the royal cosmographer, relates in his *Cró: ica del Emperador Carlos V* that the emperor ordered a member of the Council of Castile and his secretary, Francisco de los Cobos, to meet with the Council of the Indies to hear Las Casas read from a manuscript then in the process of preparation. Las Casas read a draft of the *Brevisima relación* in which he directly accused certain individuals, including Fernando Cortés and Pedro de Alvarado, of complicity and tyrannical behavior. At the same time, he offered his solution—essentialy that contained within the *Octavo remedio*—to add more pressure. Moreover, as Santa Cruz reports, Las Casas's accusation of corruption within the Council of Indies led to an investigation of the Council ordered personally by the emperor.[59] Members of the Council of Castile replaced all the councillors, including the president, Fray García de Loaysa, Archbishop of Seville. Two officials eventually were dismissed and forced to return bribes. The investigation ruined García de Loaysa's career and damaged that of Francisco de Cobos, the royal secretary.[60] Subsequently, a reconstituted Council of the Indies, favorable to Las Casas, assumed control. The far-reaching verbal and written attacks made by the energetic priest and his allies resulted in Carlos V's formal approval on November 20, 1542, of a comprehensive set of laws dealing with the treatment of the Indian.[61] The New Laws marked the high point of the Indianist movement.

The New Laws

The government's reactive nature dictated a problem-specific response; thus the New Laws focused on the encomienda, slavery, and administration. As Las Casas had protested that officials failed to devote sufficient time to Indian affairs, the new regulations ordered the Council of the Indies to follow a set schedule and procedures. In a similar fashion, the high courts in the Indies received instructions to investigate and punish those responsible for mistreating Indians. The New Laws prohibited the use of the "just war" concept as an excuse for enslavement, and furthermore declared that those illegally enslaved must be freed. The Crown ordered royal officials to release Indians held by them in any form of personal bondage and, in a direct attack on the encomienda, prohibited future grants of tributary Indians. Article 35, the most unpalatable restriction, provided that on the death of the incumbent holder of an encomienda the grant reverted to the Crown. The inhabitants of the islands, whose plight was used repeatedly by Las Casas to substantiate his case, were relieved of all tribute burdens; in new discoveries, the royal governor would set the tribute. Predictably, several of the horrendous examples employed by Las Casas received attention. Use of porters would be permitted only when absolutely necessary and under strict regulation. Pearl fisheries, described by Las Casas as subjecting Indians to a most "infernal and desperate life," could not employ forced labor.[62] The essentially reactive nature of the process assured a match between the points emphasized by Las Casas and others, and the New Laws. Lascasian scholar Lewis Hanke observed that the regulations might well have been drafted by the good father himself.[63] Characteristic of such enactments, the New Laws did not serve as a pattern or guide for subsequent action on the issue. The influence of the notion that the law reflected rather than created justice is evident. Each article stood alone as an individual reflection of the philosophical matrix.

The victory would be short-lived; counterattacks by different groups, including encomenderos and their influential supporters, began to undo the new regulations almost immediately. Spanish settlers insisted that they could not survive without the institution of the encomienda. Allegedly, even those who did not hold one received help from those who did, and abolition would force them all to return to Spain.[64] Las Casas had assured the Emperor that once freed of the institution the Indians would be most grateful and loyal, but the idea of a European withdrawal must have been disquieting. Clerical supporters warned that the missionary church depended on the involuntary assignment of Indians. Fray Toribio de Motolinía, who inveighed against Las Casas's exaggerated condemnation of mistreatment of the native population, declared that an encomienda provided one of the few means of forcing the Indian to be productive.[65] The Bishop of Mexico, Juan de Zumárraga, although he supported Las Casas on many points, defended the encomienda, as did the provincials of the various orders. Zumárraga himself held an encomienda, as well as Indian and black slaves.[66]

Financial inducements reinforced rhetorical and political pressure. Encomenderos offered the emperor, and subsequently Felipe II, large sums of money in return for revoking the New Laws.[67] Predictably, the Crown responded by attempting to balance conflicting demands in a fashion that reflected the relative strength of the factions. In 1545 it eliminated article 35, and the following year annulled the regulation that called for releasing Indians from an encomendero guilty of mistreating his wards.[68] Reacting to overwhelming pressure, the Crown ordered Viceroy Antonio de Mendoza to investigate the demands of the conquistadores and placate them with grants of Indians.[69] Small wonder the Mexico City Council set aside a holiday to celebrate the victory.[70] The Crown reacted to the counterattack in the same problem-specific fashion as the original action.

The process of legitimization through debate did not run its full course until the official disputation between Bartolomé de Las Casas and Juan Ginés de Supúlveda in 1550–1551. The Crown convened the Valladolid meeting as a consequence of Las Casas's attack on Sepúlveda's treatise, *Democrates alter, sive de justas belli causi apud Indos* (On the Just Cause of War on the Indians), as well as the issue of new conquests. Sepúlveda's work, written with the encouragement of Cardinal García de Loaysa, defended the concept of just war, as well as the political and social subordination of the aboriginal population. Las Casas attacked this interpretation, and raised the as yet unresolved issue of further conquest. He demanded moreover that expansion be stopped until a proper method of extending the king's domains could be decided upon. The Crown ordered that the controversy be settled before a body of learned clerics and officials. In fact, the political stakes were not high, and many panel members participated reluctantly.[71] Both Sepúlveda and Las Casas claimed to support the monarch's legitimate right to rule in the New World. It became a question of method rather than of the continued existence of royal authority. Las Casas proposed to "open the gates" to legal claims based upon solid, strong, truly Catholic, and truly Christian, grounds.[72] Although his argument inherently contained a threat that the monarchy might forfeit authority, that feature could no longer be stressed after the debates surrounding the New Laws. The disputation concluded with both men claiming victory. In reality the Crown, free to pick and choose arguments to suit its needs, won. Sepúlveda's position, because of its harshness, had limited utility except in the negative sense of supplying the foil for the positive justification supplied by Las Casas. The official meeting in Valladolid proved to be the last significant debate involving the legitimacy of Spanish rule. Philosophically, the monarchy had met the challenge and turned it to its own advantage. In the end, Las Casas served to legitimize colonial authority. The fact that the rejection of Sepúlveda's argument marked the end of his public career provided a momentary illusion of victory for his opponent.[73]

Although defused, the issue lingered on as reassured encomenderos pressed for perpetuity of title as well as civil and criminal jurisdiction. A financially overcommitted Carlos V in 1555 charged his son with exploring the matter. Prince Felipe, then in England as a result of his marriage to Mary I, ordered the Council of the Indies to prepare a *consulta* (written report) on the question. The councillors expressed the opinion that in the case of Peru unrest made it advisable to hold out the prospect of perpetuity of title as an incentive rather than actually grant it.[74] Nevertheless, the following year Felipe, then king, ordered the council to decide how perpetuity should be implemented and to select four commissioners to negotiate sales.[75] The council responded that grants made to three or four hundred individuals would anger an even larger number of settlers who could be expected to react violently. An additional point, more tactical than sincere, was whether such concession might result in perpetual slavery for the Indians. Raising the political stakes, the members of the Council of the Indies wondered whether the original papal grants allowed the assignment of civil and criminal jurisdiction to individuals. Furthermore, the councillors asserted that Indian caciques, as *señores naturales*, retained first instance jurisdictional authority; therefore the Crown could not alienate what it did not possess. The Council of the Indies suggested that because so few stood to gain, the issue of the common good needed to be examined and decided upon by a Peruvian cortes.[76] Some form of perpetuity without jurisdiction was more acceptable as a means of pacifying settlers.[77] As a result of opposition when the commissioners arrived in Peru, jurisdiction was no longer contemplated.

The difficulty of arriving at a definite decision on perpetuity threatened to repoliticize the encomienda issue—a danger underscored by the gathering of caciques in Lima during the summer of 1559. The caciques appointed Las Casas and Domingo de Santo Tomás as their representatives to lay the entire issue of the encomienda before the pope, the king, and the Council of the Indies. Their actions complicated matters beyond the original purpose of fattening the depleted royal coffers. Las Casas and Santo Tomás petitioned Felipe II, offering 100,000 ducats over any sum offered by the encomenderos if the monarch would agree to incorporate encomiendas into the Crown. Among other unsettling requests, they asked that the Indians be allowed to convoke a representative assembly along the lines of a Castilian cortes, as they allegedly had under the Incas.[78] The extent of opposition, as well as the variety of plans raised, made it clear that a simple financial transaction could not be arranged. No one side had sufficient strength to press the issue decisively and the Crown lost serious interest, although discussions continued into the next century.[79]

Actual enforcement of the restrictions placed on the encomienda as a result of the legislation of 1542–1543 (the New Laws) depended upon political factors. As a consequence, the degree of enforcement varied widely from one region to another. New Spain's viceroy, Antonio de Mendoza not only suspended the New Laws pending clarification, allegedly because of the possibility of revolt, but also continued to receive illegal personal service and provisions from tributaries. In Peru premature implementation led to a serious revolt that required strenuous military and political efforts to contain. Alonso López de Cerrato, in contrast, succeeded in enforcing the New Laws in Santo Domingo. The Crown, as was to be expected, offered no real support, but Cerrato, in the absence of sufficiently powerful interest groups and by force of his personality, freed illegally held slaves and insisted on other reforms. A pleased Las Casas referred to him as a "most righteous and great judge."[80] Even then, total enforcement could not be achieved. A weary Cerrato begged to be allowed to retire to Spain, but the Crown ordered him to assume the presidency of the Audiencia de los Confines, itself a creation of the New Laws. In Central America, Cerrato once again succeeded to a remarkable degree. European settlers, unable to muster sufficient political strength, held him personally responsible for the reforms. As they sensed, the Crown itself would have settled for simple acknowledgment of its jurisdiction.[81]

Under the circumstances, repetition of prohibitions designed to emphasize royal authority and linked to specific cases could be expected. A disillusioned Las Casas declared in 1563 that Satan invented laws to conceal the actual evil that continued without restraint.[82] A subsequent example of the politics of enforcement is provided by the experience of Bishop Antonio de San Miguel of the Chilean see of La Imperial in 1568. Almost immediately on arrival, he pressured the Audiencia to enforce the laws governing Indian-European relations. With considerable reluctance, the judges dispatched two inspectors to examine and correct the abuses inflicted upon the population by encomenderos. Both inspectors attempted to institute reforms and levy fines on those guilty of violation of the laws. Predictably, those adversely affected appealed to the Audiencia, which considered their petition for two years and took no action either on the collection of fines or on the reforms ordered by the inspectors. An outraged San Miguel advised the king to abolish the Audiencia. Eventually, the bishop succeeded in getting a royal order directing the Audiencia to revise tribute schedules and enforce the laws. The politically astute judges ordered yet another investigation. In disgust, San Miguel wrote the king in 1575 that the judges of the Audiencia fulfilled their obligation to the monarch by issuing a new tribute scale, and then countermanded it to satisfy the encomenderos.

Even when Felipe II abolished the Audiencia, and appointed Rodrigo de Quiroga governor, the political balance remained the same. Governor Quiroga advocated continued personal service, arguing that primitive Indians could not be expected to respond to any other form of taxation. For a brief period starting in 1580, a new governor outlawed personal service; by 1583, however, Alonso de Sotomayor, his replacement, permitted it again.[83] Obligatory personal service lingered on as a reflection of the political power of the Chilean encomenderos, regardless of decrees and angry clerics.[84]

As is characteristic of a reactive regime, issues tended to diminish slowly in importance. The encomienda remained an issue throughout the sixteenth century until, little by little, it became relatively innocuous and insignificant. Changing conditions, more than any action by the Crown, affected the socioeconomic position of the aboriginal population. The emergence of complex colonial societies and economies contributed to the end of the issue of exploitation as an imperial political problem.[85] Individuals and Indian communities entered into direct arrangements with employers. Workers and employers in Guatemala as early as the 1540s labored under notarized contracts setting forth working conditions as well as compensation.[86] Even in other parts of late sixteenth-century Central America, where frontier conditions still prevailed, the condition of labor improved and wage compensation became the norm.[87] Astute employers realized that heavy-handed coercion had a negative impact on the quality and reliability of labor. In a system that was more acceptable and closer to Indian customs, bosses known as *capitanes cuadrillas*, organized work groups, freeing the employer of the need to supervise the work force and enabling workers to bargain for better wages and conditions. In addition, reluctant acceptance by Indian communities of a regulated temporary assignment of labor under the *repartimiento* system made it possible to assign labor when deemed necessary.[88] Population decline and the resultant competition for workers also had an effect on the treatment of labor. Casual abuse of increasingly valuable resources could prove costly to employers, but a combination of mutual obligation and advantage induced cooperation.[89] In Peru, Diego Maldonado, one of the wealthiest encomenderos, distributed gifts and food to establish a sense of obligation. On occasion Maldonado could be ruthless, but he understood that force provided fewer benefits than voluntary arrangements.[90]

Mining, a labor-intensive as well as speculative industry, rapidly developed incentives to attract and retain workers. In New Spain entrepreneurs, by effectively adjusting to the labor market, sustained the silver boom of 1615 and 1633 in Zacatecas, one in Parral in the 1630s and one in Sombrerete that lasted for twenty years into the 1690s.[91] Even in Peru, where the mining *mita* of officially assigned labor provided a subsidy into the eighteenth century, the bulk of production depended upon free labor. In many respects, mine workers constituted a favored labor elite, although the ups and downs of the industry provided little social or job security and working conditions were unpleasant, unhealthy, and dangerous. Well aware of their contribution, mine workers tenaciously defended their customary rights. Attempts to modify or end the partido system, which allowed an individual to collect a certain amount of ore after his quota had been met, generally received an angry and hostile response. A sense of mutual dependency normally tempered the attitude of both workers and owners and poor labor relations could mean disaster for an insensitive or overly grasping employer. An unattended mine produced nothing and risked flooding, so administrators of large-scale operations preferred to deploy two shifts and maintain twenty-four hour operations.[92] As a variety of methods for obtaining labor emerged, employers increasingly objected to the control exercised by officials through the repartimiento. Official assignment of labor gave corregidores and alcaldes mayores the power to withhold as well as assign, and to compete with private agriculturalists and others for labor.

Once the transition to voluntary labor had been accomplished, the issue of coercion no longer posed a problem that might jeopardize legitimacy. Although abuses continued, they were perceived to involve persons not entire groups, and the needs of the abused could be met by the individual granting of relief.[93] Theoretically, group paternalism remained, however, and served to emphasize Crown concern for the weak as well as for the common good. Thus, a special Indian tribunal, the *Juzgado de Indios* (1571, Mexico; 1603, Peru) heard appeals and complaints against local officials. The attempt to draw even the poorer elements into the controlled judicial arena led to the appointment of a lawyer paid by the Crown to assist Indian litigants. Subsequently, each municipality was urged to designate an attorney paid out of local funds for the purpose. In addition, an *abogado de pobres* (lawyer for the poor) attached to each Audiencia provided legal services financed from court revenues.[94] The arrangement provided a controlled outlet for social frustration. In a governing system dependent on distributive justice, lawyers seldom performed to the clear advantage of their assigned clients; yet from the standpoint of both the monarchy and the individual, they served a useful purpose. By providing access to the legal system, the Crown defused issues before they went beyond the individual or community level.

By the end of the first century of Spanish rule, the legitimacy question had been successfully separated from the issue of Indian abuse. This fact is no better illustrated than in Melchor Calderón's (1599) *Tratado de la importancia y utilidad que hay en dar por esclaves a los Indios rebelados de Chile* (Treatise on the Importance and Utility of Enslaving the Rebellious Indians of Chile). A resident of Chile since 1555, treasurer of the cathedral in Santiago, and known for his friendly relations with the aboriginal population, Calderón composed his treatise following the violent uprising of 1598-1599. Although he conceded that abuse had sparked the violence, he maintained that the Indians, who had formally recognized the king, engaged in an unjust war against the Europeans. He reasoned that a ruler did not forfeit dominion simply because of the valid grievances of his subjects. Only if a monarch failed to provide his subjects access to justice or refused to address their complaints would violent action be warranted. As this was not the case, the rebellion constituted treason against legitimate authority.[95] Mitigating circumstances, including exploitation resulting from a lapse in good government, or even the failure of the regime to function as philosophically mandated, might well be taken into consideration, but not the legitimacy of imperial authority.

Conclusion

The clash of personalities and the rhetorical and persuasive genius of the various protagonists should not obscure the extent to which the political process and concrete results conformed to the philosophical matrix of the Castilian monarchy. All factions manipulated the system in accordance with a shared ideal perception of the monarchy. Moral questions, because spiritual well-being constituted an important responsibility of the monarchy, had a direct political connection. As a result of the fusion of moral and political concerns, discussions and debates over policy often appear sanctimonious to the modern mind.[96] The monarchy and others constantly sought the reinforcement of moral principle. Yet, without pressure from insistent interest groups, issues were unlikely to receive serious attention. Consequently, exaggeration to the point of hyperbole played an important role, and questions tended to be simplified and made absolute. Although political theorists, such as Palacio Rubios and others, often carefully reviewed pro and con aspects before proceeding to pronounce their judgment, political actors, including Las Casas and his opponents, avoided uncertainty in their efforts to press a particular solution. In the political process, loud voices and graphic examples served as weapons.[97] Thus, Spaniards sourly, but not without some justification, noted that many "muy ladino" (acculturated) natives filed outrageous and overblown charges with the hope of attracting at least the support of a reforming friar, if not a bishop.[98]

While officials reacted to demands to establish or recognize an acceptable balance between conflicting interests within a distinct philosophical context, a uniform balance throughout Spanish America could not be expected, nor did it exist. The balance struck in a frontier or marginal region differed from that in Peru or New Spain.[99] Yet, local or regional interest groups could not strike an arbitrary balance. Moreover, the process remained subject to continuous adjustment. Enforcement provided an opportunity to make refinements in conformity with the current political strength of a particular group, and thus rectify miscalculations. Unless the interested parties continued to press their demands, enforcement was likely to be sporadic. Unenforced laws served as mute testimony of past struggles won only on the policy-making level. The actual political strength of the protagonists, based upon and reinforced by principles contained within the philosophical matrix, in the end determined the result.[100]

4

The Governing Ideology of the Bourbon State

IN THE EIGHTEENTH CENTURY, with the ascension of Felipe V, the first of the Spanish Bourbon monarchs, a different approach to problems became evident. The change, not abrupt or complete, reached its apogee during the reign of Carlos III (1759-1788). A different perception of the state and its potential altered the nature and intent of the monarchy. New ideas, coupled with new analytical methods, engendered confidence among high-ranking officials who believed it possible to elaborate and implement comprehensive schemes to stimulate Spain's economy. At the same time, the new secular point of view forced the state to advance other reasons for its position within society. Implied benevolence, an important part of the traditional philosophical matrix, would not be laid aside, but its impulse had to be shifted from a remote divine source to a definite material foundation. As a consequence, an economic justification developed that linked the state to the prosperity and well-being of the individual.

At what point Spanish economic thought shifted from mercantilism to physiocratic, and subsequently to liberal economics, is not as significant as the development of a political ideology that relied so heavily on economic factors. Physiocratic economic ideas provided a secular link between the state and the people. Although physiocratic thought permeated mercantilism much earlier, by the latter part of the eighteenth century it became more conscious and important throughout Europe. Yet, mercantilism was not displaced until the turn of the century, and even then continued to have a lingering influence. Physiocratic doctrine postulated a series of natural economic laws established by some remote cause that could be uncovered and then implemented. The new formulation emphasized material well-being.[1] Thus the political economy, and the advice of economic theorists, became more important than the religio-political elements and the rumination of philosophers.

The shift toward a material justification of authority had Iberian roots at least as far back as Juan de Mariana. His views, expressed in the latter half of the sixteenth and early seventeenth centuries, appear similar to those advanced later by the physiocrats. To Mariana, agriculture supported everything and therefore proper and full use of the land should be encouraged, or, if necessary, the land should be expropriated and cultivated by the government itself. Further, farmers should be permitted to select the crops that returned the most profits. He recognized the negative affects of high tariffs and monopolies. He advocated the recruitment of foreign craftsmen and the need for government economic intervention, even to the extent of providing employment on needed public projects in times of depression. Yet Mariana never separated moral and economic objectives. Only if his ideas are isolated from his general perspective do they seem modern. The expansion of commerce and trade that followed on the heels of the Portuguese voyages, and the establishment of the Spanish American empire, represented to Mariana the growing friendship and charity between all the nations involved in far-flung commerce.[2] Never attracted to material possessions, Mariana did not envision the Western world's struggle over resources.

The need to concoct a remedy for Spain's perceived economic malaise also attracted the imaginative energy of other seventeenth-century theorists. The so-called *arbitristas*, while suggesting solutions ranging from cutting expenditures, tax relief, repopulation, internal improvements, and the stimulation of industry and agriculture, did not comprehend fully the interlocking nature of the country's problems. Consequently, most focused on one or two issues in isolation. The lack of comprehensive planning and a broad perspective doomed such plans to failure.[3] Nevertheless, a number of individuals moved toward a new pattern of thought. Miguel Alvarez Osorio, for example, presented Carlos II with a number of memorials that indicated a detailed knowledge of the economy, including agriculture, industry, finance, and commerce. Approaching his topic in a deliberate, scientific, and analytical fashion, Alvarez Osorio linked agriculture, industry and public administration, including education, foreshadowing eighteenth-century reformers.[4] His views on state intervention went beyond mercantilism to suggest a remolding of society. While he could not rid himself of the flights of fancy that undermined much of the work of the arbitristas, his expansive inquiries represented an intellectual contribution. The Count of Campomanes reprinted Alvarez Osorio's discourses in 1775. A number of his contemporaries deserved similar credit.[5]

In the early eighteenth century, the decisive move toward a material basis for royal authority is evident in Father Juan de Cabrera's instructive *Crisis política* (1719) in which he demonstrated the growing strength of the belief that the state should take primary and active responsibility for the prosperity of its subjects.[6] Cabrera pointedly noted that the government, before worrying about the needs of the treasury, should attend to the prosperity of its factories.[7] The task of implementing the natural economic order required a strong state to rearrange existing, but harmful, accommodations and provide for proper functioning of the newly discovered or appreciated economic laws. The state remained protected from the charge of arbitrary action by the notion that it implemented the natural economic order as it became known, rather than actually fabricating it. In the late eighteenth century, Gaspar Melchor de Jovellanos, one of the most influential enlightened thinkers, defined happiness as "that state of abundance and comfort which a good government ought to procure for its subjects.)[8] By the early nineteenth century, Alvaro Florez Estrada's flat statement that "the only greatness of a prince consists of his promoting by every possible means the prosperity of his nation" could be accepted by most educated Spaniards.[9]

The critical thought of the eighteenth century rested upon an analytical method that stressed intellectual unity. The interlocking nature of knowledge made it possible to think in terms of systems that could be projected toward a determined goal. This conception of knowledge differed from that inherent in the medieval concept of the Great Chain of Being, although that image also included a perception of unity. While the Great Chain of Being linked every speck of creation from the lowest to the divine, it did not suggest that man could unravel, or even comprehend, such plenitude. Nevertheless, man through reason mounted the ladder of understanding toward truth and the contemplation of divine goodness.[10] In contrast, the eighteenth-century chain of reason moved horizontally in a secular search for the links that bound worldly knowledge together. Materialism proceeded to isolate and devalue spirituality. Reforms, aimed at the coprosperity of the monarchy and the people, changed the economic structure as well as the organization of the state.

Formulation of an Ideology of Change

Benito Gerónimo Feijóo y Montenegro, (1676-1764) a professor of theology and a Benedictine monk, popularized the new method and critical spirit in Spain. His *Teatro crítico universal*, published in nine volumes, reached the public in 1739, soon to be followed by another five volumes under the title of *Cartas eruditas*. Feijóo believed in the progress of science as exemplified by Francis Bacon, René Descartes, and Isaac Newton. The experimental and critical methodology of the Enlightenment as cautiously championed by Feijóo could be accepted, if not fully, at least as worthy of discussion. His adroitness at sidestepping troubling aspects of the new knowledge while introducing the skepticism necessary to guide his readers to a critical conclusion led to bolder steps in subsequent decades.[11]

As a transitional theoretician, Feijóo retained traditional values at the same time he espoused new ideas. He attacked Machiavelli's conception of the state, and upheld the notion that the monarch, as a divine agent, ruled because God so commanded.[12] Yet his view of the best type of ruler reflected the Enlightenment's antiheroic materialism. He posited two archtypes, the peaceful prince (*el príncipe pacífico*) and the prince-conqueror (*el príncipe conquistador*). The peaceful prince pursued peace and economic development, stressed education, encouraged research in the sciences and useful arts, promoted an active commerce, and provided for the security and comfort of his subjects—in effect, a "great and glorious king." The prince-conqueror, however, exerted a negative influence.[13] While accepting the formative influence of a country's unique historical development, Feijóo rejected the defeatist notion that the human spirit and ingenuity varied from people to people. Backwardness did not have to be fatalistically accepted, nor could the destructive notion that inferiority was grounded in inherent character defects be permitted to block reforms. The historical reality, subjected to critical analysis to identify the cause of decline, could itself suggest the remedy. Feijóo advocated an active and positive stance rather than acceptance of Spanish incapacity.[14]

The perception of a progressively unfolding and interrelated fund of knowledge demanded firm direction. Compartmentalization of activities had to be broken down and placed within a broader perceptual pattern. The state found itself pressed to accept managerial responsibilities and control by the particular configuration of ideas elaborated by a series of influential theorists.[15] One of these, Melchor de Macanaz (1670-1760) went straight to the point in his advice to Felipe V. He flatly rejected the notion that the well-being of the state existed apart from that of its subject. After all, he noted, rich American mines counted for little when the exchequer remained weak and the king's vassals miserable.[16] Taxes should increase only with the wealth of the king's subjects, and if that declined, so should the levies. The monarch's duty was to attack nonproductive elements that monopolized as well as wasted assets. Moreover, Melchor de Macanaz advised the king to set an example for the grandes and others of wealth by becoming the nation's principal businessman (*comerciante*).[17]

Typical of economic thought in the early eighteenth century, the ideas of Melchor de Macanaz were both archaic and progressive. He supported sumptuary laws and decried extravagance but did not appreciate the need to stimulate consumption as an incentive to produce. As a mercantilist, he viewed immigration as a drain on the mother country. More positively, he suggested the formation of private and publicly supported patriotic societies to stimulate industrial and agricultural development—an idea subsequently implemented by the Count of Campomanes.

Tax policy provided a consistent opportunity to present extensive reform programs. Bernardo Francisco Aznar, under the direction of the Marqués de Campoflorido, Secretary of the Treasury, composed a critique in 1724 entitled *Discurso que formó tocante a la Real Hacienda y administración de ella.* (Discourse on the administration of the Royal treasury). Aznar's report, published in 1727, catalogued the bewildering array of regional and local taxes. Reflecting the thinking of officials charged with revenue collection, he warned against partial and superficial adjustments, and advocated rational and comprehensive tax reduction. His memorial cautioned the monarch against state industrial or commercial concerns, allegedly because such activities detracted from the royal dignity.[18] The ideal modern ruler functioned at a higher level, actively creating internal conditions conducive to industrial development while leaving the actual operations of such concerns to private individuals.[19]

The widely held perception that the country supported too many parasites resulted in demands that the government break their hold on the nation. Once the nonproductive groups engendered by Spain's particular historical experience had been identified, the state would have to alter the circumstances that perpetuated them. Consequently, the monarchy attempted to ennoble commercial activities and pressure a swollen, and often semi-impoverished, aristocracy into productive enterprises. Economists pressed for the development of a *nobleza comerciante* (commercially involved nobility) and replacement of the archaic notion that the aristocracy's primary function was to bear arms in defense of the Crown.[20] A redefined nobility would be forced to justify its privileges on the strength of its economic contribution or risk slipping into the ranks of commoners. Efforts to create a productive nobility raised the status of commoners already engaged in commercial activities.

Melchor de Macanaz advised Felipe V to ennoble them formally as an incentive, as did Gerónimo de Uztáriz. Valentín de Foronda (1751-1820) subsequently argued in 1778 that so many benefits accrued to the state from the commercial activities of particular commoners that they deserved noble privileges.[21] The monarchy, although anxious to remove any stigma connected with commerce, shied away from bestowing noble status on enterprising commoners for fear they might give up their productive activities. The extension of quasi-noble status, by bestowing privileges associated with the aristocracy, seemed politically safer and more reasonable.[22]

Elaboration of an ideology designed to strengthen the political economy and commercial activity in the face of institutional obstacles, traditional attitudes and customs, and foreign contraband competition required time and a number of false starts. Scholasticism in its principle variations remained influential through the reign of Carlos III.[23] As a consequence, officials often accepted traditional methods in one area of concern while employing a modern innovative approach elsewhere. Such ambiguity is evident in the thinking of the secretary of the Junta de Comercio, Gerónimo de Uztáriz (1670-1732), subsequently a member of the Consejo de Hacienda and the Cámara de Indias. He had traveled extensively throughout Europe and England and established a reputation as an expert on European economic affairs. Although Uztáriz depended upon mercantilism to provide the theoretical framework, his pragmatism contributed to the development of liberal economics. In his *Teórica y práctica del comercio y de marina* (1724), written the year before he became a member of the junta, he addressed immediate problems and outlined long-range objectives. His ideas mixed nascent laissez-faire thought with demands for decisive state intervention.

Gerónimo de Uztáriz believed that backward industrial conditions resulted from inadequate protection from foreign competition; yet he warned against overprotection, privileges, and outmoded taxes that discouraged productivity as well as commerce.[24] He attacked the creation of monopoly trading companies, then under discussion, because of their official and privileged nature, asserting that broad and general initiative should be stimulated instead.[25] He viewed as futile all regulations and laws that ran counter to the natural course of trade. Lower prices, and reduced customs duties, would do more to drive out contraband traders than unrealistic regulations and monopoly companies. Uztáriz, drawing upon F. Huet's discussion of Dutch commerce, characterized Spain's economic attitude at that time as passive and maintained that, as a result, much of the fruits of trade and commerce were falling into foreign hands. According to the economist, an active policy designed to change the structure would profit all. Subsequently, the notion of active verses passive commercial policies became popular. Gaspar Melchor de Jovellanos repeated the characterization in his *Economía civil* (1776), as did a treasury official in New Spain, Ramón de Posada, in his 1781 *Teórica y práctica informé sobre el comercio de harina* (Theory and Practice; Report in the Commerce of Flour.[26] In addition, to direct state action, Uztáriz suggested that consulados or regional juntas de comercio under the jurisdiction of the Junta General de Comercio be created to encourage commercial and supporting activities. He also urged the establishment of royal academies of science, fine arts, and architecture.[27] Uztáriz obviously influenced superintendent of the mint Fernando Josef Mangino's proposal to establish the Academy of San Carlos in Mexico. The previously established (1770) school of surgery in Mexico City also reflected his recommendations.[28]

A similar line of thought is evident in the writings of Bernardo de Ulloa, an admirer of Gerónimo de Uztáriz. Ulloa's 1740 *Restablecimiento de las fábricas y comercio español* (Revival of Spanish Industry of Commerce) placed the burden of change on the state. Besides the now familiar call for tax reduction, he advocated opening the Philippine trade to all Spanish ports as a means of bringing about an economic resurgence. Interestingly, he did not suggest that America be included in this liberalized trade scheme. In common with many economists, Ulloa was obsessed with the problem of contraband trade in the empire. He called for state investment when necessary, particularly in transportation. The proposal implied the need for state strong enough to dismantle restrictions and move toward definite economic goals. An image of a powerful government, intervening against its now archaic corporate parts, is inescapable.[29]

José del Campillo y Cossío (1693-1743), Felipe V's Minister of State, Navy, War, and the Indies, epitomized early eighteenth-century political economists. Campillo became one of the most influential commentators on Spain's ills. His early writings reflected the frustration, even panic, that gripped thoughtful individuals when they contemplated the situation. In his 1741 *Lo que hay de más y de menos en España*, he presented a generous list of what the country lacked, balanced by a bitter enumeration of abundant, but negative elements. According to Campillo, the country suffered from a lack of agriculture, defenses, commerce, diligence, discipline, education, factories, government, hospices, inventiveness, justice, learned men, good bureaucrats, ships, public works, population, artisan guilds, small farms, reality, intellectuals, wheat, and finally, virtue. On the other side of Campillo's grim ledger, Spain supposedly had an excessive amount of debauchery (*abandono*), idle gentry (*bastones*), contributions, elegance of carriage, poor writers, friars, thefts, Indies, judges, laws, prostitutes, inept businessmen, idle, privileges, complaints, laxity, excessive pride, taxes, and vice. Campillo's list suggested a stream of consciousness and word association indicative of a bitter and deep pessimism.[30] Complementing this grim accounting was his *España despierta*, which proposed remedies but offered no new approaches. Campillo's major work, the *Nuevo sistema*, in contrast, represented one of the first comprehensive reform plans that drew on the Enlightenment's critical method. Campillo accepted the idea that diversified trade stimulated both consumption and production. Individual self-interest, rationally pursued, would engender a positive mixture of enterprises. The *Nuevo sistema* asserted that commerce maintained the body politic in the same fashion as the blood's circulation benefited the body.[31] Campillo defined a good government as one that provided its people with the means to enrich themselves and, as a natural but secondary consequence, the state. The government should direct the country's resources toward beneficial ends and should invest in transportation and the introduction of new technology. He supported the development of colonial industries that did not compete with those of the mother country.[32]

Campillo insisted that both Spain and the Indies needed reform designed to stimulate development. Tax policy should be used to influence domestic as well as foreign trade, and encourage the poor to produce and consume. In addition, by removing the artificial restrictions that stifled his natural instinct, the Indian could be transformed into a self-motivated producer and consumer. Campillo advocated encouraging an equality of class, not race. To facilitate a fusion, authorities should urge Indians to adopt European dress.[33] The state had the obligation to manage the economy for the "universal benefit of all classes," stimulate industry, agriculture, and artisans' skills, and advance everyone's interest "from the king to the lowest day laborer."[34] Campillo called for a general inspection of the empire to determine possibilities, and the establishment of the intendant system of political organization. Subsequently, Carlos III proceeded to implement reforms in the manner suggested by Campillo.[35] A Junta Tecnica composed of specialists was established in 1764 and given the task of implementing the new economic thought. Their report, submitted in February 1765, advocated the termination of Cádiz's monopoly on the colonial trade, removal of excessive customs duties and taxes, and abandonment of the outmoded convoy system.[36]

The integrated perspective, or systems approach to reform, was further advanced by Francisco Roma y Rosell, an economist, attorney for the poor of the Audiencia, and member of the Royal Conference of

Physics and Agriculture of Barcelona. Roma linked diverse elements in a "chain." Agriculture, industry, commerce, and population formed major segments linked together, but each also formed its own chain. A monarchy with an archaic "link" in the chain, like a machine with an inoperative part, could not function. A state must have an operational plan that defined its objectives, facilitated their attainment, and assured the utility of its actions.[37]

Although the state assumed responsibility and direction, individual initiative, responding to opportunities created by reforms, played a major role. Bernardo Ward in his *Proyecto económico* (written in 1754, but published in 1779) observed that just as a river begins with a few drops, prosperity depends on the activities of many individuals attending to their own interests. The state might assist, but the task itself had to be shared.[38] Moreover, if the monarchy persuaded individuals to venture the capital hidden in private strongboxes, Spain could reap ten times the profit derived from the Indies. Cultivation of the soil and economic development depended on the active circulation of currency. Ward viewed money as an instrument of circulation and credit subject to positive and negative political manipulation. Too much money in circulation raised prices and wages but also had the positive effect of making credit inexpensive. Although the use of credit by the state itself might be marginally productive or harmful, it was unquestionably useful in the hands of private individuals. Ten pesos, according to Ward, going through ten hands generated as much benefit as one hundred going through two.[39] Commerce, divided by Ward into useful and prejudicial or active and passive, allegedly depended on a sound monetary policy. The government's responsibilities included dismantling privileged monopolies, artisan guilds, restricted associations, special taxes collected by individual cities or localities on commercial activity, and anything else that impeded individual enterprises. Furthermore, the bureaucracy needed to be consolidated and centralized.

As for the American colonies, Ward, drawing on Campillo, proposed a general inspection and strengthening of colonial governments preparatory to the establishment of a new economic order. Ward shared Campillo's sense of frustration with Spain's inability to profit from its empire—a frustration that engendered a hostile attitude toward the Indies. He asserted that colonial governance had fallen into the hands of a bastard caste of second-rate politicians.[40] Like Campillo, Ward advocated providing Indians with land and assistance, and freeing them from negative and initiative-stifling supervision. He differed from Campillo on the question of colonial industry, recommending that factories not be permitted. He suggested, however, if Cádiz merchants failed to understand the need for mutually beneficial reforms, the Crown should then permit the establishment of New World factories—at least the royal treasury would receive increased revenue.[41] Supposedly, tax and customs reduction, together with free navigations, would make Spanish goods cheap and attractive; thus both the mother country and the colonies stood to benefit.

Once the retrogressive nature of the empire had been established by political economists, confirmation soon followed. Colonial officials under increasing pressure offered excuses and explanations that confirmed the preconceived notions of colonial vices held by enlightened ministers. Manuel de Amat, Viceroy of Peru (1766-1776), who conducted his administration in the traditional fashion, nevertheless explained his government's deficiencies in terms acceptable to Madrid. Viceroy Amat, aware that Madrid viewed colonial officials as corrupt and economically parasitic, associated himself with the new ideology by attacking the traditional governing structure from the provincial corregidores to the Audiencia. He alleged that with few and notable exceptions, they thought of little but their own interests.[42] Amat's criticism centered on economic issues, addressing political factors only to the extent they had a negative impact on the economy. In a similar fashion, a corregidor struggled to identify himself with the new critical attitude. Almost as an article of faith, he declared his belief that the true happiness of a kingdom rested on a large and expanding population dedicated to active commerce—hardly a novel idea, but one sure to find approval among enlightened officials who responded to a mixture of mercantilism, physiocratic ideas, and proto-utilitarian economic notions. The corregidor observed that priests and local officials misdirected the Indian population, and as a consequence they lived in poverty and continued to experience a sad and wasteful decline. Sweepingly he characterized Peru as a region given over to destructive and insatiable greed.[43]

Jorge Juan y Santacilia and Antonio de Ulloa, son of the economist Bernardo de Ulloa, were two of the most influential official reporters on American problems in the mid-eighteenth century. Both young lieutenants, educated at the elite Naval Academy, they personified the new man intellectually molded by the scientific thought of the Enlightenment and expected to contribute to Spain's moderization. Felipe V assigned both officers to the expedition dispatched by the French Academy of Science to measure a degree of the meridian at the Kingdom of Quito (Ecuador).[44] Upon their return to Europe, the Marqués de Ensenada ordered them to report on the state of the region. Their report (1749), an internal document, offered a frank, brutal assessment of the political and social situation, as well as a series of recommended reforms. Inclined to label as archaic or corrupt practices that conflicted with the rational economic goals contained within the official ideology, they approached their task as men of the Enlightenment. They had little patience with the various forms of accommodation that had developed, or with the perceived economic mismanagement over which the colonial authorities presided. Like other individuals trained in the scientific fashion, they believed that a problem, once identified, should be resolved rationally and immediately.[45] Juan and Ulloa appeared to be apolitical men adrift in the traditional sea of Hapsburg philosophical notions where political consideration took precedence over economic matters. Their rational, economically oriented frame of reference was narrow and the degree of flexibility and accommodation they believed proper correspondingly limited.

The first issue dealt within their report was the contraband trade—a problem that political economists believed robbed Spain of the advantages of its empire. Juan and Ulloa soon confirmed this view. They portrayed illicit trade as the dominant economic force in the region, and one which in turn corrupted the government. Royal officials responsible for regulating trade accepted bribes and competed with each other to attract the greatest volume of illegal trade to their particular ports. Even the viceroy in Lima claimed to be powerless to stop the flood of contraband into the capital. Merchants introduced smuggled goods openly into the city at high noon. The Marqués de Villagarcía (1736-1745) reportedly dispatched an honest dedicated agent to the coast to stop the illegal traffic only to have him co-opted, as was his immediate successor. Finally, the viceroy sent the *alcalde de corte*, who returned the corregidor and other officials to Lima to stand trial. When the case came before the Audiencia, the charges had been watered down to the extent they scarcely merited even a small fine.[46] The report pictured an active trade that stretched from Peru to Panama, New Spain, and Manila, but which provided few benefits for the mother country. Juan and Ulloa avoided drawing the conclusion that trade flowed in natural directions and responded to circumstances over which Spain had little control, although they proposed that a more rational and calculated introduction of merchandise, and the buildup of the merchant marine, might help.

Evident in the report is the concern expressed by José del Campillo and others that the resources of the empire had been badly used and allowed to fall into the hands of a few who extracted large profit without attention to the general prosperity. Supposedly, an "utter absence of reason" contributed to the wide variety of exploitive abuses.[47] An ignorant and miserable population, subjected to parasitic practices, could not effectively produce or consume. Corregidores not only profitably manipulated tribute collection but also engaged in lucrative forced trade (*repartimiento de comercio*) with the population. Allied with powerful merchants they excluded others, controlled the sale and rental of mule transport, and otherwise dominated economic activity. The report identified the enemies of well-being and true prosperity as a corrupt bureaucracy, a parasitic dissolute clergy, illegal commerce, a society split into factions, and an exploitive economy that discouraged production and consumption and increased the likelihood of revolt. Juan and Ulloa presented a picture of a society that had perverted the colonial government and turned it to its own advantage.

The two observers approached actual abuses in a manner that suggested the remedies. Selection and definition of the problem in enlightened terms led logically to predictable solutions. The report constituted an eighteenth-century formulation of reality. The economic solutions proposed included the exclusion of all corregidores from commerce and the amalgamation or elimination of small corregimientos. They rejected the notion that Indian sloth and indolence required coercive direction, suggesting that self-interest as well as the return of a proportion of Indian land would be sufficient. Juan and Ulloa addressed economic problems; political issues had importance only as they adversely affected material prospects.

While many officials appeared to accept the frequent civil disruptions, riots, and even localized rebellion as almost a natural state of affairs, the report viewed them as proof of the urgency of reform.[48] Addressing perceived political problems, Juan and Ulloa recommended that laws be drawn precisely so as to eliminate flexibility and that legislation be reduced to regulations. In line with this suggestion, they recommended that the viceroy's independent "sovereignty" be curtailed, coverting him from a politician into a bureaucratic administrator. The report complained that Peruvians confused the viceroy with the king to the extent that "he must feel himself a king in his own right."[49] Juan and Ulloa offered welcome confirmation, based on direct knowledge, of the soundness of the views of Madrid's enlightened ministers. Their report represented a significant step toward the implementation of the new ideology in the empire.

Pedro Rodríguez de Campomanes, the Count of Campomanes (1723-1803), became one of the most influential proponents of the new political economy. A scholar and publicist, he published and circulated the works of the earlier economists. He accepted the idea that the state had to be an active intervenor in certain areas, and in others encourage and permit private initiative to function without interference. The Count emphasized the interrelated nature of the task and the need to identify errors systematically and objectively and then correct them.[50] The state had the responsibility to free the internal economy from the sterile grip of powerful, but regressive elements. For example, he viewed the *mesta* (sheep raisers' guild) and its right to reserve common pasture as a major obstacle to the development of a self-interested and prosperous peasantly. Campomanes cited the village of Espinar as an example of a potentially prosperous community if the commons could be enclosed, the livestock divided, and the capital raised from land sales invested in small-scale textile production.[51]

In 1765 Campomanes published his *Tratado de la regalía de amortización* under the auspices of the Council of Castile. In the Tratado he attacked clerical property as a barrier to the generation and circulation of wealth. Initiative and self-interest required a fluid rather than a static concept of wealth. Artisan guilds, in a similar fashion, appeared to discourage innovation and initiative. Economic societies, enthusiastically supported by the Count, were proposed as a counterbalance to the guilds. Such groups, only loosely linked to the government that served as their patron, would be responsible for introducing new technology and otherwise encouraging individuals to pursue their own self-interest. The state itself could discourage counter-productive customs by educating the public on the evils of idleness, excessive holidays, alcohol consumption, and poor work habits, all of which increased production costs.[52]

Campomanes shared the general view of the empire based on José del Campillo's analysis and the confirmation provided by Juan and Ulloa's report. Cádiz's merchants and their American trade monopoly had ruined both internal manufacturing and colonial commerce. While Spain had every right to reserve colonial trade for itself, it had to be administered in a rational fashion; thus negative taxes and restrictive practices could not be continued. Nevertheless, liberty of commerce had to be reconciled with the needs of the metropolis. The Indies, according to Campomanes's vision, would have to play the major role in Spain's economic and political resurgence, and thus trade must be within a Spanish system.[53] In the *Discurso sobre la educación popular* (1775), Campomanes examined the problems of trans-Atlantic trade. The ideas he expressed there appeared three years later in the *Reglamento de comercio libre* that ended Cádiz's monopoly and opened an expanded number of peninsula ports to direct colonial contact.

The movement toward an economic formulation of authority remained uneven and ambivalent. Baltasar Melchor Gaspar María de Jovellanos (1774-1811), an important theorist although less influential on an official level than Campomanes, exhibited some of the intellectual contradictions of the new attitude. Influenced by Adam Smith, John

Locke, and Adam Ferguson among others, and determined to follow reason, Jovellanos reflected the economic pragmatism of the Spanish Enlightenment. At the same time, he expressed such traditional values as the medieval concept of an organic society and the notion of virtue and merit, and was a defender of the monarchical system. His contradictions, as well as those of his colleagues, were a result not only of the strength of the traditional philosophical matrix but also of the fact that the ideology, because of its inherent nature as a limited set of ideas, could not always define a satisfactory reality, allowing traditional notions to reassert themselves.

Jovellanos blamed the nation's decline on a government consisting of lawyers and a magistracy without any understanding of its office or of history or science.[54] He attacked the notion of judicial balance because it appeared unable to provide the leadership necessary to implement an active ideology. Mirroring the age, Jovellanos linked material prosperity and power. The state set policy, while the true productive source of strength lay with the nation's workers and their skills. Public instruction encouraged by the government enabled individuals to pursue self-interest and ultimately benefit the nation.[55] State responsibilities, however, had to be implemented without destroying individual liberty. In common with most theorists, Jovellanos conceived of liberty and self-interest as pertaining only to the individual. Corporate groups free to follow their collective self-interest tended to become obstacles indulging in monopoly and other negative practices. The state thus had to move against corporate groups and block their natural tendency to kill individual initiative.[56] Jovellanos's best-known contribution to economic thought, the *Informe en el expediente de ley agraria* (1795), published under the auspices of Madrid's Economic Society, placed the obstacles to prosperity into three categories—political, moral, and natural. If the first two could be effectively deal with, the third would result in natural perfection.[57] Productive elements ought to be able to expect liberty, enlightenment, and assistance—in short, a favorable atmosphere for the free exercise of individual self-interest.

The elaborations of an economic justification of authority did not depend solely upon critiques circulated among small groups of officials, or upon more widely circulated books. Periodicals directed at the literate population indoctrinated a broader constituency in the basic outlines of the new thought and the changing political perspectives it engendered. Starting in a timid fashion, periodicals soon became a major element in the formulation of an ideology of change. One of the first efforts, the *Diario de los literatos* (1735), died almost at birth, followed by the equally fleeting *Mercurio histórico y político de Madrid*. In 1755 Juan Enrique

Graef published the *Discursos mercuriales*, exposing his readers to informative articles dealing with agriculture and commerce. Subsequently, Francisco Mariano Nipho edited a series of state-subsidized periodicals. The proto-modern state of Spanish journalism began after 1750. Nipho's *Diario noticioso, curioso-erudito y comercial, público y económico* (1758) provided the first daily coverage.[58] In 1761 Joseph Clavijo y Faxardo, who subsequently translated the Comte de Buffon's work, issued *El pensador*, using his pen to beat mercilessly the idle aristocracy and taunt those who accused others of heresy simply because they espoused new ideas.[59] In a similar fashion *El censor* (1781) published by Luis Cañuelo ridiculed elements opposed to the new thought. *El censor* inspired *El apologista universal* (1786) by the Augustinian monk Pedro Centeno, *El corresponsal de censor*, and other publications. Two important periodicals dedicated to spreading useful knowledge were the *Correo literario de la Europa* (1780-81, 1786-87) and the *Espiritu de los mejores diarios literatos que se publica en Europa* (1787-91). Another influential publication, the *Semanario erudito* (1781) published by Antonio Valladares de Sotomayor, made available the latest criticism and analysis dealing with political and administrative affairs, industry, commerce, and modern morals, often employing Spain's own history and thinkers to make the point.[60]

Growing recognition of the role of newspapers in the spread of knowledge stimulated journalism within the empire. *La gaceta de la Havana*, patterned after the *Diario de los avisos* of Madrid, began publication in May 1764. The same year a weekly, *El pensador*, edited by two lawyers, entered the field. While both proved short-lived, they paved the way for other efforts.[61] In new Spain, José Antonio de Alzate y Ramírez's *El diario literario de Mexico* (1768) lasted only three months. He returned to journalism in 1772 with an equally fleeting effort, the *Asuntos varios sobre ciencias y artes*, the same year José Ignacio Bartolache edited the *Mercurio Volante con noticias importantes y curiosas sobre física y medicina*. A fourteen-year hiatus followed before Alzate tried again in 1787-88, this time under the title *Observaciones sobre la física, historia natural y artes útiles*.[62] His final effort, the *Gaceta de literatura de Mexico* (1788-95), indicated the increasing maturity of the colonial press. The outpouring of knowledge emphasized the interrelated nature and potential usefulness of all knowledge.[63]

The transitory nature of many publications may be explained by marketing and circulation problems and the need to stay within certain bounds. For example, the Marqués de Croix suppressed Alzate's first journalistic effort allegedly because of offensive material. Whether he objected to the topic of the issue in question, which dealt with the theater, or a phrase that could be interpreted as a slight against the viceroy himself, is not clear. The same fate awaited Alzate's next effort, suppressed by order of Viceroy Bucareli. Subsequently, the viceroy, aware that Alzate had prepared an essay on cochineal at the request of José Antonio Areche, soon to make an uncertain reputation as an enlightened reformer, asked for an expanded version. Obviously, the line between constructive criticism or useful knowledge so pleasing to those in authority and unacceptable notions could not be easily identified by the energetic scientist. Ironically, his last venture into print also came to an end in 1795 after he criticized Viceroy Revillagigedo.[64] The state reserved the right to judge the utility of journalistic efforts. Yet, the willingness of the state to tolerate, encourage, and even financially support a number of newspapers indicated an appreciation of the press's ability to mold opinion. While some confusion continued to exist as to whether newspapers constituted literature or simply written communication, the directive impact of journalism on the public had been recognized.[65]

Newspapers emphasized indoctrination rather than originality. José Baquíjano in Peru demonstrated the general lack of creativity; his articles often contained paragraphs taken directly from Hume, Quesnay, Adam Smith, and others.[66] It is apparent that many supported journalism as a means of indicating their attachment to modernity as well as official policy. Educated individuals, desirous of demonstrating their support, hastened to subscribe. Manuel del Socorro Rodríguez, editor of the *Papel periódico de la ciudad de Santafé de Bogotá* (1791-97) proudly published a subscription list that included the viceroy, the archbishop, members of the Audiencia, a host of royal administrators, and the noted scientist José Celestino Mutis. Newspaper editors viewed their efforts as a civic contribution. The founders of the bi-weekly *Mercurio peruano* in late 1790 all expected some sign of royal favor in acknowledgment of their contribution.[67] Alzate, no doubt wisely, dedicated his second newspaper to the king in the most flattering terms as "Carlos the wise, Carlos the prudent, Carlos our sovereign," and in a more traditional fashion, "Carlos the father of his vassals."[68]

The Problem Defined

By the latter half of the eighteenth century, both the problems as well as the proposed solutions had fallen into a set pattern. A regressive and crippling tax system, poor administrative organization, archaic attitudes, parasitic corporate and privileged groups, lack of industry and commerce, an impoverished and sparse population—all were noted and lamented. Most of the proposed solutions depended on the active state's ability to change the existing structure. More importantly, the point was made that the state's legitimate existence rested on the responsibility of assuring material well-being. In the projected economic rejuvenation, the empire played a key role. While restrictions needed to be lifted within the empire, few advocated throwing the empire open to the world economy.[69]

The dangers inherent in an aggressive state did not go unappreciated. The anonymous author of the *Cartas político-económicas al Conde de Lerena* (1787-89) bluntly observed that all-encompassing authority risked great evils, but the malaise that possessed the land could only be cured by overwhelming power.[70] As the Count of Floridablanca noted, in order to do one good thing, four hundred bad situations had to be undone.[71] The perception of political economists of the magnitude of the task at hand demanded a strong authority to stimulate confidence and develop a sense of mutual advantage arising from individual self-interest, as appeared to be the case in England.[72] Thus, while a strong monarchy might be best for Spain at the moment, in the future the situation could well be different. The *Cartas político-económicas*, reflecting the influence of Rousseau, noted that the social pact implied a mutual arrangement; if a society decided that its form of government might lead to ruin, it had the authority to change it.

The logical implications for the monarchical structure of government were understood and discussed privately by enlightened theorists. They became and remained regalists out of utility, not principle, a position Sánchez Agesta aptly called "hipocresía táctica."[73] They shared a loyalty to an ideology that subordinated political considerations, including the monarchy itself, to material progress. The preception that the problem and its solution constituted a unified whole pressed the state to implement corrective measures. If the state failed to take action, it became part of the problem.

Ideologues constantly searched for confirmation of their operational principles, and some devised models to demonstrate cause and effect. State factories provided a concrete example of this tendency.[74] Such establishments, while reducing dependence on foreign sources of supply, served as technical displays to introduce and diffuse modern methods. The government lured foreign artisans and technicians with lucrative contracts. Foreigners provided the nucleus for the largest such operation, the royal factory at Guadajara, which functioned until 1820.[75] Although state enterprises received active support throughout the century, they failed to prosper. Mismanagement and operating deficits forced the closing, leasing, or even outright ceding of many of these ventures.[76] Nevertheless, attempts by the state to eliminate or at least lessen the obstacles to the introduction of new technology did have an effect.

The same motivation lay behind the establishment of New Spain's mining tribunal. Mexican mining analysts had long urged the Crown to become actively involved. Royal officials, aware that mining functioned as the economic engine of the region's prosperity, and fortified with the ideological confidence of the era, moved to rationalize the industry. Officials suspected that new methods designed to increase productivity required not only encouragement but also pressure. Characteristic of the ideology, the mining tribunal embodied the directive rationalism of the enlightened state.[77]

On the political level, the perceived need for a powerful state prompted the dismantling of the conciliar system of government. Structural changes represented the rationalization of the governing system in conformity with the new ideology. The virtues of the traditional system— corporate balance, maintenance of the status quo, and predictability— became, if not vices, no longer desirable. While change would have occurred even if the Spanish Hapsburg dynasty had not been extinguished, in 1700 the introduction of the French Bourbon monarchy under Felipe V (1700-1746) accelerated existing tendencies. Innovations could not have succeeded, however, had they not coincided with philosophical changes already under way. With a tendency to vacillate, and troubled with mental instability, Felipe fortunately had only to go along with the reform movement. Baltasar Patiño, who became his principal minister in 1726, guided such efforts.

Even before Patiño assumed direction, structural changes opened the way for implementation of an active policy. Drawing upon the political advantage achieved as a result of the successful outcome of the War of the Spanish Succession, the Crown established a more unified and administratively centralized government. The new regime extended the Castilian system into Aragón and Valencia in 1707, and into Catalonia in 1716. Aragón continued to have a separate legal code, but administered by the monarchy. Only Navarre and the Basque region retained their historic privileges, although royal authority was strengthened.[78] New procedures, introduced by French officials brought in for that purpose, changed the relationship between the state and its subjects. The process was not without setbacks. Premature establishment in 1718 of a new type of provincial administrator, the intendant, modeled on the French system, provoked such a reaction from the traditional bureaucratic structure that it had to be suspended. The ordinance of 1718 attempted to invest the new administrative system with Iberian historical roots, claiming that it had originated in Spain, been employed effectively in other nations, and was now being resurrected in its country of origin.[79] Manipulation of history failed to camouflage its more immediate antecedents. Eventually, Fernando VI succeeded in reestablishing the intendant system in 1749.[80]

By 1714 the conciliar governing system began to give way to a ministerial structure. Felipe V established the Ministry of Marine and the Indies, among others, only to suppress it the following year. Nevertheless, the Council of the Indies did not regain its old authority, but received instructions to reserve significant matters for direct disposition by the king of his appointed agent (via reservada). Finally, in 1721 the Crown reestablished the Ministry of Marine and the Indies. Its minister combined much of the authority of the Council of the Indies and the Case de Contratación. Fernando VI, in 1754 and 1755, established the five secretariats of State and Foreign Relations, Justice and Ecclesiastical Affairs, War, Treasury, and Marine and the Indies. In 1787 Charles III divided Marine and the Indies into two, and added a seventh, that of Navigation and Commerce. The division of Marine and the Indies lasted only a few years before both were suppressed, and their duties distributed among the remaining ministries. After 1790 the Council of the Indies functioned mainly as a supreme colonial appellate judicial tribunal, the same year the Casa de Contratación was abolished completely. Specialized concerns fell to ministers who acted as autonomous executives directly responsible to the king.[81]

Each of these high officials carried the title of Secretario de Estado y del Despacho Universal of a particular secretariat (Secretary of State of the universal office of. . .). One individual might control three or four of these positions, as did Baltasar Patiño, José del Campillo, the Marqués de la Ensenada, and others; therefore, it is correct to identify such individuals as prime ministers. A minister might also be a member, and on occasion even president, of one of the councils, thereby bridging the new and traditional governing structures.[82] The need for cooperation among the various ministries led to the creation of a joint junta. Until 1787 the junta functioned in an irregular and ad hoc fashion. After that date, however, Carlos III authorized the formal establishment of a Junta de Estado—in modern terms, a cabinet.[83] Councils continued to perform administrative and advisory functions but progressively lost influence. Understandably, the Conde de Floridablanca hailed the creation of the Junta de Estado as Carlos III's greatest reform.[84]

The material justification of authority directly affected the relationship between the people and a restructured monarchy. The notion that political justification rested upon economic utility transformed the monarchy from a mystical and spiritual institution into one based on performance. The de facto severing of the state's link with the divine left the monarch at the mercy of his subjects, now free to insist on material results. The positive assumption that the monarchy reflected divine benevolence, even if not immediately recognizable, no longer provided political support. Economic progress and material well-being became the yardstick, and the state became accountable. Concrete criteria emerged for evaluating a government's effectiveness that touched on its right to rule. The most Catholic monarch became the *comerciante principal* — from vicar of God to the custodian of material progress. The elevation of individual self-interest moved the monarch from the center of the economic and political universe to the periphery. Moreover, the goal became more important than the type of state. The monarchy's continued existence depended on its ability to attain set objectives.

An ideology of change based on economic criteria depersonalized royal service. The head of state no longer served as the focus of government service. Even court etiquette came under criticism as a useless display that in effect made the king a slave to formalities.[85] Although traditional formal rhetoric and terminology continued to be used, a psychological leveling undermined the monarch as a personal authority symbol. The changing attitude toward ceremony reflected an antipolitical rationalism that progressively weakened Crown mystique. Fittingly, in the latter part of the century, the Mexican *Protomedicato* (medical board) offered a lecture and two published reports on inflamatory obstructions of the liver in honor of Carlos IV's elevation to the throne.[86] While ideologically correct, such flattery contrasted sharply with past glorification of royal benevolence and divine justice. Personal loyalty and mutual obligation, major features of the Hapsburg system, became unimportant. Officials ceased functioning primarily as the king's agents and became responsible for performance standards dictated by the established ideology. Administrative restructuring resulted in an increasingly vertical organizational structural and a high degree of standardization. The ad hoc type of administration of officials who perceived themselves as having a personal commission from the king had to be eliminated. The tendency to view change as a natural process that did not vary significantly from one nation or region to the other reenforced the movement toward administrative homogeneity. Providing that historical differences could be laid aside, the process functioned everywhere in the same fashion.

It became the state's responsibility to assure that historical factors did not impede the functioning of beneficial processes. Thus Ramón de

Posada, fiscal of the Audiencia of Mexico, referred to the implementation of "those natural principles dictated by reason."[87] The New World's historical experience posed only a tactical problem. The viceregal system in Spanish America, elaborated to meet the needs of a different philosophy, appeared to be an archaic obstacle. Personal and horizontally organized, it seemed to be the institutional antithesis of the new ideology. Inevitably, the political structure and internal social organization of Spanish America was viewed as a major reason that the mother country failed to profit.

Reformers felt impelled to take action. Campomanes asserted that timidity in attacking abuses could be explained only as a consequence of a lack of understanding of the causes of the evils, or a desire not to offend those who maintained the abuses.[88] Disdainful of traditional elements, the reformers believed that their aggressive rationality could transform the Spanish world. Opponents, rather than being perceived as practioners of different ideas, represented the problem's regressive human dimension. Thus vocal Christian moralists, who tirelessly denounced the new eighteenth-century man as a dangerous and radical enemy of the old mystical order, could be shrugged off by the secular devotees of the new ideology.

A similarly unsympathetic attitude characterized the response of reformers toward American hostility to externally imposed reforms. They dismissed New World doubts as further proof of the educational backwardness they sought to correct. Little attention was paid to potentially dangerous philosophical and intellectual opposition. Many who perceived themselves under pressure resorted to humor in an effort at least to prick the pride of those sent to rescue them. Thus the anonymous author of the 1779 *Amor del tiempo* (Love of the Times) received publication permission from "Don Knowledge, Councilor of Reason and Attorney of Disillusionment in the year of caprice...by order of Don Liberty."[89] In Quito, Eugenio Espejo produced in 1781 a widely known satirical piece in which he gleefully took on José de Gálvez and Carlos III, characterizing the latter as a playing card (*barajas*) king. Although the prime suspect, Espejo stoutly denied involvement and escaped punishment.[90] Such attacks angered the authorities, but opposition within the political structure itself posed more immediate difficulties.[91] Many colonial officials, including viceroys, resented the subordination of politics within the emerging administrative system. While distant enlightened officials approached internal opposition as a technical or structural problem, those on the scene struggled with political ramifications. Madrid did not fully appreciate their reactions. Consequently, the Marqués de la Ensenada, as Secretary of the Indies, War and Treasury, in

1751 pressed for the recruitment into government services of university students not associated with traditional elements. University *manteistas*, perceived to be sympathetic to the new knowledge and hence more innovative, could provide a counterbalance for the traditionalists associated with the *colegios mayores*.[92] Eventually, Ensenada believed, the entire administrative structure would fall under their influence.

The grand design, to modernize the Spanish world, required a series of related decisions that followed a conscious pattern under the direction of ideologically motivated officials. Powerful enlightened individuals, described by Juan Marichal as "intellectual executives," launched consistent reforms and pressed for administrative sovereignty.[93] They may have overestimated the force of innovative ideas, but it is evident that confidence in the state's ability to effect change in accordance with a concrete pattern designed to achieve overall goals permeated the thinking of officials. Consequently, as Stanley Payne observed, the program that emerged, particularly between 1760 and 1780, provided reform objectives for the next 150 years.[94]

5

Ideology and Reality

BOURBON INNOVATORS SUBORDINATED POLITICS TO rational criteria and sought to formulate objectives and goals in advance of a crisis. Rather than allowing events or external parties to define problems and solutions, enlightened reformers created their own reality, designated the issue, and indicated the steps to be taken. Balance as an important political objective fell before the ideology of the active state, and those who did not subscribe to the new thought became obstacles to be removed, not accommodated. A rational scientific approach made manipulative political skills suspect, and in certain cases corrupt. While such skills might be employed on an individual basis, provided an acceptable goal remained in view, they no longer functioned as an approved part of an open-ended political process. Administrative direction had to be maintained, in contrast to the constant backing and filling that characterized Hapsburg politics.

In the early decades of the new century, a partially articulated ideology had only a limited and indirect influence on the empire. Nevertheless, a changing political vocabulary presaged the new approach, as the term "dominion" (*dominio*) increasingly replaced "kingdom" (*reino*) in reference to both Spain and the Indies.[1] Initially, officials shifted between traditional political accommodation and the pursuit of rational goals. Early eighteenth-century ambiguity is particularly evident in commercial policies. Thus, the merchant community succeeded in securing further advantageous restrictions on colonial trade, including prohibition of American merchants from serving as agents or consignees of Spanish houses, or investing their own assets in the colonial export trade.[2] While such restrictions could not reverse economic reality, they demonstrated the power of exporters to demand them as well as official readiness to comply. More positively, Felipe V ended Seville's grip on colonial commerce by transferring the Casa de Contratación from that city to Cádiz in 1717. Although Cádiz had pressured the Crown to do so for some time, the shift represented the beginning of the rationalization of the trade structure.

The hesitant ambiguity of the early decades eventually gave way to an active economic policy. José del Campillo's grand design asserted that the American empire required the same type of reforms as Spain. His two-stage plan called for a general inspection (*visita*), establishment of a new administrative system, and sweeping economic change. Subsequently, in 1746, three years after Campillo's death, Felipe VI requested the opinion of the viceroys of New Spain and Peru on the advisability of structural reforms.[3] A series of inspections beginning with Cuba and Louisiana in 1763, New Spain in 1765, Peru in 1777, and other areas of the empire, provided the data to confirm the need for reform. The ideological perspective of Crown ministers made the findings predictable.[4]

The two political and economic poles of the empire, Mexico and Peru, appeared to possess resources that, if properly managed, could provide the means to rebuild the Spanish system. From Madrid's perspective, however, a small American elite, supported and abetted by an archaic and easily manipulated political structure, maintained a regressive hold on the colonial economy. Supposedly, this entrenched and privileged group controlled a disproportionate share of the wealth, blocked the true economic potential of the empire from being developed by more aggressive elements, and allowed many areas to languish in backwardness—a situation that resulted in great wealth for the few at the expense of the Indians, misdirected lower classes, and royal revenue. The official assessment contained a mixture of substance and fantasy, both of which could be employed to justify change.

José de Gálvez, one of the architects of the eighteenth-century ideology, molded, implemented, and directed it in the American environment, first as visitador in New Spain (1765-71) and subsequently as Minister of the Indies (1776-87). As visitador he appointed an intendant in Sinaloa, and permitted the governor of Veracruz to exercise limited intendant functions.[5] Gálvez even tentatively selected individuals to fill the proposed positions. Colonial opposition caused delays, however, and made Madrid move with more care. In 1776 Venezuela became an intendancy.[6] The establishment of two new viceroyalties, New Granada and Río de La Plata, weakened the traditional Viceroyalty of Peru. In 1782 copies of the proposed intendant regulation circulated secretly among high colonial officials in the Viceroyalty of La Plata. It suggested, among other things, the use of the title governor-intendant to preserve the notion that the old structure remained intact.[7] Two years later, Peru experienced administrative reorganization, and finally in 1786-87 the intendant system went into effect in New Spain. By the 1790s the intendants functioned throughout the empire, including the Philippines. The new regional executives received a salary that exceeded that of Audiencia judges and other high officials of the traditional governing structure.[8] The intendants, although technically inserted into the traditional viceregal system, in fact functioned differently. They served not as political officials but as administrative chiefs, and ideally acted as ideological agents rather than regional politicians.[9]

The staged introduction of the new administrative structure did not mean that the intendancy as an institution had been perfected. Enlightened reformers, because of their perception of the colonial reality, viewed the visita not as an investigative stage but as an opportunity to seize control of the traditional structure and move it in the desired direction.[10] José de Gálvez compressed José del Campillo's original proposal for a two-stage process into a single step of implementation of reforms during the visitation itself.[11] Gálvez and his agents believed it imperative to take immediate action and resolve operational problems later.[12]

Trade Reforms

The revitalization of commerce provided the first ideological objective. Although France pressured Felipe V to form a joint stock company with direct access to New World markets, officials had no intention of unnecessarily relinquishing trade advantages. France, in spite of some temporary success, in the end had to be content with a profitable contraband trade.[13] Rather than conceding controlled internationalization of commerce, officials sought to restructure Spain's access to American wealth.

Spain, unlike other European powers, had not established or permitted the organization of powerful trading companies in spite of considerable debate. Under the influence of scholastic economics, most theorists viewed monopoly as incompatible with the needs of distributive justice. Even the guild system, although allowed to function, did not escape censure for its monopolistic tendencies.[14] Moreover, the success of foreign companies in the seventeenth century appeared to rest on quasi-sovereign authority. Hapsburg Spain could not vest extraordinary powers in a private company to the same extent as had been done for the

Dutch East or West Indies companies or the English East India company. Overriding the structure of viceroys, Audiencias, and other institutions directly affected the notion of royal jurisdiction upon which the Crown rested its authority. Eugenio de Castro, a proponent of monopoly companies in the 1660s, who well understood the philosophical obstacles, asserted correctly that the Council of the Indies would prefer to ruin the empire rather than risk infringement on its jurisdiction. Subsequently, he endeavoured to convince officials that the legal foundations of the monarchy could be made compatible with monopoly companies.[15] Ambrose Daubenten, the French consul in Seville at the turn of the century, who also advised the Spanish king, observed that companies flourished only in countries like England and Holland because the former was almost, and the latter was actually, a republic. In France and Spain, such organizations could not enjoy the same authority because of the very nature of the monarchy.[16] That such entities violated philosophical notions constituted only part of the problem. When coupled with the question of foreign participation, technical matters, and internal opposition, it is understandable why Spain failed to follow the example of other European powers.[17]

In the eighteenth century, however, willingness to direct the economy overrode the issue of jurisdiction. Growing confidence in the ability to direct and control change, impatience with traditional barriers, and the desire for immediate action inclined officials toward pragmatism. Consequently, the Junta de Comercio demonstrated the growing receptivity to commercial companies. In 1701 the Junta asserted that it always had regarded companies, modeled along the lines of those chartered by other nations, to be an effective method.[18] This view was supported by an influential economist, Gaspar Naranjo y Romero, who suggested the formation of several in 1703. Even Uztáriz, who attacked monopolies, did not totally rule them out. Nevertheless, the delivery of monopoly functions into the hands of stock companies, even when the state retained directive authority, conflicted with the perceived need to stimulate broad private initiative. Thus, privileged, as distinct from monopolistic, organizations appeared more acceptable. Such organizations depended upon officials to set objectives and tailor concessions to encourage them. Tax advantages, rather than monopoly, provided incentives.

In the empire, the most successful company, the *Real Compañía Guipuscoana de Caracas*, nevertheless exercised monopoly control. Yet, article five of its charter, conceded the Caracas company in 1728, made it clear that the state would not be bound by private monopoly powers: "I will concede, if I find it well, to [other]...vassals similar licenses for Caracas, with equal or distinct circumstances according [to]...my royal will."[19] Although Felipe V legally recognized the company's de facto monopoly in 1742, from 1753 on the Crown began to reduce its powers. Officials increasingly favored limited companies designed to attain a certain goal, although even limited privileged enterprises came under criticism.[20] As the Duke of Sotomayor argued in 1749, such companies, whether domestic or colonial, caused more injury than benefit.[21] In fact, privileged companies enjoyed scant success. For example, the *Cinco Mayores Gremios* of Madrid, formed by merchant guilds in 1763, survived only after repeated modifications and eventually fell into the hands of creditors.

In America, the movement toward unrestricted trade made privileged companies even less useful. As early as 1752, the Crown tentatively indicated its intention of modifying trade restrictions in a cédula ordering colonial officials to examine interregional trade and the possibility of new beneficial regulations.[22] Finally, in 1765 the Crown permitted Cuba, Santo Domingo, Puerto Rica, Margarita, and Trinidad to trade with an expanded number of Spanish ports, as well as simplifying and lowering taxes. Gradually, other areas fell under the new system: Louisiana in 1768, Campeche and Yucatán in 1770, Santa Marta in 1776, and in 1776 all areas except New Spain and Venezuela, which remained outside the general regulations until 1789. Meanwhile, intercolonial trade became legal in 1774. The result proved gratifying. New Spain's trade with the mother country increased in value from 13,268,847 pesos in 1787 to 20,600,267 in 1795. For the whole of Spanish America, it may have increased as much as 700 percent between 1778 and 1788, and with New Spain's contribution after 1789 the result appeared miraculous.[23]

While enlightened reformers agreed on the need to eliminate obstacles to productive individual self-interest, they hesitated to relinquish a directive role. They entertained a strong suspicion that the elements they hoped would become productive, including the Indian and the merchant, might, unless pressed, lapse into idleness or passive and marginal trading activities. As the Marqués de la Ensenada noted, "the French and English are born traders (*comerciantes de corazón*) while ours are [merchants] out of necessity."[24]

The Island Model

Cuba, its normal socioeconomic rhythm disrupted by war and occupation, provided the ideal testing ground to move theory into practice. When the Count of Ricla and Field Marshal Alejandro O'Reilly arrived in Havana in 1763 to arrange with the British occupation forces for the return of the island, they carried instructions not only to investigate why it fell to the enemy but also to assess Cuba's future contribution to the well-being of the empire. Officials, well aware that the open trade carried on during the occupation had been both extensive and profitable, reflected that prior to the war the island contributed little, and indeed consumed resources transferred from New Spain. Madrid had no desire to see post-occupation Cuba return to its former fiscally dependent position.[25] Thus, the island served as a pilot project, not only undergoing the recommended visitation but also economic reforms and the establishment of the intendancy system. Defense of the island against future military pressure made action a matter of some urgency. Unless the economy could be restructured and stimulated, sufficient funds to maintain a trained militia, reinforced by regular units, would not be available. Consequently, royal instructions provided that fiscal and military affairs be placed under an intendant in a fashion similar to that of Castilian intendants. The Cuban ordinance (1764) drew heavily upon Spanish regulations with a few modifications.[26]

In keeping with the ideology's unified perception of cause and effect, officials linked economic reforms with increased taxes and tightened revenue collection. The combination of expanded trade channels and the sugar boom succeeded in stimulating the Cuban economy and providing the needed revenues. Growing prosperity, military privileges, and status elicited the support of the elite, who watched with satisfaction as plantings increased from 10,000 acres in 1763 to 160,000 acres by 1792. Such economic strength had a direct bearing on Spanish military successes in the Gulf of Mexico during the American Revolution.[27] To enlightened planners, the island's response to their initiatives confirmed the utility of a goal-oriented ideology. They tended to underestimate the impact of the sugar boom in their desire to see a causal effect. Nevertheless, even with an expanding economy, the response to political reorganization, as distinct from fiscal or commercial modifications, indicated stress. In 1769 Antonio María de Bucareli y Ursúa, Captain-General of Cuba, and an individual who responded to the political needs of the colonial elite, suggested that the intendancy system in Cuba be abolished and the old structure reinstated.[28] Bucareli in Cuba, and later as viceroy in Mexico, understood the reluctance of the colonial population to abandon a political system and adopt an ideologically based administrative structure.

New Spain's Ideological Reorganization

In Mexico, the reform period began with the arrival of José de Gálvez in 1765. The general outlines of the conflict between the old philosophy and the new ideology may be seen in the visitador's orders. Gálvez carried separate sets of instructions one from the Council of the Indies as a body, and the other issued over the signature of Julian de Arriaga, Secretary of Marine and the Indies, who also served as president of that body.[29] Arriaga, a respected conservative member of the old guard, reluctantly allowed his authority to be manipulated by the king's enlightened advisors. Consequently, his directive and active orders reflected an approach that he did not agree with philosophically. The making of Arriaga into a tool of the new ideology was a minor victory on the road to reform. The Secretary's instructions indicated the areas to be examined and emphasized Gálvez's duty to take remedial action. Although, theoretically, modifications and changes had to be ordered by the colonial chief executive, "the viceroy will concur efficaciously" (art. 32). Gálvez received authority to remove, replace, or reduce the number of officials, and to name appropriate subordinate officials (arts. 8 and 28). Any judicial disputes arising from his decisions could be appealed only to the royal person, bypassing the normal procedure through the Council of the Indies (art. 29). The Secretary, responding to the opinion that the absence of powerful middle-level regional administrators stymied reforms, directed Gálvez to ascertain whether the intendant system, already operating in Spain, should be introduced in Mexico (art. 31). The decision as to what remedies should be employed appeared to lie with Gálvez. In contrast, the instructions of the Council of the Indies stressed the investigative and information-gathering role—to "inform" and proceed against "wrongdoing." The Council instructed Gálvez to bring specific charges in a formal manner and to prove them in conformity with the Laws of the Indies, with appeals to the Council whenever permissible.[30]

José de Gálvez, with a preconceived notion of what he would find, arrived with the remedy in mind. The visitador ignored reality, or opinion not in accord with his own perceptions. He refused to acknowledge Mexico's obvious prosperity, which produced the New World's first millionaires, as well as its importance in the world economic system. Gálvez claimed that the colonial government had allowed the country to degenerate to the same extent as Spain during the worst days of Carlos II.[31] Thus, the situation in New Spain, as he perceived it, required fundamental changes. The ideology elaborated a standard cure that required a uniform disease. According to Gálvez, the methods that had cured the head (*cabeza*) should now be applied to the colonial parts. Ironically, not only did the visitador employ a medieval analogy to make his point, but he also submitted the plan to the bishops of Mexico and Puebla for their comments, employing a traditional method of gaining consensus political support.[32] Predictably, he attacked the viceregal structure, hoping to replace it with a system of commandancies and a powerful secondary level of intendants. Following the demands of the new ideology for vertical and uniform political organization, the horizontally organized administrative system that had served for over 250 years could not be permitted to continue unmodified.

The obstacles—including entrenched traditional officials, a powerful monopoly-linked merchant community, contraband trade, and the general desire of Spanish-Americans to manipulate or adjust their own internal situation—did not deter reform-minded innovators. While Hapsburg agents would have viewed the creation of such powerful opposition as both a policy failure and a crisis, eighteenth-century officials accepted it as part of the larger problem of administrative and economic rationalization. As a consequence, conflict between reformers and those who adhered to the traditional political philosophy began immediately. Even before Gálvez left the port of Veracruz, cooperation between the visitador and the viceroy became strained. Acting on his own authority, Gálvez dispatched a warship to Laguna de Terminos in Campeche in response to information of smuggling activities.[33] The viceroy, the Marqués de Cruillas, schooled in the traditional political philosophy that required attention to prerogatives, quickly reacted. He viewed Gálvez's action as a dangerous infringement by one corporate unit on another which could not go unchallenged. Cruillas failed to understand that the new ideology rejected the concept of balance. He referred the conflict to the viceregal fiscal and promised to abide by that official's competency determination. A judicial investigation of the law and prior procedure, aimed at deciding the appropriate balance, seemed entirely reasonable to the viceroy. Gálvez, however, rejected the idea, claiming that he represented the highest authority in such matters and had no intention of accepting a subordinate official's judgment.[34]

A stalemate, never desirable, appeared even less so because of Spain's intervention in the Seven Years War. Conclusion of peace in 1763 brought territorial problems, and continued uncertainty in the face of British military and commercial power. The failure to cooperate with the visitador, and the generally unsettling international situation, resulted in the viceroy's replacement. Arriaga, acting for Carlos III, selected a loyal soldier, the Marqués de Croix, as the new viceroy. When the Marqués de Croix landed at Veracruz in July 1766, he brought with him orders to cooperate fully with José de Gálvez.[35] Viceroy Croix understood that his task was to implement the modification decided upon by the visitador. As a result, Gálvez could be confident of support on both sides of the Atlantic. The use of military men in administrative positions soon became a notable feature of the reform movement. The notion that they would obey orders rather than make considered political judgments underlaid the preference for army officers.[36]

Madrid's innovators needed certain types of obstacles to justify their actions. Moreover, they sought to demonstrate their control and ability to effect sweeping change. Conveniently, the Jesuits provided a suitable target. The expulsion of the Society of Jesus from all Spanish domains in 1767 supplied an important psychological victory at the beginning of the campaign for colonial reform. The Jesuits represented most of the vices against which the reformers rallied. As they were highly visible, with landholdings throughout the American empire, including an extensive mission system in Paraguay, and heavily involved in education, the idea of Jesuit power seemed creditable. As an international order, they posed a perceived security threat in an age when the border between Spanish and Portuguese territory had become important. In addition, in view of the intellectual struggle, Jesuit colleges that trained and influenced the colonial elite had become suspect. While the Jesuits did not reject all aspects of the critical method, they clung to values in conflict with the new secular materialism. Their pragmatic adaptability seemed a crafty perversion, even caricature of enlightened thought. Moreover, they subscribed to the political theories of Suárez, which opposed the arbitrary imposition of change and the tyrannical exercise of authority. To Madrid's determined planners, such notions appeared subversive.

The official perception of the Society of Jesus contained the optimum mix of fact and fancy to focus the psychological attention of enlightened innovators. Jesuitphobia constituted an emotional state difficult for those not caught up in the fabrication of enlightened ideology and its required reordering of reality to appreciate.[37] The simultaneous expulsion of the Society from all Spanish dependencies, carried out with the utmost secrecy in obedience to sealed orders, indicates the level of paranoia engendered. Its successful accomplishment, despite rumors of armed resistance, represented an important ideological victory—bold, decisive, and sweeping. Such action would have been unthinkable during the Hapsburg era.

Although the Society surrendered to royal authority with only a whimper, the expulsion resulted in civil disturbances, particularly in New Spain. Significantly, the lower classes, least affected by the removal, reacted. They responded not so much in defense of the Jesuits as against an apparently arbitrary, and thus inexplicable, act by the state. Reflecting their disdain for the political process, enlightened reformers did not prepare the population for change. The principle of predictability, so important under the Hapsburgs, had been flagrantly violated. The combination of recent pressures on the lower classes, of military service and new fiscal burdens, and then the sudden forceful sweep of the state against the Jesuits, proved too much to bear. A series of revolts erupted. In response, a confident, even arrogant Gálvez quickly moved to suppress the reaction. He blamed other factors, including the alleged reluctance of regional officials to deal with problems.[38] In fact, the colonial kingdoms had become the object of reform on a nonparticipatory basis. Even in regions where the expulsion proved popular, such as Paraguay, where the ouster ended the control of the Jesuits over labor, the decision clearly stemmed from considerations other than the desires of the population. Among enlightened officials, the expulsion of the Jesuits acted to bolster their confidence that the structure could be altered to suit their specifications.

Disdain for consensus politics also characterized the approach to administrative modifications. Gálvez's provisional restructuring and centralization of fiscal administration, under the supervision of the governor of Veracruz, foreshadowed the soon-to-be implemented separation of fiscal authority from the traditional corporate and political structure. Subsequently, the visitador instituted fiscal reforms in Mexico City over the protest of the merchant guild (*consulado*), which complained of their effect and questioned their legality. In response to the consulado's petition, the Council of the Indies recommended in its consulta of February 10, 1768, that the change be voided. Tomás Ortíz de Landazuri, contador of the Council, argued that Gálvez had not uncovered any actual violation of fundamental law. He noted that the visitador's measures appeared to be directed at the total transformation of fiscal affairs, and their organization along lines employed in Spain.[39] Shrewdly, Ortíz de Landazuri identified the pattern of decisions that moved toward predetermined ideological goals. The Marqués de Croix indeed received authority to establish intendancies as early as 1769, although such authorization proved premature.[40]

Finally, in 1776 José de Gálvez became Secretary of Marine and the Indies. The same year, the Crown appointed salaried directors in New Spain's major urban centers to collect excise taxes, whereas Veracruz, the country's principal port, had its own tax superintendent.[41] In addition, the appointment of a regent directly under the viceroy, who functioned as the administrative head of the Audiencia and also assumed the powers of the senior judge, affected the authority of the two major colonial political institutions. The following year, the Crown ordered the viceroy to establish a junta to examine the number of officials in each alcaldía, recommend the elimination of superfluous units, map and rank each jurisdiction, and propose which should be included in different intendancies.[42]

The South American Offensive

In Peru, reform attempts went forward with equal swiftness. Gálvez personally selected José Antonio Areche to undertake the preliminary review. Appointed Visitador-General in 1776, Areche had bureaucratic experience that included the posts of *Fiscal del Crimen* of the Audiencia of Mexico and head of its *Fiscalia de lo Civil*.[43] During Gálvez's Mexican mission, Areche's dedication had impressed the future minister. The fact that he had no experience in Peru mattered little; it seemed to be a question of implementing rational universal ideas. The ideology made no allowances for regional variations. Areche had served an apprenticeship under Gálvez during the Mexican visita; therefore he understood the goals and difficulties involved.

In reality, the Viceroyalty of Peru, centered around Lima, was in the latter stages of a difficult economic realignment. The commercial growth of regional centers, and a flourishing contraband trade posed major problems. Buenos Aires drained wealth and commerce away from traditional channels, forcing a serious economic contraction in Peru. From the seventeenth century on, the Consulado of Lima complained of the effects of contraband and characterized Buenos Aires as a nest of smugglers. Merchants in Buenos Aires in return accused the Peruvians of usury and speculation. In the end, Lima could not retain its hold on the South American economy in the face of geography and an emerging world economic system that pulled commerce through Buenos Aires.[44] Consequently, traditional and marginal sources of profit, such as the forced trade conducted by regional officials (*repartimiento de comercio*), became important. Whereas New Spain's visita had operated within a dynamic and expanding economy, in Peru Areche faced at best a static situation.

Moreover, establishment of the independent Viceroyalty of La Plata with its capital in Buenos Aires in 1776-77 detached Upper Peru (Bolivia) and Asunción (Paraguay) from the Peruvian viceroyalty, making it impossible for the elite to control artificially the flow of trade and commerce. While Chile technically remained within the Viceroyalty of Peru, the economic bonds that had tied the region to Peru in the sixteenth and seventeenth centuries had weakened considerably. The increasing volume of French contraband, as well as direct ship contact with Buenos Aires and other areas, pulled Chile away from its traditional Peruvian market, and introduced a measure of competition previously absent.[45] The Audiencia of Lima counted itself fortunate to have retained jurisdiction over Arequipa, arguing that it constituted an economic dependency. In fact, most of Arequipa's wine and brandy trade flowed naturally toward Cuzco, not Lima. Political boundaries could not alter reality.[46] Change, in a political and economic sense, appeared to benefit all except Lima. Paradoxically, Peruvian merchants, while fearful of externally mandated change, hoped for some economic improvement. Thus, their initial attitude toward the visita was ambivalent.

Visitador Areche sailed from Acapulco on March 21, 1777, to take up his duties. In addition to the title of Visitador-General, he carried an appointment as Intendant of the Army, and, in order to indicate further support, the Crown conferred upon him a place on the Council of the Indies, as well as the prestigious Order of Carlos III. His staff consisted of individuals drawn from bureaucratic circles in New Spain; consequently, the visita had aspects of a Mexican mission to Peru.[47] He carried with him three separate sets of instructions. Predictably, the instructions of the Council of the Indies dealt with the judicial administration, another set of instructions signed by the king concentrated on financial affairs, and the third document touched on important political problems.[48] His confidential instructions contained an analysis of Peruvian society apparently drawn from Juan and Ulloa's 1749 report. Thus, Areche arrived in Lima with an already formulated perception of the Peruvian situation. Shortly after his arrival, he wrote a former colleague, Fernando Mangino, Superintendant-General of the Treasury in Mexico, of how Peru differed from New Spain: "where there is usually justice, here [in Peru] tyranny is common...[it] is being ruined by the lack of honest judges, forced Indian labor, and forced trade...corregidores are concerned solely with their own interests....Here everything is private, nothing for the public good."[49] Areche's exaggeration is reminiscent of José de Gálvez's sweeping judgment of corregidores in Mexico as "two hundred wretches, who, with their empty title of judges, have come to constitute an independent judicial sphere, wherein, driven by greed, they work out their own fortunes at the expense of the royal treasury and the ruin of the people."[50]

The visitador's attempts to reform the Audiencia soon united a conservative elite and the viceregal government in opposition. Audiencia judges, tied to local families through marriage and economic interests, resisted reform efforts. Cries of outrage, and violent resistance to the establishment of a customs house in Arequipa, along with demonstrations in Tarma, Huailas, and Cuzco, constituted a political problem for the viceroy. Not surprisingly, Viceroy Manuel Guirior, who viewed Areche himself as a problem, withdrew his cooperation and resisted the visitador's reforms. Areche in turn accused the viceroy of catering to the elite and valuing their friendship and esteem to the point of failing to fulfill his duties.[51] While he could not resist harsh words about the viceroy's personality, the visitador suggested, as had Juan and Ulloa, that the nature of the viceregal office itself constituted the major obstacle.[52] Areche's correspondence demonstrated the inevitable conflict between two different governing philosophies. He viewed the viceroy as too anxious to accommodate a politically manipulative elite, while Guirior perceived his own actions as a reasonable compromise that conciliated a potentially disruptive alienated element. Areche, in common with those who subscribed to the official ideology, equated compromise with timidity, a weakness that sacrificed rational reforms to a disastrous status quo. José de Gálvez accepted Areche's version of the stalemate and replaced the viceroy.[53]

The new viceroy Agustín de Jáuregui had a military background. Before his appointment to Lima in 1780, he served as Captain-General of Chile.[54] Nevertheless, Jáuregui, also too sensitive to politics in Areche's view, soon came under attack. When the University of San Marcos held a sumptuous reception for the new viceroy, the politically ambitious Peruvian José Baquíjano made the mistake of lauding the viceroy as an official who realized that actions could not be taken against the people's will and recognized that particular groups had their own needs. Such rhetorical flourishes that drew their inspirations from the traditional philosophical matrix clashed with the official ideology. Areche chose to make an issue of the *Eulogy*, and arranged to have it suppressed. The visitador used the episode as an example of how viceroys had allowed things to get out of hand.[55] Although Madrid accepted Areche's assessment, his unrestrained complaints eventually cast doubts on his competence. Consequently, Gálvez abruptly replaced the visitador in 1781 with Jorge Escobedo, who carried the visita to its conclusion.

The rebellion of Túpac Amaru complicated reform attempts and had a lingering influence. Unlike the expulsion of the Jesuits, and the relatively easy suppression of the disorders it triggered, the revolt that began in 1780 and endured until 1783 had not been orchestrated, nor could it be manipulated easily for political purposes. Although eventually suppressed, it indicated that Madrid could not fully control the situation at the same time as it weakened the structure in order to implement change. The revolt caused anxiety as it rippled across Peru and Upper Peru, reaching Tucumán in modern Argentina, and northward into New Granada. It became a topic of worried conversation throughout the empire. It is is not clear to what extent its leader, José Gabriel Condorcanqui, who took the name Túpac Amaru to indicate direct Inca descent, responded to the unsettling climate of change. He considered himself to be an educated individual and a supporter of knowledge; consequently, it is unlikely that he was unaware of the issues being hotly discussed in Lima. Before leading the revolt, he attempted to manipulate the viceregal structure to provide relief from the mita and the activities of abusive officials.[56] As a politically active individual, he could hardly have overlooked the implications of the visita.

The rebellion had aspects of an attempt to secure concessions from a partially discredited and weakened colonial regime by elements not necessarily subjected to vexatious burdens or practices. This possibility is supported by indications that provinces with low repartimiento levels, and several not subject to mita labor, nevertheless joined the insurrection, while Aymaraes and Paucartambo, provinces where repartimiento levels exceeded the norm, remained loyal.[57] Moreover, Túpac Amaru's advisors and army included mestizos, criollos, and even a few Spaniards.[58] José de Gálvez confidentially informed then viceroy-designate Teodoro de Croix, who replaced Jáuregui, that the colonial elite had plotted the rebellion as early as 1776 to coincide with the visitation. It is evident that criollo elements in Cuzco, including Bishop Juan Manuel Peralta y Moscoso, an Arequipa native, appeared ambivalent about the revolt—not a reassuring demonstration of loyalty in the opinion of nervous imperial officials. Gálvez also suggested that the failure of the Audiencia of Lima to act in the early stages could be explained in terms of their own interests. Regardless of Gálvez's private opinion, an open break had to be avoided and general loyalty assumed.[59]

The elimination of abusive practices and parasitic corregidores, a stated goal of Túpac Amaru, also were major reform objectives.[60] Moreover, Túpac Amaru's criticism of the viceregal system corresponded, to a large extent, with that of enlightened reformers. Although Túpac Amaru adroitly used resentment caused by the increased fiscal burdens imposed by Areche, he continued to proclaim to his multiracial followers his desire for a negotiated settlement based on the reforms he had intially proposed.[61] Consequently, Minister Gálvez publicly expressed the view that the rebellion constituted a reaction to an already officially recognized exploitive socioeconomic system and archaic governing structure. Gálvez therefore responded positively to the opinion of the commander of military operations, Gabriel de Avilés, that certain administrative demands of Túpac Amaru, including the establishment of a separate Audiencia at Cuzco, made sense.[62] Characteristically, Gálvez declared his intention of delivering Peru "in one stroke from anarchy, confusion, and disorder," implying that it could be done before other elements seized control of the direction of change.[63] The impending introduction of the intendant system would provide the bold and decisive administrative remedy.[64]

As previously noted, Teodoro de Croix replaced Viceroy Jáuregui. A military man schooled on New Spain's Indian frontier, and with political experience gained under his uncle, the Marqués de Croix, he appeared to be a good choice. The Minister of the Indies hoped that he would not be influenced unduly by the Lima elite in contrast to his immediate predecessors.[65] Croix thus played the same role in Peru as had his uncle in Mexico during that region's visitation—immobilizing the traditional structure while the visitador laid the basis for sweeping reforms. Nevertheless, although Croix cooperated during the visita, he became a critic of the new system after its implementation.

Reaction to Desovereignization

The desire to create an administrative empire, uniformly structured, depoliticized, and subject to rational direction, resulted in a different attitude toward public office—in particular, the sale of Audiencia posts. Colonial high courts and the judicial function traditionally provided a political arena within which a viable balance between imperial needs and local concerns could be achieved. The influence of the judges reached far beyond the court itself. Audiencia members received innumerable separate commissions, such as auditor of war, assessor of the tribunal of accounts, positions on various pension funds or pious trusts, and other lucrative or prestigious duties. Virtually every aspect of socioeconomic life fell under their influence to some extent.[66] Unlike the viceroy, the judges worked within an institution that possessed a sense of continuity and an organic connection with a particular region.

The Hapsburgs attempted to restrain the court's natural regionalism without destroying its useful political function. Such restrictions proved only marginally effective in the face of constant pressure for "de facto home rule."[67] Eager office seekers, including Huamán Poma noted earlier, often employed philosophical arguments to make their claims. For example, Pedro de Bolívar de la Redonda, a lawyer from Cartagena de Indias, published in 1667 a detailed plea for regional privileges. Bolívar, with his own career in mind, asserted that natives had legal rights to all offices within their own patrias.[68] Even the renowned legal commentator, Juan de Solórzano y Pereyra, although personally against native son appointments, acknowledged that they had some claim.[69] Restrictions violated the implied right of preference inherent in the notion of kingdoms. Before the issue could be resolved, a financially pressed monarchy defused it by selling public office, including Audiencia positions to native sons, as well as exemption from vexatious restrictions.[70]

Eighteenth-century reformers, however, responding to their own ideological perspective, struggled to reverse a policy they believed to be corrupt. After 1713 the Crown almost exclusively appointed Europeans to colonial Audiencias. Consequently, by 1725 native sons no longer dominated any of the American courts. Although military expenses after 1750 required the resumption of sales, the imperial government tightened the enforcement of the regulations. A strong disdain for colonial bureaucrats as a group reinforced Madrid's desire to reconstitute the Audiencias. Reality, however, made it impossible to exclude Americans. Even José de Gálvez, who made no secret of his harsh opinion of local officials, admitted that some native son judges performed well.[71] Rigorous selection, direction, and careful placement offered a solution to the perceived problem. Carlos III's decree of February 21, 1776, which encouraged colonial inhabitants to seek employment within the general imperial structure, including Spanish offices, represented a major step toward bureaucratic amalgamation. The elevation of the Council of the Indies in 1776 to the same status as that of the Council of Castile also encouraged new career patterns. Yet, equality of appointment on the imperial level did not end the desire to serve within one's own region. Consequently, Mexico City's municipal council continued to insist that natives deserved such appointments.[72] Reformers in Madrid firmly rejected such demands.

The eighteenth-century ideology took bureaucratic form in the Ordinances of Intendants, designed to implement José del Campillo's proposed reforms. New Spain's ordinance became the model and eventually went into force in other parts of the empire. In 1787 the Crown ordered the collection of all copies of the Buenos Aires regulations in Guatemala and the substitution of New Spain's document. The same year, Venezuela adopted the Mexican ordinance, followed by Louisiana in 1789, and Cuba in 1791. In Peru, Río de la Plata, and Chile, Madrid ordered that the ordinance of Buenos Aires, under which they functioned, be brought into conformity with that of New Spain.[73] The notion, characteristic of eighteenth-century political economists, that only powerful officials could overcome retrograde elements permeated the document. Nevertheless, reality demanded continuation of the viceroy as the king's personal representative, as well as politico-judicial function of the Audiencia (art. 2). Even the new territorial entities of New Granada (1739) and la Plata (1776) had to be organized as viceroyalties. As both a concession to the viceroy, who represented the traditional structure, and an attempt to fuse the two systems in the public perception, the regulations required him to countersign the intendant's title of appointment. This symbolic gesture only thinly veiled the fact that Madrid selected the intendants and empowered them with independent authority (art. 3). The coexistence of the traditional structure along with the new guaranteed conflict, confusion, and resentment. Juan José de Vértiz y

Salcedo, Viceroy of la Plata, expressed the opinion that the intendant's independence diminished his own status and thus made it difficult to function. In response to Vértiz's political concern, Madrid soothingly replied that he should have no fear in that he continued to represent the king in his very person.[74]

Colonial modification undermined not only the position of viceroys and governors but also of virtually every other official and institution, including the Audiencias. Whereas alcaldes mayores had been subject to Audiencia supervision, intendants and their subdelegates fell under the treasury, with only marginal authority vested in the court. Further disrupting traditional lines of authority, intendants also acted as vice-patrons of the Church. Viceroys and governors retained authority within their capitals and other designated regions, but intendants had supervisory responsibility over regional administrative aspects, including clerical presentation. Consequently, the provincial clergy dealt with these officials rather than with distant viceroys or governors. The shift of supervisory focus emphasized the subordination of politico-judicial functions to fiscal and administrative responsibilities. In addition, the creation in 1776 of the office of regent to serve as the administrative chief of the high courts in place of the viceroy and senior judge brought Audiencias under more administrative control. The new position weakened the bond between the courts and the viceroys. The Audiencia of Cuzco, established in 1787, not only reduced the Lima court's jurisdiction and prestige but also functioned under a regent-intendant. Earlier, within the office of the viceroy itself, the Crown had assumed appointment and removal powers over the viceroy's private secretary—a move justified on the grounds that many secretaries demonstrated little aptitude, had limited experience, and on occasion performed in a scandalous manner. The professionalization of the post in 1742 eliminated a political ally and confidant of the colonial chief of state.[75] Although a viceroy might lobby successfully for the appointment of a particular individual, control over the secretary had been lost. To cap the new structure, the regulations provided for the appointment of an administrative superintendent, who acted as an intendant in his own region and also exercised executive authority over all the other intendants in fiscal and economic matters. The superintendent, directly responsible to the Minister of the Indies, constituted an administrative viceroy.

The natural conflict of interest between a viceroy and the demands of the new ideology could be disruptive as well as politically dangerous. Even those who understood Madrid's objectives often found themselves in opposition once confronted with the actual colonial reality. For example, Viceroy Manuel Antonio Flores of New Granada, an educated and enlightened individual with extensive experience, including a tour of

duty with the Frontier Demarcation Commission that sought to determine the boundary between Portuguese and Spanish America, understood the official ideology. Nevertheless, once charged with the conser-
vation of New Granada, he appreciated the need to rally regional
support. In contrast, Visitador Juan Francisco Gutiérrez de Piñeres,
ordered to implement fiscal measures, paid little heed to such sensibili-
ties. His relentless pursuit of fiscal objectives made him appear arrogant,
arbitrary, and inflexible, in spite of the fact that on other matters he could
be accommodating.[76] The viceroy, aware that the imposition of reforms
eroded political cooperation and that force would have to be used in the
absence of a willingness to make accommodations, advised the formation of a disciplined militia. As had been the case in Peru, José de Gálvez
consistently sided with the visitador. As a consequence, Flores, frustrated
and politically immobilized, used the pretext of coastal defense to turn
over most of his authority to the visitador and repair to the coast,
resolving the conflict by withdrawing from the arena. The viceroy's
timing proved flawless. Gutiérrez de Piñeres as de facto executive faced
the comunero revolt of 1780-81, a violent and bitter confrontation that
drove him from power, whereas Flores survived subsequently to become
viceroy of New Spain.[77]

Ironically, the nature of the office behind which the reformers
worked pushed viceroys into becoming adversaries of the reforms. For
example Peruvian viceroy Croix cooperated in the implementation of the
intendant system but eventually became a bitter critic and advocated a
return to the old system. He reacted in a fashion indicative of the high
level of frustration of individuals caught in an untenable position. When
the municipal council of Lima in 1787 requested his permission to elect a
new *alcalde ordinario*, Croix accused the council of "real contempt" for
his authority, alleging that they had already decided upon the appointment and treated the procedure as a mere formality. Petulantly, he
demanded they recognize his position and possession of the monarch's
complete authority and power. In fact, the ordinance of intendants gave
the power to confirm to intendants, and indeed viceroys had been
advised not to interfere in municipal elections. Nevertheless, as a result
of the fuss, Croix received the right to confirm in the capital while
intendants exercised it elsewhere.

In another seemingly trivial issue, Croix resisted the loss of power.
When Superintendent Escobedo imposed a tax on Indian woolen goods
without consulting the viceroy, Croix vigorously objected. As a result,
Madrid allowed the viceroy to absorb the superintendent's power in the
capital while Escobedo returned to Spain to assume a position on the
Council of the Indies.[78] Croix's reaction to seemingly trivial slights served

his political purposes well. His opposition resulted in the suppression of all superintendencies.

Croix's successor as viceroy, Fray Francisco Gil de Toboada y Lemos, previously viceroy of New Granada adopted a less hostile view. He recommended adjustments within the general framework, which in effect, however, also returned authority to the traditional level. Publicly he supported the notion that the king not only served as God's temporal representative but also exercised office by divine right—a position contrary to the medieval political thought that constituted the strength of the philosophical matrix inherited by the New World empire.[79] Yet Gil's protestations concerning unquestioned obedience to the king did not deter him from acting as a politician in the traditional sense. As superintendent, Viceroy Gil weakened the control exercised by the intendants over their subordinates. Originally, the subdelegados, as an extension of the intendant's authority, served at the pleasure of that official with the approval of the junta superior and the superintendent. Inevitably, subdelegados removed from office appealed to the junta now chaired by the viceroy. A favorable reception at the top destroyed the intendant's control over his local assistants and in effect disrupted the intended organizational structure. In addition, the viceroy ordered superintendents to submit a list of three candidates so that he could make the final choice, although he retained the right to make a selection without reference to the intendant's list. Gil also proposed setting a five-year term for subdelegados. He justified his proposals on the grounds that as the kingdom's supreme authority he needed the power to appoint and dismiss. The viceroy's proposals received royal approval in January of 1792, allowing the viceregal chief of state to dominate the selection process. The new procedure amounted to a partial repoliticalization of regional administration. Consequently, Gil's successor, Ambrosio O'Higgins, the Marqués de Osorno, could dismiss earlier conflict as a result of change itself.[80] Yet, it must be noted that because of Teodoro de Croix's opposition, Peruvian viceroys worked within a modified system structurally closer to that of pre-intendancy days.

A similar reaction to the dual system occurred in New Spain. Antonio Bucareli y Ursúa, the first post-visita viceroy, found it equally difficult to serve as a compliant instrument. Aware that the Gálvez visitation constituted only a preliminary step in the complete transformation of the colonial government, he deplored the inevitable "confusion which reigns between a half new system and the old." While Bucareli admitted his preference for the "old way," he struggled to avoid an automatic rejection of innovation.[81] Nevertheless, he believed it his duty to counter ideological modification that ignored the actual reality.

The role Madrid expected him to play became evident when Bucareli received a copy of Gálvez's *Plan de Intendencia* along with instructions on how it should be implemented, rather than asking him if it should be put in place. The viceroy nevertheless urged Madrid to proceed slowly and with moderation so as to avoid the possible failure of bold and sweeping reforms. He suggested that the degeneration of the traditional structure had caused the problem and therefore its restoration, coupled with strict attention to laws and regulations already in existence, would provide a logical remedy rather than an untried costly new system.[82]

Viceroy Bucareli's complaints appear less shrill than those of his post-visita Peruvian counterpart because he did not have to contend with essentially autonomous intendants, which were not in place in New Spain until 1786-87. He could rely also upon important individuals within the viceroyalty to support his general position. For example, the Conde de Tepa, an Audiencia judge, attacked the notion of a uniformly structured empire.[83] He thus opposed one of Campillo's major reform recommendations. A more pragmatic argument came from Pedro Muñoz de Villavicencio. In a persuasive structural analysis, he noted that Spain with its well-developed infrastructure of regional officials and municipalities, as well as a reasonably homogeneous population, could benefit from the intendancy system. In contrast, he observed that Mexico, with many different and culturally distinct Indian groups and a mixed population scattered over a wide region with relatively few cities and villas each with extensive territorial dependencies, could not support the proposed new structure. Compared to Europe, the region had fewer governors, viceroys, and all the supporting officials that one took for granted in Spain. Consequently, he voiced doubts that only twelve intendants could perform effectively. The main point, the lack of an extensive political-administrative structure, deserved serious consideration.[84]

Opposition to institutional change encouraged a type of official deviousness. "Hypocresía táctica" evolved into obfuscation that over time undermined Madrid's credibility in the American empire. In New Spain, for example, Gálvez secretly separated treasury affairs from the viceregal office during the interim viceregency of Martín de Mayorga (1779-83), who assumed that post on Bucareli's death. Gálvez placed one of his confidants, Pedro Antonio de Cossío, an individual with some bureaucratic experience and commercial ties within the Veracruz merchant community, in charge of finance. Cossío publicly served as secretary of Cámara and virreinato while behind the scenes he exercised financial authority formally vested in the viceroy's office. Until Gálvez lost confidence in Cossío, New Spain in effect had two financial executives, one public and the other a secret agent of the new ideology.[85] The experiment foreshadowed the creation of an independent superintendency noted earlier. Subsequently, Gálvez's program of reform in New Spain moved forward almost as a family affair. His brother, Matías de Gálvez, served briefly as viceroy (1783-84), to be followed by his nephew, Bernardo de Gálvez (1785-86). The minister of the Indies had full confidence that his talented nephew would be able to launch the new administrative system in Mexico. Unfortunately, the finely crafted Ordinance of Intendants of New Spain received final approval on December 4, 1786, only four days prior to the untimely death of Bernardo de Gálvez. As a consequence, the Archbishop Alonso Nuñez de Haro, who served as interim chief executive (1787), implemented the changes. The archbishop-viceroy proceeded with diligence, but Gálvez had hoped for a more aggressive start. Nuñez de Haro, a humanist, hardly sympathized with Madrid's ideology.[86]

Doubts about Madrid's intentions, coupled with the movement away from the government's traditional role as arbitrator, caused political resentment and apprehension, particularly after the establishment of intendancies. A manuscript entitled *Justa repulsa del reglamento de intendencias* (1787), circulated among sympathizers, contained an array of philosophical arguments against the system. Its anonymous author bitterly attacked both the innovations and the mentality that led to them.[87] His opinion represented the thinking of the most rabid opponents of innovation. The Justa Repulsa rejected the narrow ideology upon which Madrid based its policies and demonstrated strong attachment to the broader philosophical matrix that supported the viceregal structure. Repeatedly, its author urged the imperial government to restore justice and religion to their proper place. Although willing to concede the importance of economic matters, the Justa Repulsa called on the state to harmonize such concerns with more abstract and spiritual values. The author recogized the increasingly secular approach of the state and lamented its effect on society. Allegedly, a series of wounds had been inflicted on New Spain's body politic, including arbitrary disregard for the law, disdain for traditional jurisdictions, and the reduction of viceregal authority and status. By expanding the power of intendants, the Crown appeared to have substituted the feet (local and regional officials) for the viceregal head, with detrimental consequences. Pro forma official statements that viceroys remained supreme were identified as propaganda that flew in the face of reality. According to the author, the viceregal office had became a mere "skeleton, a body without a soul or life" (art. 31). Resentment against externally imposed reforms is evident in the author's rhetorical questions. Why had New Spain's historical development been disregarded when formulating policy? After so many years, was radical change (*trastorno universal*) needed? What of all the labor of wise officials expended over the centuries? The Justa Repulsa sarcastically noted that enlightened officials, enamored of change (*amigos de novedades*) proceeded as if colonial inhabitants lived in total darkness oblivious of their own situation (arts. 37, 39). The author viewed administrative uniformity as contrary to historical circumstances and the laws of the Indies. In a manner similar to the seventeenth-century jurist Solórzano, the Justa Repulsa defended diversity and implied that the heedless and arbitrary attempt to force all into one mold constituted an act of violence and violated the (unwritten) constitution (arts. 43, 48). The author warned that "nothing violent can be permanent" (art. 53). A government, according to the Justa Repulsa, should act like a "padre de familia" (art. 269).

The second Conde de Revillagigedo, Juan Vicente de Güemes Pacheco, because of the rapid turnover of viceroys immediately following the implementation of the intendant system, provided the first sustained viceregal reaction. Unlike his immediate predecessor, Manuel Antonio Flores (1787–89) who, turning over the government, expressed serious misgivings and fear of a financial collapse unless the old system was reestablished, Revillagigedo approached the intendant system in a less reactionary fashion.[88] An eighteenth-century man in an intellectual and emotional sense, he believed in rational change, accepted innovation, and disliked politics.[89] Archbishop Alonso Nuñez de Haro's description of the viceroy Revillagigedo could just as easily be applied to other enlightened officials, including José de Gálvez, José Antonio Areche, and Pedro Antonio de Cossío. According to the archbishop, Revillagigedo disdained the work of his predecessors and made changes apparently without reflection and study. Moreover, once decided on a course of action, he could not be dissuaded or contradicted. To the conservative cleric, such boldness and tendency to take action indicated a lack of prudence. In his criticism, Nuñez de Haro made what he obviously believed to be a devastating charge that the viceroy approved of the French Revolution, although not its excesses, and subscribed to all the enlightened notions of the liberty of man. It is clear that the viceroy shared Madrid's enlightened ideology.[90] Nevertheless, placed in charge of the colonial governing system, the count responded predictably. While not petulant or strident, he asserted that both the creation of the office of regent, which removed the viceroy from actual administrative control over the Audiencia, and the intendant system had weakened executive authority, power, and prestige. Yet, rather than a return to the old system, he advised subordinating all the intendants to the viceroy—

in effect integrating the new and old systems at the top. In his instructions to his successor, he expressed his disappointment in a system that had initially appeared so promising. Revillagigedo observed that because it interfered with the traditional jurisdiction of virtually all officials, opposition had become widespread.[91] The move toward an administrative regime without the elements of sovereignty that characterized the viceregal structure made political manipulation difficult and in some cases impossible.

6

A Faltering Ideology

THE *REPARTIMIENTO DE COMERCIO* ISSUE symbolized the official ideology's ultimate inability to overcome reality. Just as the encomienda system two centuries earlier focused on broader concerns, the repartimiento constituted an ideological test. Involving local officials, who worked closely with merchant houses marketing local production, extending credit, distributing food stuffs, mules, and manufactured goods, it cut across all socioeconomic levels. Alcaldes mayores, corregidores, and subsequently subdelegados used their authority to ensure the smooth functioning of the system. In the absence of other sources of credit, the repartimientos appeared indispensable if marginal areas were to contribute to the colonial economy. Such artificial markets indicated the weak nature of provincial trade. In contrast, in areas of intense economic activity, particularly urban centers and their surrounding regions, voluntary transactions predominated, although payment in kind occurred in spite of regulations to the contrary.[1]

Fragile markets forced into existence required controlled access in order not to exhaust the population's ability to meet involuntary obligations. With the repartimientos' subsequent legalization in 1751, efforts to exclude others rested on this realization, as well as on the fact that poorly paid local officials depended on the trade. The regulations provided for juntas chaired by the various viceroys to set prices and determine the nature and quantity of goods to be distributed. The Peruvian junta elaborated an official scale in 1753 after an assessment of each province's wealth and needs. Mules constituted the bulk of the value of the repartimientos.[2] While viewed as useful items by the junta in areas that employed llamas, the forced purchase of mules served only to enrich the corregidor. In Mexico City, the junta waited until 1763 before deciding to take secret testimony in order to determine the type and quantity of goods to be introduced.[3]

In spite of efforts to direct and control the system, local officials, because they had direct political and economic influence in their jurisidiction, arranged things as they pleased. Mandatory acceptance of goods often became exploitive, draining capital from a region and perpetuating economic marginality. The extent of credit dependency became a controversial issue. Francisco de Polanco, Bishop of Chiapas (1778), contested the "myth" that only alcaldes could provide the necessary agricultural credit, noting that local businessmen, familiar with both the region and the people, could extend assistance. In a manner reminiscent of another age, he charged that the repartimiento violated canon, civil, and moral law. In 1793 Viceroy Revillagigedo expressed the opinion that Indians had become so accustomed to repartimiento credit that even when they had sufficient money they preferred drawing on it.[4] He failed to consider the possibility that the "ignorantes" might have developed a rational financial strategy both for managing their own resources and manipulating their creditors.

The mixed benefits and liabilities of the repartimiento de comercio provided abundant ammunition for both defenders and detractors. It constituted a closed economic system defended on the grounds that it pressed an otherwise indifferent population, and marginal regions, into the commercial structure quite apart from the profits of those involved.[5] Such an arrangement contradicted the ideological premise that individuals, free to follow their own interests, would produce and consume more—to the state's benefit and prosperity. Gálvez correctly charged the alcaldes mayores and corregidores with impeding free commerce. Typically, he inflated the vices of a controlled and marginal economic system to the point that those who directed the repartimiento became the "scourge of provinces, and the usurpers of the royal treasury."[6] Instances of abusive practices by corregidores, caciques, clerics, hacendados, and others provided seemingly endless confirmation of the repartimiento's evils. The rural population, regardless of ethnic background, had been drawn into the system to varying degrees; consequently, complaints came from virtually every region. On the Peruvian coast, a culturally mestizo area, forced distribution met with resistance, including that of hacienda owners who moved to protect their own interests. Nevertheless, distributors pressed their trade to the extent possible in all areas.

Sales tax avoidance and irritating cases of illegal appropriation of funds by officials to speculate in goods provided additional justification for Madrid's hostile attitude.[7] Removing officials from commerce, encouraging an open market, and providing incentives appeared to be a rational solution. Accordingly, the nature of the Indian once again became a consideration. Enlightened officials did not rule out coercion if, after the proper conditions had been created, individuals did not respond positively. In New Spain, Ramón de Posada, expressing the official position, observed that "the faculty to trade...common to all... benefits society and the individual...and each may dispose freely of property according to their will and convenience." Yet, reflecting the directive freedom inherent in the ideology, he added that individuals were not free to waste their assets.[8] Posada appeared to mirror the contradictory tensions of Lockean political philosophy. The failure to use resources, including labor, productively was contrary to God's will and therefore could not be tolerated. In this case, Posada substituted the state for the deity.[9]

The Ordinance of Intendants sought to end the repartimiento and move toward free exchange. It also authorized the compensated expropriation of uncultivated private holdings and distribution of royal land to Indian and others "for their own profit"(art. 61). Subsequently, Viceroy Revillagigedo recommended an examination of titles to ensure that large inefficient holdings had not usurped Indian land, and that the available arable land was in production. The regulation instructed intendants to monitor commodities in order to facilitate production and marketing (art. 71). Nevertheless, production and commerce "must always be free," and producers should be encouraged by prices to continue their "useful occupations" (art. 71).

The Ordinance severed the legal connection between local officials and merchant houses. As a result, as predicted by many individuals, including Viceroy Antonio María de Bucareli, local administration, now less profitable, became less desirable.[10] Officials did their best to circumvent the restrictions and dispatched alarming reports of impending economic collapse. Those who profited from the old system mounted a campaign to convince Madrid to permit its reinstatement. Under the Hapsburg system, a compromise would have been struck; however, ideological innovators, not responsive to the traditional political process, favored enforcement.

In Peru, lack of cooperation from merchants, subdelegates, and others made the transition to a new economic system difficult. Many feared that a drying up of credit would jeopardize agricultural production and threaten revenues. Moreover, Indians desperate for credit might fall into the hands of hacienda owners and clerics who in effect would impose the old abusive practices unhindered by competition from local officials now barred from trade. Others, however, asserted that with the end of exploitation the rural population could retain sufficient capital to continue productive activities. The Crown, to assure an orderly transition, ordered the extension of government credit in the form of mules and agricultural supplies. Eventually, private sources of regulated credit would then replace royal assistance. While the extension of government credit had to be requested, the program reestablished the connection between local officials and agricultural credits, although its voluntary nature was emphasized in the designation of such loans as *socorros* (assistance). In the end, inadequate salaries and the difficulty of supervising local officials, as well as the disasterous economic condition of Peru, defeated the reforms. Obviously one of the major reform objectives, the replacement of officials involved in commercial activities, had failed, a fact that had become notoriously public. Even Audiencia members blatantly ignored the laws and regulations designed to curb such activities. An investigation of the Audiencia in 1810 discovered that several judges administered haciendas and other businesses. One individual even traded with the Philippines. Another judge combined business with pleasure having left his wife and children to live with a lower class woman in his bread shop. Such conduct appeared to be the equivalent of dancing on José de Gálvez's grave.[11]

In Mexico the situation and process differed. New Spain's booming economy engendered competition. A new and vigorous commercial community contested the hold of traditional merchants. Consequently, Juan Antonio Riaño, the intendant of Valladolid, assured his superiors that with the end of the repartimiento his region would experience no shortage of willing traders.[12] The major obstacles appeared more political than economic. Businessman Manuel Urquijo complained that Miahuatlan's subdelegate not only competed with him but also used his authority to threaten those who engaged in trade. In a similar fashion, a merchant in Tehuantepec whose interests ranged throughout the region protested attempts by the subdelegate to monopolize trade. A series of viceregal orders did little to stop the conflict between aggressive businessmen and local officials, and their commercial allies.[13] Over the long term, the growing importance of urban consumption and the subsequent rise in prices made controlled commerce archaic. Meanwhile, supporters of unrestricted commerce faced the opposition of merchant houses and their allies within the bureaucracy.[14] As a consequence, no firm consensus on the issue emerged. The fluid struggle over the repartimiento needed to be tilted toward open commerce. Yet, in spite of reasonably favorable circumstances, the innovators failed.

The inability to deal decisively with the repartimiento issue may be traced to several factors. Fiscal weakness made it all but impossible to respond to the recognized need to place subdelegates on a reasonable salary. Belatedly, the Ordinance of 1803 addressed the problem, but it never went into effect. In Peru, because of the general economic decline, reform could not be accepted. War and the British navy dashed the brief export recovery of 1790-96, and the economy continued to slide into the next century. A weak internal market offered few opportunities, and the repartimiento remained important to a commercial community worried about survival. Providing Peruvian subdelegates with sufficient support would not have changed the grim economic reality that made marginal activities vital.

The absence of agreement among intendants as to whether the Indian could adjust to the new system also enervated implementation. In Mexico, several intendants insisted, as did Antonio de Mora y Peysal of Antequera de Oaxaca (1787-1808), that the natives appeared "sufficiently rational" to organize themselves productively, but others, including Felipe Cleere of Zacatecas (1787-92) and the intendant of Veracruz, Pablo de Corbalán (1788-91), favored a modified repartimiento.[15] In Oaxaca, treasury official Francisco Antonio Villarrusa Rivera, known for dispassionate impartiality, submitted a report on April 22, 1793, that defended forced repartimientos on the basis of negative view of the Indian mentality.[16] The ambivalence of those charged with suppressing the repartimiento blunted enforcement. Another factor arose as a natural consequence of the preceding ones. Viceroys, given such uncertainty, attempted to establish a balance between conflicting demands. Predictably, they titled their accommodation toward the most powerful interests, although the need to conciliate differing opinions led viceroys to propose modified versions of the repartimiento. The evident divergence between what imperial authorities directed and the actual situation further undermined credibility.

By the end of the eighteenth century, a resurgent political process had become evident in New Spain. Viceroy Marqués de Branciforte (1794-98), faced with the repartimiento issue, identified the interest groups involved and accommodated them. After consultation with the Consulado of Mexico, a center of traditional sentiment, the viceroy permitted reintroduction of the repartimiento under the supervision of the intendants, and on a nonmonopolistic basis. Subdelegates and independent traders theoretically could participate, while their clients remained free to enter such arrangements as they found convenient. A modified repartimiento appeared to be a viable arrangement that met, at least partially, the demands of those groups most concerned. It provided credit, did not exclude others, offered assurances that the rural population would continue to produce as well as to sustain the market, and permitted voluntary participation.[17] Nevertheless, the Council of the Indies queried Miguel José de Azanza (1798-1800), Branciforte's replacement, as to why the repartimiento continued to function in violation of the ordinance. In defense, Azanza noted a royal decree that ordered him to proceed with prudence and toleration.[18] Whereas the viceroy resorted to a traditional formula to justify his action, the Council of the Indies, then dominated by individuals with experience in the American empire, reacted ideologically and viewed the issue as a technical problem.[19] When former viceroy Branciforte arrived back in Spain, he endeavored to persuade the council to support a modified repartimiento. Nevertheless, the Council of the Indies continued to favor suppression, recommending resolving the issue by placing the subdelegates on an adequate salary.[20]

The eighteenth-century ideology had reached a state of operational paralysis. Jorge de Escobedo, former visitor-general in Peru, then a member of the Council of the Indies, charged with some bitterness in 1801 that virtually everyone participated in the repartimiento, including the parish priest.[21] In 1807 the Council of the Indies recognized its own impotence when it decided not to issue further prohibitions of the repartimiento, in spite of the resurgence, because it had already done so repeatedly without effect.[22] An unofficial accommodation had been reached, but one that violated Madrid's ideology. Enlightened reformers, by adopting a narrow goal-directed ideology, had attempted to end the process of continuous adjustment that sustained the monarchy's authority during the sixteenth and seventeenth centuries. Rather than drawing strength from political accommodation, they could only admit weakness. Ironically, given freedom to arrange reasonable compromises, colonial officials could have achieved at least some of Madrid's goals. Ambrosio O'Higgins, as Captain-General of Chile (1788-95), for example, cultivated the support of the Cabildo of Santiago, as well as that of influential families. As a result of his willingness to compromise, he accomplished some of his objectives in return for various concessions to local interests. Instinctively more of a politician than an ideologue, O'Higgins ignored instructions and shaded his reports accordingly.[23] In recognition of his success, he moved on to the Peruvian vice-regal post.

The Last Gasp

While the repartimiento problem constituted a debilitating drain on the credibility of ministerial innovators, and ultimately symbolized failure, change continued with more success in other less contested areas. Even after Gálvez's death in 1787, and that of Carlos III the following year, the pace slowed, but did not stop. A month after the death of the minister of the Indies, the Crown divided his duties between two ministries—Grace and Justice, and War. In 1790 Carlos IV ordered the appropriate ministries to incorporate American affairs. An integrated approach to knowledge, and the downgrading of political considerations, made geographically based institutions archaic. In a similar fashion, the tendency of enlightened officials to think in terms of unified administrative regulations, rather than individual legislation that reflected abstract justice, prompted an attempt to reform colonial law and devise a legal code. The need was manifest to replace the seemingly hopelessly muddled and collectively incoherent *Recopilación de Leyes de los Reynos de las Indias*. As a compilation of individual laws issued over the centuries in response to specific problems, it constituted historical evidence of the innumerable political contests and accommodations that characterized the Hapsburg state. The *Recopilación* did not include laws framed after the reign of Carlos II (1665-1700). The first volume of a new American code, the *Nuevo código de leyes de Indias*, received royal approval in 1792. Nevertheless, widespread opposition defeated the project. Carlos IV, responding politically, ignored the code's ideological unity and ordered that each law required an individual decree in order to take effect.[24]

A politically less sensitive issue involved the reorganization of New Spain's mining tribunal and its definitive establishment on a sound basis. Authorized in 1776, the tribunal experienced prolonged organizational difficulties unresolved at the death of Carlos III. Director-General Fausto de Elhuyar, selected by José de Gálvez, arrived in Veracruz in August of 1788, with a team of German mining experts, a year after the death of his patron. Without the active interest and intervention of the new regime, the organization probably would have continued in a state of unproductive confusion, regardless of the enthusiasm and boundless energy of the director-general. Happily, the government of Carlos IV supported the tribunal's activities and approved the budget for the School of Mines. Royal support enabled the organization to pursue the objective first elaborated in the provisional phase and in the Ordinance of 1783. Mining engineers trained by the School of Mines, which opened formally in 1792, assumed important positions in the industry, including that of administrator of the famed Valenciana mine. A royal order in 1798 instructed officials to fill the position of mining director in Guatemala, Peru, Chile, and Buenos Aires with graduates of the Mexican school.[25] Madrid continued to think in terms of spreading rational methods and new technology.

The creation of new commercial organizations provided more evidence of lingering momentum. Although plans to establish a series of consulados had been laid under Carlos III, his successor Carlos IV presided over their foundation. The new organizations, while they included guild features and emphasized judicial regulation, also served as development corporations. Eighteenth-century consulados responded more to the spirit of the Society of the Friends of the Country than to that of the guild tradition. Bourbon interest in economic growth brought into question the effectiveness of the two traditional consulados of Mexico City (established 1594) and Lima (established 1613). Although both these organizations appointed provincial delegations (*diputaciónes*) in other regions and ports, the practice proved less than successful. Conflicting interests caused tension between local elements and consulados. Often the very structure of trade differed markedly from one region to another. Lima, for example, established a delegation in the distant port city of Buenos Aires in 1756 in an effort to control the contraband trade, which benefited local merchants but injured those in Peru.[26] Buenos Aires cared little about the socioeconomic structure of Peru, nor did it see the repartimiento de comercio in the same light as Lima's merchants. Consequently, in 1778 the Crown indicated its intention of creating new independent consulados.

The *Reglamento...para el comercio libre* (1778) required that in the ports covered by the regulations preliminary steps must be taken to form merchant organizations to stimulate production and trade. In the meantime, local authorities functioned as consulados in judicial matters, subject to appeal to the Council of the Indies.[27] Actual establishment of new consulados in the last decade of the century represented the final major reform. Caracas and Guatemala established merchant guilds in 1793, followed by Buenos Aires and Havana the next year, and finally, in 1795, Cartagena, Santiago (Chile), Guadalajara, and Veracruz founded consulados. The new merchant associations demonstrated a vitality that sharply contrasted with that of Mexico City and Lima. Unavoidably associated with the restrictive past, the traditional consulados appeared stodgy, whereas nascent organizations, in the process of formation and role definition, seemed dynamic. For example, enthusiastic merchants in the port city of Veracruz responded aggressively to the Crown's charge to do everything possible to advance agriculture and the introduction of useful machinery and tools. Jalapa, the inland distribution center, fell within its jurisdiction.[28] In a similar fashion in Guatemala the new organization quickly responded to its own economic interests. Guatemalan merchants moved to control the price of domestic production and direct the region's development to their advantage. They soon succeeded in breaking the hold of the old economic elite and merchant power became dominant.[29] In contrast, in Mexico City and Lima, the changed terms of trade, as well as the new consulados, caused a shakeout of merchants unable to unwilling to make adjustments.[30] Nevertheless, Mexico City, and even Lima in spite of its economic problems, served as major political centers and capital markets as well as important centers of urban consumption. Viceregal capitals continued to support an influential merchant community, albeit on a different basis than in the past.

On a regional level, the instructions issued to the Marqués de Branciforte on assuming New Spain's viceregal authority (1794-98) provide further evidence of the tendency toward uniformity and the end of paternalism. The new viceroy received orders to examine the possibility of suppressing the Juzgado de Indios and turning its general responsibilities over to other officials, including the intendants. Earlier, in 1776, Carlos III ordered the absorption of the separate office of Protector of Indians by the Audiencia's criminal fiscal.[31] While monetary considerations played a part in the suggested abolition of the Indian court as well as the Juzgado General de Bienes de Difuntos (probate court), no savings were contemplated. Revenue previously assigned to the Indian court could be used to fund local courts staffed with trained lawyers.[32] The Crown thought in terms of diverting existing funds to provide reasonable salaries at the lower levels. Administrative rationalization remained the goal.

A potentially important indication of the desire for uniformity was the proposed restructuring of the Tribunal del Protomedicato de Mexico along the lines of that of Madrid.[33] Even more significantly, royal instructions directed Branciforte to stimulate education at all levels as well as to bring higher education into conformity with recent changes in Spain.[34] Branciforte's instructions do not indicate a ideological retreat.

Branciforte's successor, Miguel José de Azanza (1798-1800) struck a symbolic yet noteworthy ideological blow against an economically restrictive paternalism when he ordered that the guild ordinances that prohibited women from manufacturing leather goods be annulled. The issue arose over the petition of Josefa de Celis, a widow with numerous children, to continue to be allowed to fabricate such items and sell them in the streets. Manufacturers claimed that this would violate the established regulation that prohibited women from engaging in guild tasks and that the poor quality of these items injured the consumer. The viceroy, totally out of sympathy with such reasoning, rejected their arguments. An analagous situation in Spain during the reign of Carlos III had been resolved by a royal order of 1784 that permitted Maria Castejón to operate a thread factory without subordination to the master examiner of the appropriate guild. The objective in both cases was the removal of obstacles to production. The Council of the Indies even considered dispatching Azanza's order to the other viceroyalties for similar action. Furthermore, it ordered that New Spain's guild ordinances be reviewed to eliminate any exclusion of women that hindered economic development.[35]

Although innovative momentum continued under Carlos IV, it is evident that the pace of change differed from previous regimes. Undoubtedly, the death of the forceful José de Gálvez and Carlos III made opposition less restrained, but the resurgent strength of the traditional political attitudes could not have been held in check even if death had not removed two principal ideological actors. Moreover, the shock of the French Revolution in 1789, and the unsettling period it ushered in that led to the Napoleonic invasion of Spain in 1808, diverted resources and attention. The urgent need to raise money to fend off foreign pressure resulted in repeated Crown requests for loans from every conceivable source. The imperial government received large sums from New Spain's mining tribunal and from consulados, as well as more modest amounts from other institutions and individuals. Early in 1794 Viceroy Revillagigedo warned Madrid that the constant draining of the colonial treasury jeopardized the viceregal government.[36] Financial dependency discouraged an arbitrary attitude. Necessity, coupled with growing realization of the limits of Madrid's power to carry through innovations, made the royal government less willing to confront resistance, although still dedicated to rationalization. Significantly, the successful innovations of the last decade of the eighteenth century did not directly involve the colonial political structure.

Conclusion

POLITICALLY, THE SPANISH WORLD FUNCTIONED as an intellectual construct. Working within the confines of a Romanized Christianity, theorists elaborated a political process and determined how conflicts would be resolved. Natural law, the knowable reflection of the celestial order, provided the foundation of the philosophical matrix that regulated society and supported the monarchy. As a divine agent, the king became the temporal interpreter of natural law and assumed the obligation to pass on its benefits to his subjects. A monarch demonstrated a divinely delegated concern for the people's spiritual and material well-being. Legitimacy arose from that obligation. Although a ruler manipulated ideas to achieve an acceptable balance within society, the philosophical matrix restricted freedom of action. Arbitrary actions in conflict with the philosophical foundations violated sociopolitical expectation and, as a result, could not gain compliance or contribute to a new balance. The concept of tyrannicide, while diligently encapsulated by wary political theorists, could be neutralized only to a limited extent. The widely accepted obligation to call injustice to the monarch's attention, which served as the initial step in the reactive political process, had the implied as well as actual potential of terminating in revolt if the monarchy failed to respond. The royal function of validating accommodations required that the king react in the accepted manner. As a consequence, a certain predictability, based on the restrictions inherent in the philosophy itself, facilitated acceptance of the king's just and proper intervention.

Hapsburg monarchs, responsive to a widely accepted philosophy, presided over a governing system characterized by flexibility and stability. While contesting interests struggled sometimes violently, they did so within the limits elaborated by political theorists. The abstract nature of the philosophical matrix provided a broad arena in which conflicts could be resolved through compromise and concession without jeopardizing the monarch's authority. The actual establishment of a viable balance required an extended period of discussion and negotiation. Accommodation, compromise, and adjustment emerged from a process that might last years, or even decades. On occasion, with the passage of time the issue became moot. Proposed solutions offered by contesting groups had to conform to philosophical requirements. Contestants professed loyalty to the same shared principles but disputed the method to be employed in their realization. As the divine agent, only the king conferred legitimacy on any arrangement. Validation that the resolution conformed to philosophical requirements had to be sought—naked power alone did not suffice.

Manipulation of moral principle served as the main method of control and also provided the means by which various interests argued for a particular balance. Thus, on the surface, a political struggle often appeared to be an exercise in hypocrisy. Nevertheless, acceptance of higher principles regulated the manner in which private goals could be achieved. The degree of compromise depended on the relative power of the interested parties, as well as the effective use of ideas.[1] Investigative hearings and the courts provided a controlled arena within which to test the strength of contending parties. Although appeals to the laws and abstract notions constituted a form of pressure, without actual power a legal victory could not be sustained. When seemingly powerless Indians forced Audiencias to recognize their communal land-holdings, they not only relied upon philosophical notions but also implied their ultimate willingness to resort to violence or some form of social disruption in defense of their expectation of justice.[2]

While any arrangement had to be viewed as reasonable and just, it is important not to confuse social acceptance with the actual reality. A political accommodation occurred, agreed to be in accord with the philosophical matrix and therefore just and proper. In reality, justice represented a distributive compromise, not the actual realization of the abstract ideal. Powerful elements, while restrained to varying degrees by philosophical notions and consequently unable to behave arbitrarily in total disregard for their weaker opponents, nevertheless could insist on a favorable balance. European-Indian relations, particularly in the early decades of the sixteenth century, demonstrate the point. Only after the Indian population rallied, and manipulated the colonial system to its advantage, could a more equitable and less oppressive adjustment take place. Accommodations, however, seldom remained static for long periods of time. While the Crown conferred legitimacy, it did not stand rigidly by a particular balance. Enforcement depended upon the power of the interested parties to sustain pressure. If they proved unable to do so, Crown decrees in their favor became inoperative. Furthermore, because all accommodation theoretically rested upon abstract notions subject to constant reinterpretation, it remained intellectually fluid.

The philosophical matrix directly influenced the functioning of the colonial government. Officials primarily served as agents regulating and monitoring, rather than directing. The viceroy acted as both the colonial chief executive and the highest magistrate. On a regional level, alcaldes mayores and corregidores combined civil and judicial duties. Any separation of these functions would have seemed both dangerous and ridiculous to Hapsburg theorists. The flexibility engendered by the philosophical matrix enabled officials to adjust to unique circumstances.

Ad hoc regulation restricted by philosophical notions assured a viable balance in a particular region, as well as wide variations between regions. What passed for a just resolution in one area might be viewed as unacceptable in another. A reactive response to a situation characterized Crown actions.[3] The absence of coercive force in Spanish America testified to the effectiveness of methods made possible by the philosophical matrix. Without much difficulty, shared principles, reinforced by cultural coercion, regulated the empire.

Within the governing structure itself, a sense of being the king's personal agent as well as a recipient of royal favor encouraged officials to act politically rather than as administrative functionaries. Emphasis on individual responsibility and mutual obligation retarded the development of an orderly hierarchy of authority. A perceived direct link between the monarch, his agents, and subjects of all ranks and social stations made a vertical structure undesirable. A simplified ladder existed that ran from the divine, to the king as temporal representative, to the people. Consequently, a viceroy, while technically the chief executive, had fragmented and limited influence and control over lower-ranking officials, as well as over society in general. Without a strong personality and manipulative skills, he could not fulfill his duties. Lower-ranking officials, well aware they possessed individual commissions and legitimacy from above, functioned independently of other appointees. As a result, the discrediting of one official, even a viceroy, did not damage the entire regime. Moreover, dispersal of authority within a horizontal structure encouraged a broad spectrum of royal representatives to mediate conflicts, as well as provided virtually endless channels of communication. Less positively, the self-contained nature of royal commissions engendered innumerable jurisdictional disputes, in part because personal charges retarded the standardization of functions. It also encouraged the use of secret instructions as well as implied special commissions.

The nature of the monarchy made it difficult to handle the personal failings of its dependents. The emphasis on compassion and forgiveness that complemented the Christian view of humans as essentially weak encouraged lapses in approved behavior. Politically, while it enabled the Crown to reconcile all manner of misconduct short of absolute treason, and thus avoid forcing individuals into intractable opposition, it made it difficult to discipline royal servants. The notion that officeholding represented a favor bestowed on an individual by a benevolent ruler compounded the problem. Making the fine distinction between venality and prudent manipulation of assets and opportunities was not easy. Lack of rigid standards, useful in political matters, had a negative effect on individual conduct. Corruption became a question of degree. While the residencia process, among other things, constantly attempted to reinforce ideal behavior, its realization proved difficult. In addition, the notion of personal patronage that tied the individual to the monarch also encouraged the development of a secondary patronage network radiating in all directions. Officials developed alliances, exchanged favors, and when necessary protected each other from charges of misconduct. Royal agents operated within a thoroughly politicized system and responded to a complex web of loyalty and mutual obligations that mitigated the consequences of personal failings.

The relationship between royal representatives and the king's subjects remained that of judge and petitioner. While the people expected to be treated justly, technically they could not demand it. Even when the laws or regulations favored them, justice remained a gift. In return, the Crown expected its subjects to be grateful in an individual sense, as well as to assume the benevolent intent of official acts. On occasion, the extension of favor by royal agents bordered on arrogance and condescension. Arbitrary and abusive officials, however, acted contrary to philosophical expectations and thus risked a withdrawal of cooperation, and even violent resistance. Crown officials and those they governed had a distinct perception of what constituted proper conduct which could not be casually violated.

In the eighteenth century, an attempt to override the established philosophical matrix created stress, and in the end failed. Enlightened officials constructed a narrow goal-oriented ideology designed to achieve material prosperity. Motivated by the obvious economic distress of the peninsula, and enthralled by the notion that the new rational scientific ideas of the age made it possible to direct affairs dispassionately toward projected material goals, Crown ministers embarked on an ambitious program. The purpose of the state shifted from the abstract spiritual and moral to concrete material objectives. Common good, reduced to material progress, laid aside mystical and moral aspects so important in previous centuries. As a consequence, the state became accountable for definite measurable performance. Late eighteenth-century Buenos Aires merchants, already part of the worldwide economic system, viewed a good monarch as one who functioned primarily as a patron of commerce and whose activities should be directed toward the expansion of trade.[4] Such an attitude represented Feijóo's *príncipe pacífico* taken to a logical and material extreme. Economic achievements became the yardstick of state utility. The Crown no longer occupied the relatively safe position made possible by its divine charge to guide the Christian community, in which the judgement of whether it succeeded or failed awaited the celestial moment. Acceptance of the new ideology made it possible for the Bourbon state to succeed or fail, a possibility not present in the Hapsburg notion of kingship.

Enlightened officials viewed politics as a nonproductive process that interfered with the implementation of rational ideas. They attempted to transform the colonial empire into an administrative organization stripped of the elements of sovereignty. The relatively simple structure of empire, so admirably suited for political maneuvering, was temporarily immobilized by the insertion of new officials responsible to a rigid ideology. The introduction of a ladder hierarchy of vertical administrative accountability made it difficult to achieve viable accommodations. Traditional political officials, in their efforts to reach acceptable compromises, found themselves hamstrung by administrative officials. An authoritarianism inherent in the official ideology demanded conformity and ruled out compromise; thus concessions could come only from those pressed to accept the new vision of reality. Directives, designed to facilitate ideological control, appeared absolutely necessary to remove traditional elements from the path of progress. Enlightened ministers held lower-level officials accountable for implementing the ideologically motivated reform program, and insisted on reliability and uniform behavior. Each activity, as part of a larger pattern, had to fit within the accepted ideological framework. Contradictory pressures had to be resisted or rationalized within the official ideology.

Decision-makers responded to restricted categories of issues that ignored the reality of complex colonial societies. Paradoxically, while the new knowledge made it possible to perceive the interrelated nature of problems and their solutions, corrective actions tended to be simplistic. Officials excluded as well as discouraged the search for alternatives that fell outside ideological boundaries. The acceptance of a limited pattern of ideas resulted in increasingly rigid behavior.[5] The unwillingness of José de Gálvez to acknowledge the fact that the empire had generated its own internal economy quite apart from Spain is evident. Madrid's refusal to listen to contradictory advice concerning its policy of suppressing the repartimiento de comercio, and the introduction of the intendant and subdelegado system, provide operational examples of the rigidity fostered by the new ideology. Contrary advice, characterized as reactionary, had little influence. Ideological arrogance encouraged those in authority to believe they had discovered the "true method." They consequently sought to end the political dialectic that had characterized Spanish America from the moment of the European arrival in the New World.

Depoliticization of the colonial governing structure, a rational objective from Madrid's standpoint, could not be accepted in the various kingdoms and dependencies of the empire. Reformers enjoyed tactical victories and succeeded in increasing royal revenues, yet ultimately met defeat. What on the surface appeared to be a successful reform, the rationalization of commerce and trade, in fact constituted an adjustment to economic forces far beyond Spain's ability to counter. When the goals of the reformers coincided with economic reality or the wishes of the colonial population, they succeeded; in other circumstances; they failed.

The official ideology clashed with the philosophical matrix and colonial expectations. Consequently, reforms stalled and experienced de facto modifications that outran Madrid's ability to admit reality. At the end of the century, innovators found themselves in a state of political paralysis, complicated by events in Europe.[6] A thoughtful student of empire aptly labeled the eighteenth as a "historically frustrated" century.[7] Lacking sufficient coercive strength, and unable to gain acceptance of their ideology, the reformers failed to achieve a perceptual revision of the colonial reality. Moreover, insistence on material self-interest as the universal motivator ignored the possibility that the American socioeconomic environment, within which individuals pursued their own interests, might lead in different directions from that envisioned in Madrid. New World mining, agricultural, and merchant entrepreneurs functioned within an economic system only technically linked to Spain.[8] Contradictions could not be papered over, nor could a dynamic bourgeoisie tied into a world economic system be persuaded by Iberocentric rationalization.[9]

An unintended consequence of the imperial government's attitude was the development of an adversary relationship. Enlightened officials viewed themselves as an elite dealing with an uncomprehending population with scant appreciation for innovations. The reformist mentality placed enlightened ministers on one side and the governed on the other. Those excluded perceived the in-group attitude as arrogance. A natural separation developed between the reformers and the governed who became the objects of change. Moreover, Madrid's innovators made few allowances for the reaction to rapid, externally imposed change.

Only in the economic sphere could change be readily understood, even by those who opposed trade rationalization. The cutting and simplification of taxes, opening of more ports, and ending of the restrictive and expensive convoy systems, resulted in lower prices and cut inflated profit margins. With a plentiful, and usually uninterrupted, supply of reasonably priced goods, a new group of traders entered commerce, much to the dismay of the less competitive. Viceroy Revillagigedo in his 1793 report on New Spain's trade noted that those unable to adjust to competition had withdrawn from trade.[10] Trade liberalization and the rapid development of a world-wide economic system created a sense of fluidity and opportunity.

As economic theorists predicted, pragmatic and self-interested traders stimulated commerce and innovation, and broadened the commercial base. A former secretary of the consulado of Veracruz, José María Quirós, demonstrated the extent to which the new commercial elements shared the economic views of imperial reformers. In a memorial of 1817, he suggested three fundamental causes of the backwardness of the Intendancy of Veracruz. Supposedly, the initial lavish division of land in the sixteenth century, along with the tyrannical attitude of large landholders and the apathy and subsistence expectations of the natives, accounted for the lack of prosperity and population. Earlier, in 1805, Veracruz's municipal council, joining with the consulado, obtained a royal order giving owners of unutilized land one year to revitalize their interest or face forced sale. Iberian economists felt that such criticism and actions were in line with their own analysis and recommendations. Nevertheless, they found themselves pushed by their own converts. Their frame of reference broadened to include the entire Western European world and, coupled with uncritical admiration of foreign economic achievements, exerted performance pressure on the Spanish state. The imperial government had to deal with economic expectations aroused by its own ideology.

Cold rationality left little room for sentimental loyalty when economic issues were at stake. Quirós, while lamenting the destruction caused by Napoleonic armies and brushing aside doubts about loyalty, made a blunt demand for further liberalization of foreign trade. He concluded by advising that the common good had to be viewed with disinterested impartiality.[11] Economic progress had to be continually accelerated. Yesterday's triumphs meant little in terms of tomorrow's profits. The expansion of Spanish exports to the New World in 1782-96 was only impressive if one ignored the low level of trade prior to the reforms. While New World exports to Spain increased in value ten times over the 1778 level it had become evident that Spain could not take advantage of the American market nor absorb the New World's production. Political ties might modify, but could not change economic realities. American economies could not be sustained by an obsolete trading system regardless of how it was reformed.[12]

Bourbon ideologues found themselves battling a truculent America. New World resistance alternately frustrated and enraged the reformers. José de Gálvez and José Antonio Areche constantly appeared to be in danger of losing emotional control over themselves. Gálvez indeed suffered some type of mental breakdown while in New Spain although he soon recovered. In their disdain for differing views, those who shared the ideology developed a Hobbesian view of the relationship between the people and the state. When reactionary violence occurred, they responded harshly in both an intellectual and physical sense. Such a response is evident in the work of Capuchin friar Joaquín de Finestrad, who wrote *Vasallo instruido en el estado del nuevo reino de Granada y sus respectivas obligaciones* (1789) in the aftermath of the suppression of the Comunero revolt. Finestrad, active in the pacification efforts, fused the traditional notion of a hierarchical natural law with a Hobbesian idea of the obligations of society. He dismissed justice as a primary consideration and put order and security first. The king's subjects, according to Finestrad, must accept orders blindly and assume that they are just and fair. Like a latter-day Montaigne confronted by colonial Huguenots, he declared that disorder and riots constituted a fate worse than tyranny.[13] Finestrad's work represented the opposite philosophical pole from the *Justa repulsa* written two years earlier.

To those who shared the ideology, compromise represented weakness. Officials well understood that opposition might delay or even defeat their objectives; yet the notion that opposing elements could play a positive role in developing or modifying them appeared to be intellectual heresy.[14] Enlightened officials perceived the existing colonial reality as essentially irrational—made so by a political process and its endless compromises and accommodations. Ideological rigidity ruled out political manipulation. Moreover, the inability to recognize de facto accommodation formally, so evident in the last decade of the century and symbolized by the repartimiento, eroded the credibility of the state and demonstrated its powerlessness.

The deliberate unbalancing of the traditional corporate structure required a different approach to enforcement. Self-policing by quasi-official corporate groups believed to be hostile to the official ideology came under attack. The authority of the old structure over other units was diminished. Both the viceroy and the Audiencia lost authority and status. At the same time, self-policing concessions to newly established and favored state institutions, such as the tobacco monopoly, playing card monopoly, postal service, gunpowder monopoly, and others, further weakened traditional authority. A multitude of administrators, subdelegates, treasurers, accountants, and other types of bureaucrats imbued with a technocratic ethos made political manipulation a frustrating experience.[15] The attitude toward the implementation of regulations and laws changed dramatically. Individual enactments constituted part of a pattern directed toward understood objectives, and thus became as important as the goal itself. The state, motivated by a goal-directed ideology, theoretically had to be an active and rigid enforcer.

The attempt to depoliticize the New World proved disruptive and caused substantial tension, even as it foundered. The empire continued to respond to the traditional philosophical matrix and make its own internal adjustments, although willing to accept economic changes that corresponded to its needs. An administrative bureaucracy, upon which Madrid pinned its hopes, failed to end the colonial political process. Ironically, the elaboration of a bureaucratic structure eventually blunts and softens change. While the active state requires a rationally organized and technically skilled bureaucracy staffed by experts, over time such officials develop their own internal ethos and interests unsympathetic to daring, risky, or sweeping change. Bureaucrats, although theoretically apolitical, in fact tend to prefer cooperation and prior consensus. Policymakers, dependent upon the expertise of administrators, eventually become captives of their supposed instrument.[16] Moreover, Spanish-American administrative expansion benefited colonial subjects eager to secure both a salary and a position of authority.[17] Over time, a complex colonial bureaucracy would serve to conciliate as well as modify externally imposed objectives, thus performing a political function. In the meantime, in the last decade of the century, the return to the old political methods could not be resisted.

Even the appointment process indicated the return of personal patronage—a development that benefited American-born aspirants for public office.[18] From 1790 on, the Crown reasserted its right to make appointments by decree, thus circumventing the body charged with screening and recommending candidates. As a result, José Baquíjano's long quest for preferment ended as he became the only native son named directly to the Audiencia of Lima in twenty years. The direct use of royal patronage constituted a political act rather than a fiscal measure.[19] Tadeo Bravo de Rivera, Lima's representative in Madrid, reported in 1802 that the Crown had decreed a virtual restitution of municipal authority and privilege. Out of gratitude, a jubilant cabildo named Secretary of State Antonio Caballero an honorary councilman and had his portrait hung in the assembly hall. Earlier, in 1800, the imperial government restored the right of annual election of alcaldes ordinarios throughout the American empire. It remained for Madrid to concede reality and formally acknowledge the continued political validity of the philosophical matrix.[20]

Spanish Americans desired political autonomy, an objective that could be met within the traditional concept of kingdoms. They understood the need for flexibility and accommodation within a general consensus of what constituted a just and proper resolution of conflict. At the same time, the colonial elite accepted the useful aspects of the Enlightenment and contributed significantly to the expansion of knowledge.[21] A broad appreciation of new ideas within colonial society is indicated, among other things, by the extent of the book trade and personal libraries. In New Spain, the Fagoaga's family library included works by Adam Smith and Buffon, as well as books in English, French, Italian, Greek, and Latin. The Marqués de Rayas demonstrated a similar taste for the new knowledge.[22] While they clung to the traditional philosophical matrix as it pertained to politics, they were not reactionaries rejecting all new currents from Europe. For example, Pantaleón Rivarola (1757-1821), a professor at the University of Córdoba, exemplified the strength of the scholastic notions in the late eighteenth century. Nevertheless, he also accepted ideas taken from Newton, Descartes, Wolff, Leibniz, Gassendi, and others. He fused the thought of Aristotle and St. Thomas with modern thinkers. He was not unique in doing so.[23] The popularity, as demonstrated in numerous editions, of the only work on civil law written by an American in the colonial period provided further evidence of the empire's attachment to the traditional matrix. Written by José María Alvarez, a Guatemalan professor of law, the *Instituciones de derecho real de castilla y de indias* (1818-20) placed the laws of the Indies within their Castilian context. His work cited canon law, the Fuero Juzgo, Fuero Real, and Siete Partidas, as well as subsequent Castilian codes, and the laws of the Indies.[24]

Repoliticization indicated the evolution of Spanish America toward a commonwealth structure. In Spain, however, the equality of all the imperial parts could not be accepted easily. Even as late as 1817, after violence had shaken the sense of unity of the Spanish world, Finance

Minister Martín Garay voiced fears that acceptance of economic equality would lead to an unnatural political monstrosity.[25] A reversal of roles, similar to that of Brazil following the removal of the Portuguese monarchy to Rio de Janiero in the face of the Napoleonic invasion appeared to be a possibility. In the Luso-Brazilian world, the original mother country slipped into a de facto colonial position. Reactionary Portuguese liberals failed to press Brazil back into an inferior position, and in the end they opted out of a structure within which Portugal could occupy only a subordinate and marginal place. In a similar fashion, the dynamic center of the Spanish world had long before passed to the American empire. For Spain, the price of recognizing reality might have been unacceptably high. It is not inconceivable that, assigned a marginal position within a commonwealth, Spain would subsequently have had to struggle for its own independence.

In the meantime, even after the political trauma induced by French pressure, and the ineffectual maneuvering of Carlos IV and Godoy, as well as the desperate scheming of the Prince of Asturias, the future Fernando VII, political bargaining remained possible. The actual Napoleonic invasion of Spain complicated the process, but did not end it. An Iberian world, uniting both the empire and the mother country, seemed feasible—with the possible exception of Buenos Aires, already afloat on the sea of international capitalism.[26] The realization that politics provided the best hope for survival prompted the Junta Central to request in January of 1809 that the American empire send delegates to Spain. While the liberals also believed that force should be used to preserve the empire, political negotiation had come back into play. Subsequently, the Constitution of 1812 attempted to reconcile the new thought of the Age of Enlightenment with the political process inherent in the philosophical matrix.

Many Americans hoped that a new negotiated arrangement would preserve political legitimacy while permitting the flexibility to make needed reforms. For example, Manuel Lorenzo Vidaurre who served as a judge of the Cuzco Audiencia pressed for acceptance of the Constitution of 1812. He constantly reminded Spain that only loyalty could hold the empire together. His desperate desire to preserve legitimacy made him at once a firm supporter of the Constitution as well as an ardent subject of the king. In 1815 he expressed the fears of many noting that America could not survive as an independent entity becasue it lacked civic virtue as well as a sense of unity. He believed that only political accommodation could save the unity of the empire and the internal stability of its parts. As late as 1820 he argued that the Constitution of 1812 formed a concordat between American Spaniards and their European couterparts.

The great Ecuadorean intellectual and champion of Spanish Americanism Vicente Rocafuerte in a similar fashion rejected any distinction
between American and European Spaniards as artificial. Rocafuerte
supported a constitutional resolution. Others such as Fernández de
Madrid, a Columbian, and the Argentine José Antonio Miralla shared his
views. All of these individuals hoped that an acceptable political structure could be worked out. Spanish liberalism failed to match the intellectual and political vision of these Spanish Americans.[27]

While hurried accommodation under pressure of foreign invasion
failed, as did reconstruction, the trend toward colonial repoliticazation
that antedated the Napoleonic disaster did not point toward a sharp
revolutionary break. The political flexibility inherent in the broad philosophical matrix reasserted itself. Consequently, American deputies to the
restored liberal Cortes submitted an autonomy plan (June 25, 1821) that
called for the division of the empire into three parts with capitals located
at Lima, Bogotá, and Mexico City, each with its own autonomous
government, a legislative branch subordinated to the Cortes, and a
regent executive selected by the king. The new political units would pay
a certain amount for the support of the Spanish government and the
common foreign debt. Trade between all units would be considered as
internal commerce. Simon Bolivar's agent described it as a plan of
"apparent emancipation."[28] The Cortes received the scheme coolly. By
rejecting the plan, the liberals dashed the last serious chance for preservation of a Spanish system.

The failure to negotiate the retention of Hispanic legitimacy within
an autonomous structure resulted in disaster for Spanish America.
Revolutionary armies in the end destroyed the legitimacy of the old
order and plunged an independent Latin America into a desperate search
for a new political system able to contain the perceived anarchy and
disorder. As the fiscal of the Audiencia of Charcas, Victoriáno de Villava
feared, democracy gave way to anarchy and tyranny. Villava, in a widely
circulated manuscript (1797), advocated a monarchy, assisted by a
supreme council, and an elected parliament to govern the empire.[29] That
moment had now passed. The elite feared an aroused lower class and the
prospect of class war, as well as the emergence of violence as the primary
political instrument. As a result, they turned their wealth and intelli-
gence toward containing and repressing those elements they feared.
They abandoned Spanish America's colonial legacy of flexible political
accommodation. Politics, responsive to a wide spectrum of interests that
served to express the ideal as well as satisfy actual demands, became a
casualty of revolution.

In the nineteenth century, Latin America's ruling elites, struggling to reestablish a sense of control, and drawn tightly into an economic system dominated by the needs of an industrialized Europe, seized on an ordered modernization as the universal panacea. They justified their fearful abandonment of flexible political accommodation by systematic denegation of their heritage, adoption of a hostile view of their own cultural resources, and a slavish devotion to what they viewed as superior models. They developed an exploitive approach toward the lower classes.[30] The victims, guilty of backwardness, forfeited political consideration. Tragically, the elites restricted the means by which viable sociopolitical accommodations could be reached. The struggle to return to a more reasonable balance continued well into the twentieth century, and in many areas remains urgent.

Notes

Introduction

1. Edmundo O'Gorman, *The Invention of America: An Inquiry into the Historical Nature of the New World and the Meaning of Its History* (Bloomington, 1961), explores the process.

2. Morse employed the term to indicate the "deep-lying matrix of thought and attitude." Richard M. Morse, "The Heritage of Latin America," in Louis Hartz, *The Founding of New Societies* (New York, 1964), p. 153. The connection between intellectuals as experts in the manipulation of symbols and tradition is discussed in S. N. Eisenstadt, "Intellectuals and Tradition," *Daedalus* (Spring, 1972), pp. 1-19.

3. John H. Kautsky, "The Question of Peasant Revolts in Traditional Empires," *Studies in Comparative International Development* (Fall-Winter, 1981), p. 23. Predictable order, respect for authority and regulation, characterizes Indian society. It should not be confused with passivity or stoicism. James D. Sexton, ed., *Son of Tecún Umán: A Maya Indian Tells His Life Story* (Tucson, 1981), demonstrates the point.

4. Otis H. Green, *Spain and the Western Tradition: The Castilian Mind in Literature from El Cid to Calderón* (Madison, 1965), vol. 3, p. 83. For a biographical study, see F. Sánchez y Escribano, *Juan de Mal Lara* (New York, 1941).

5. Linz suggests that Spanish philosopher-scholar Francisco de Vitoria represented the archetypial institutionalizer. Juan J. Linz, "Intellectual Roles in Sixteenth and Seventeenth-Century Spain," *Daedalus* (Summer, 1972), p. 88. Leszek Kolakowski, *Marxism and Beyond: On Historical Understanding and Individual Responsibility* (London, 1968), p. 179.

6. Janet L. Nelson, "Inauguration Rituals," in P. H. Sawyer and I. N. Wood, eds., *Early Medieval Kingship* (Leeds, 1977), p. 51. Defining one's position within a legal code appears to be an extension of this tendency.

7. Cervantes de Salazar's *Crónica de la Conquista de Nueva España* obligingly claimed that the Aztecs as barbarians violated natural law and imposed a tyrannical rule over the land. Jorge Hugo Díaz Thomé, "Francisco Cervantes de Salazar y su crónica de la conquista de Nueva España," in *Estudios de historiógrafía de la Nueva España* (Mexico, 1945), pp. 15-47. Earlier he fabricated a noble genealogy for Cortés and the legend of the conqueror burning his ships behind him to link him with Greco-Roman heroes. Enrique Anderson Imbert, *Spanish American Literature: A History* (Detroit, 1963), p. 35.

8. Roberto Levillier, *Don Francisco de Toledo, supremo organizador del Perú: su vida, su obra (1515-1582)* (Buenos Aires, 1935-1942), vol. 2, pp. 182-195.

9. Lewis Hanke, *The Spanish Struggle for Justice in the Conquest of America* (Philadelphia, 1949), p. 170.

10. Juan Matienzo, *Gobierno del Perú* (Buenos Aires, 1910), pp. 12-13. Garcilaso de la Vega, El Inca, *Royal Commentaries of the Incas and General History of Peru*, trans. Harold V. Livermore (Austin, 1966).

11. Huamán Poma (Don Felipe Huamán Poma de Ayala), *Letters to a King*, trans. Christopher Dilke (New York, 1978), p. 127. Poma demonstrated a knowledge of the ideas of Las Casas, Domingo de Santo Tomás, and others, and referred to the latest books published in Spain and America. Roléna Adorno, "Las otras fuentes de Guaman Poma: sus lecturas castellanas," *Histórica* (Lima, December 1978), pp. 138-155.

12. Instances of adjustments are noted in Steve J. Stern, "The Rise and Fall of Indian-White Alliances: A Regional View of 'Conquest' History," *Hispanic American Historical Review* (August 1981), pp. 461-491. Rafael Varon Gabai, *Curacas y encomenderos: acomadomiento nativo en Huaras, siglos XVI y XVII* (Lima, 1980), pp. 88-93, noted the development in Peru of "curacas coloniales" (caciques) skilled in the manipulation of European political concepts. Proceedings of the Indian municipal council of Tlaxcala (New Spain) written in Nahuatl demonstrated the remarkable adjustment to the new imperial situation. James Lockhart, Frances Berdan, Arthur J. O. Anderson, *The Tlaxcalan Actas: A Compendium of the Records of the Cabildo of Tlaxcala (1545-1627)* (Salt Lake City, 1986).

13. See the table in Juan J. Linz "Intellectual Roles in Sixteenth and Seventeenth Century Spain," *Daedalus* (Summer, 1972), p. 74.

14. Henry Kamen, *The Spanish Inquisition* (New York, 1965), pp. 67-103, attempted the difficult task of assessing that organization's impact on the circulation of books and ideas.

15. Irving A. Leonard, *Books of the Brave: Being an Account of Books and of Men in the Spanish Conquest and Settlement of the Sixteenth-Century New World* (New York, 1964), pp. 183-257.

16. Guillermo Furlong, *Nacimiento y desarrollo de la filosofía en el Río de la Plata, 1536-1810* (Buenos Aires, 1952), p. 101.

17. For a list of philosophical works, see Bernabé Navarro B., *La introducción de la filosofía moderna en México* (México, 1948), pp. 287-305. A bibliography has been compiled by Walter Bernard Redmond, *Bibliography of Philosophy in the Iberian Colonies of America* (The Hague, 1972). For the situation at a provincial institution, the University of Córdoba (est. 1622-1623), see Furlong, *Nacimiento*, pp. 95-109.

18. O. Carlos Stoetzer, *The Scholastic Roots of the Spanish American Revolution* (New York, 1979), p. 40.

19. Quoted in Charles A. Beard, "Introduction," in J. B. Bury, *The Idea of Progress: An Inquiry into Its Growth and Origin* (New York, 1955), p. xii.

20. Shils noted that "the past does not have to be remembered by all who reenact it, the deposit is carried forward by a chain of transmission and reception. To become a tradition, however, and to remain a tradition, a pattern of assertion or action must be entered into memory." Edward Shils, *Tradition* (London, 1981), p. 167.

21. Destutt de Tracy coined the term *ideology* in 1796 to designate a pattern of rational scientific ideas employed to make policy decisions and effect sweeping reforms. David Braybrooke, "Ideology," in Paul Edwards, ed., *The Encyclopedia of Philosophy* (New York, 1967), vol. 4, p. 125.

22. For example, Claudio Véliz, *The Centralist Tradition of Latin America* (Princeton, 1980), p. 71, suggests that "the centralism of the formative decades... survived as a significant factor throughout the colonial period, and the nineteenth century and is with us today." Lingering attitudes are traced by Woodrow Borah, "Legacies of the Past: Colonial," in James W. Wilkie, Michael C. Meyer, and Edna Monzón de Wilkie, eds., *Contemporary Mexico: Papers of the IV International Congress of Mexican History* (Los Angeles, 1976), pp. 29-37.

23. G. K. Chesterton, *Chaucer* (London, 1959), p. 10. Chesterton wrote as a frustrated populist rather than as a historian. Margaret Canovan, *G. K. Chesterton: Radical Populist* (New York, 1977).

I: *Monarchy as an Intellectual Construct*

1. Walter Ullman, *A History of Political Thought: The Middle Ages* (Middlesex, 1970), p. 21. "El fuero real de España," *Los códigos españoles concordados y anotados*, vol. 1, 2d ed. (Madrid, 1872), lib. 1, tit. 11, pt. 2.

2. Michael Wilks, *The Problem of Sovereignty in the Later Middle Ages* (Cambridge, 1963), pp. 18, 57.

3. Ibid., p. 39.

4. Roger Collins, "Julian of Toledo and Royal Succession in Late Seventh-Century Spain," in P. H. Sawyer and I. N. Wood, eds., *Early Medieval Kingship* (Leeds, 1977), p. 48.

5. P. D. King, *Law and Society in the Visigothic Kingdom* (Cambridge, Mass., 1972), p. 29.

6. The Visigothic Church was "virtually a department of state" and the bishops "supine supporters of the king." E. A. Thompson, *The Goths in Spain* (Oxford, 1969), pp. 281, 316.

7. Charles Homer Haskins, *The Renaissance of the Twelfth Century* (Cambridge, Mass., 1927), pp. 284-290.

8. David Knowles, *The Evolution of Medieval Thought* (London, 1962), p. 264. Aquinas observed that a state could "not be considered just unless it is established for the common good of the people." Quentin Skinner, *The Foundations of Modern Political Thought* (Cambridge, 1978), vol. 1, p. 58.

9. "Fuero juzgo," *Los códigos españoles concordados y anotados*, vol. 1, 2d ed. (Madrid, 1872), tit. 1.

10. Peter Linehan, *The Spanish Church and the Papacy in the Thirteenth Century* (Cambridge, 1971), pp. 322-334.

11. John A. Watt, *The Theory of Papal Monarchy in the Thirteenth Century* (London, 1965), p. 72.

12. Ibid., pp. 62-63. Thirteenth-century canonists did not dismiss the notion of a duality of authority but encompassed it within a perception of the overarching unity of Christendom—a position that provided flexibility as well as theoretical contradictions.

13. Ullmann, p. 137.

14. Ibid., p. 179. José María Font Rius, *Instituciónes medievales españolas: la organización política, económica y social de los reinos cristianos de la reconquesta* (Madrid, 1949), p. 26. The Siete Partidas employed identical language noting that each king served as the vicar of God with the task of maintaining the community in justice and truth in temporal matters. Furthermore, the king, placed on earth in God's place, is called the heart and soul of the people. *Las siete partidas del rey Alfonso El Sabio contejadas con varios codices antiguos por la real academia de la história* (Madrid, 1972), pt. II, tit. 1, ley 5. Bonifacio VIII acknowledged the principle of two swords, but insisted that temporal authority must be subordinate to spiritual. He claimed that the Vicar of Christ (the pope) possessed both types of authority. T. S. R. Boase, *Boniface VIII* (London, 1933), p. 459.

15. Etienne Gibson, *Dante the Philosopher* (London, 1948), pp. 191-194. It has been suggested that Dante's *Monarchy* did not represent his mature thoughts. For the purpose of this study, the fact that he developed such a concept under political pressure is the important factor. The idea itself can be traced back to Gelasius's division of labor between the priest and the ruler. Only Christ had been both, although Gelasius assigned the pope final authority in a Christian society. Ullmann, p. 43.

16. Marsiglio of Padua, *The Defender of Peace* (New York, 1956), p. 155.

17. Arthur S. McGrade, *The Political Thought of William of Ockham* (Cambridge, 1974), pp. 134-140, 161-164.

18. Wilks, p. 91.

19. Don Juan's theories appear to have been derived from Aquinas. Don Juan Manuel, *Libro de los estados*, ed. R. B. Tate and I. R. MacPherson (Oxford, 1974), pp. xviii, xxi.

20. J. H. Elliott, *Imperial Spain, 1469-1716* (London, 1963), p. 90.

21. Skinner, vol. 2, p. 89.

22. Phyllis Doyle, *A History of Political Thought* (London, 1963), p. 126. Moral laxity, and inability to rationalize the devastation caused by the Black Death, weakened clerical influence. Subsequently, the Great Schism, and the failure of the conciliar movement to introduce successfully new methods of governance further crippled clerical authority. The failure strengthened the alternative—the politically supreme monarchy functioning within an independent nation-state.

23. Bellarmine's *The Supreme Pontiff* asserted that just as Christ avoided temporal dominion so should his vicar on earth. Skinner, vol. 2, p. 180.

24. Ibid.

25. J. Lynch, "Philip II and the Papacy," *Transactions of the Royal Historical Society*, 5th series, vol. 2 (1961), pp. 25-26.

26. Referring to Felipe II, the pope noted, "The preservation of the Catholic religion which is the principal aim of the Pope is only a pretext for His Majesty whose principal aim is the security and aggrandizement of his dominions." Quoted in Lynch, p. 23.

27. J. H. Fernández-Santamaria, *The State, War and Peace: Spanish Political Thought in the Renaissance, 1516-1559* (Cambridge, 1977), pp. 51-54.

28. Guillermo Furlong, *Nacimiento y desarrollo de la filosofía en el Río de la Plata, 1536-1810* (Buenos Aires, 1952), p. 79.

29. Albert William Levi, *Humanism and Politics: Studies in the Relationship of Power and Value in the Western Tradition* (Bloomington, 1969), p. 25.

30. Desiderius Erasmus, *The Education of a Christian Prince*, trans. Lester K. Born (New York, 1936), p. 170.

31. Ibid., p. 162.

32. Ibid., p. 159.

33. Ibid., p. 212.

34. Ibid., p. 211. Humanists did not react negatively to all change and innovation. Comparative language study advanced their historical consciousness and led to recognition that change inevitably occurred. Ancient models, renovated and adapted, thus contributed to the contemporary world. Unnecessary change, however, disrupted or even destroyed. Sara Stever Gravelle, "Humanist Attitudes to Convention and Innovation in the Fifteenth Century," *The Journal of Medieval and Renaissance Studies*, (Fall, 1981), pp. 193-209.

35. Erasmus, p. 175.

36. Reijo Wilenius, *The Social and Political Theory of Francisco Suárez* (Helsinki, 1963), p. 15.

37. Skinner, vol. 2, p. 149.

38. José Gallegos Rocafull, *El hombre y el mundo de los teólogos españoles de los siglos de oro* (México, 1946), p. 183.

39. Lutheran theorists, responding to prospects of an armed attempt to force them back into the Church, theorized that St. Paul had commanded obedience only to magistrates who performed their specified duty. If they overstepped their authority, duly ordained inferior magistrates could resist illegal force. Richard R. Benert, "Lutheran Resistance Theory and the Imperial Constitution," *Il pensiero politico* (1973), pp. 17-36.

40. Francisco de Vitoria, "De potestate ecclesiae" (the Power of the Church), in Luis G. Alonso Getino, *Relecciones teológicas de maestro fray Francisco de Vitoria*, 3 vols. (Madrid, 1933-1936), vol. 2, p. 132. While Vitoria essentially agreed with William of Ockham, Jean Gerson, John Mair, and Jacques Almain, that a ruler remained within the community and responded to its needs, he viewed political authority as both a divine and human creation. Therefore, man alone could not dispense with rulers because to do so violated natural law. Krieger notes the changing nature and focus of authority over time. Leonard Krieger, "The Idea of Authority in the West," *The American Historical Review* (April 1977), pp. 249-270.

41. Skinner, vol. 2, p. 161.
42. Lynch, p. 26.
43. E. N. Van Kleffens, *Hispanic Law Until the End of the Middle Ages* (Edinburgh, 1968), p. 168.
44. *El fuero real*, lib. 1, intro.
45. Heinrich Mitters, *The State in the Middle Ages: A Comparative Constitutional History of Feudal Europe* (Amsterdam, 1975), p. 389.
46. It became a functioning code in 1348 with the "Ordenamiento de Alcalá," *Los códigos españoles concordados y anotados*, vol. 1 (Madrid, 1847), tit. 28.
47. *Siete partidas*, pt. 1, tit. 1, ley 5.
48. *Siete partidas*, pt. 1, tit. 1, leyes 9, 10.
49. *Siete partidas*, pt. 2, tit. 10, ley 1.
50. *Siete partidas*, pt. 2, tit. 10, ley 2.
51. Robert S. Chamberlain, "The Concept of the Señor Natural As Revealed by Castilian Law and Administrative Documents," *Hispanic American Historical Review* (May 1939), p. 132.
52. *El fuero real*, lib. 1, tit. 2.
53. *Siete partidas*, pt. 2, tit. 1, ley 7. Lewy, pp. 40-41.
54. Fernández-Santamaria, p. 78.
55. Francisco de Vitoria, *Relecciones de Indios y del derecho de la guerra* (Madrid, 1928), p. 186.
56. Examples of squabbling may be drawn from all parts of the empire. In sixteenth-century Quito, a priest issued letters of excommunication to those in arrears. John Preston Moore, *The Cabildo in Peru under the Hapsburgs* (Durham, 1954), pp. 216-218.
57. Missionaries often protested subjecting the Indian to the tithe, or negotiated time-limited exemptions. In independent Ecuador, the abolition of the tribute almost caused a financial collapse. Mark Van Aken, "The Lingering Death of Indian Tribute in Ecuador," *Hispanic American Historical Review* (August 1981), p. 441; Linda Alexander Rodríguez, *The Search for Public Policy: Regional Politics and Government Finances in Ecuador, 1830-1940* (Berkeley, 1985), pp. 62-64.
58. Robert S. Smith, "Sales Taxes in New Spain, 1595-1700," *Hispanic American Historical Review* (February 1948), pp. 2-37. For details on collection, see Clarence Haring, "Early Spanish Colonial Exchequer," *American Historical Review* (1917-1918), pp. 779-796. Moore, *The Cabildo under the Hapsburgs*, pp. 251-252. José María Vargas, *La economía política del Ecuador durante la colonia* (Quito, 1957), pp. 300-302.
59. Skinner, vol. 2, p. 126. Machiavelli's defense of the ability of the people as a whole to restrain a state turned the hierarchy upside down with the statement that "not without good reason is the voice of the populace likened to that of God." Niccolò Machiavelli, *The Discourses*, trans. Leslie J. Wilkes (Harmondsworth, 1970), p. 255.
60. Adalberto López, *The Revolt of the Comuneros, 1721-1735: A Study in the Colonial History of Paraguay* (Cambridge, Massachusetts, 1976), p. 61.
61. Skinner, vol. 2, pp. 177-178.

62. John Laures, *The Political Economy of Juan de Mariana* (New York, 1928), pp. 43-44, 64.

63. Adalberto López, pp. 112-113, 116-117.

64. Bodin, while ruling out active resistance, allowed the right to disobey a law that violated natural law. Jean Bodin, *The Six Books of the Commonweal* (Cambridge, Mass., 1967), pp. 214-221, 324. Michel de Montaigne, "Essays," *The Complete Works of Montaigne*, trans. Donald M. Frame (London, 1957), p. 506.

65. Skinner, vol. 2, p. 338.

66. Luis Sánchez Agesta, *El pensamiento político del despotismo ilustrado* (Madrid, 1953), p. 112.

67. John Tate Lanning, *Academic Culture in the Spanish Colonies* (Oxford, 1940), p. 31.

68. Julio Alemparte, *El Cabildo en Chile colonial*, 2d ed. (Santiago, 1966), p. 357.

69. *Siete partidas*, pt. 7, tit. 32, intro.

70. *Siete partidas*, pt. 7, tit. 32, ley 3.

71. *Siete partidas*, pt. 7, tit. 32, ley 8. Erasmus noted that a prince "should always be more prone to pardon than punish." In a manner similar to God, he must be slow to extract vengeance. Erasmus, p. 231.

72. King, pp. 36, 44.

73. *Siete partidas*, pt. 1, tit. 1, ley 16.

74. *Fuero juzgo*, lib. 4, tit. 2; *Fuero real*, lib. 1, tit. 6.

75. *Novísima recopilación de las leyes de España*, lib. 3, tit. 2, ley 1.

76. Ullmann stated that "faith and the law stand to each other in the relationship of cause and effect." Ullmann, 101.

77. The king legislated as the highest authority but, even though he had no political superiors, he remained part of the community and subject to its laws, being at the same time above and within the community. Luis Sánchez Agesta, *El concepto del estado en el pensamiento español del siglo XVI* (Madrid, 1959), p. 45.

78. Skinner, vol. 1, p. 62.

79. Mariana confronted the problem head on in two chapters, one entitled "¿Es mayor el poder de rey, o el de la república?" Juan de Mariana, "Del Rey y de la Institución Real," *Biblioteca de autores Españoles*, "Obras del Padre Juan de Mariana," vol. 2 (Madrid, 1909), pp. 485-491. Aquinas stated that a ruler did not have a formal obligation to obey positive law. Skinner, vol. 1, p. 62.

80. *Siete partidas*, pt. 2, tit. 13, ley 5; *Ordenamiento*, lib. 6, tit. 1, ley 5. Walter Howe, *The Mining Guild of New Spain and Its Tribunal General, 1770-1821* (New York, 1968), p. 3. Roberto Moreno, "Las Instituciones de la industria minera Novohispaña," in *La minería en Mexico, estudios sobre su desarrollo histórico* (México, 1978), pp. 70-71.

81. Skinner, vol. 2, p. 117.

82. Ibid.

83. Lewy, p. 59. Mariana's ideas on taxation and consent influenced the struggle between the English parliament and the Stuarts. Laures, p. 50.

84. Bodin, p. 653.

85. Kamen, pp. 159-160.

86. Antonio Ortíz Domínguez, "Ventas y exenciones de lugares durante el reinado de Felipe IV," *Anuario de historia del derecho español* (Madrid 1964), pp. 163-207.

87. For the text, see W. Eugene Shiels, *King and Church: The Rise and Fall of the Patronato Real* (Chicago, 1961), pp. 78-81.

88. *Recopilación*, lib. 3, tit. 1, ley 1.

89. Jaime Eyzaguirre, *Ideario y ruta de la emancipación chilena*, 2d ed. (Santiago, 1957), p. 22.

90. Juan de Solórzano y Pereyra, "Política indiana," lib. 4, cap. 19, num. 31 and 37; lib. 5, cap. 16, num. 12 and cap. 8, 12; lib. 6, cap. 12, num. 2 and 4.

91. Jerónimo Castillo de Bobadilla, *Política para corregidores y señores de vasallos en tiempo de paz y de guerra* (Medina del Campo, 1608), p. 675.

92. The concessions made to Cortés in 1529, including sěnorio over "vasallos y pueblos" did not constitute feudal alienation. The Crown restricted and reserved power. Although Cortés aspired to full jurisdiction, royal officials stood firm. His privileges were not as important as structural and institutional arrangements. Juan Friede, "El Privilegio de vasallos otorgado a Hernan Cortés," in Bernardo García Martínez et al., eds., *Historia y sociedad en el mundo de habla española: homenaje a José Miranda* (México, 1970), pp. 69-78.

93. The rate of alienation is suggested by the number of large grants (*mercedes de tierras*) made by the municipal council and viceroy of Mexico. Between December 1, 1525, and July 13, 1528, the Cabildo made 23 major grants and an infinite number of smaller ones, while Viceroy Mendoza, in 1542 and 1543, conceded some 218 major grants. José Miranda, *La función económica del encomendero en los orígenes del régimen colonial (Nueva España, 1525-1531)* (México, 1965), pp. 26-27.

94. Because both the Iberian concept of authority and that implied by New World proprietary rights functioned, scholars disagree on whether the Indies were colonies or separate entities. See, for example, Ricardo Levine, *Las Indias no eran colonias* (Buenos Aires, 1951). Mario Góngora noted that Solórzano y Pereyra drew comparisons with Roman colonies, which were not colonies in the modern economic sense. Mario Góngora, *El estado en el derecho indiano: Epoca de fundación, 1492-1570* (Santiago, 1951). O. Carlos Stoetzer, *The Scholastic Roots of the Spanish American Revolution* (New York, 1970), pp. 2-3.

2: The Structural Reflection

1. A mob constituted a temporary corporate group formed to press a particular demand; when met by either force or acquiescence, the mob disbanded. All sides in the confrontation had an interest in the preservation of authority to validate the outcome.

2. Juan de Solórzano y Pereyra, "Política Indiana," *Biblioteca de autores Españoles* (Madrid, 1978), lib. 5, cap. 15, 31. Nestor Meza Villalobos, *La conciencia política chilena durante la monarquía* (Santiago, 1958), p. 111.

3. Quoted in Frederick B. Pike, "The Municipality and the System of Checks and Balances in Spanish America," *The Americas* (Oct. 1958), p. 156.

4. *Recopilación de leyes de los reynos de las Indias* (Madrid, 1791), lib. 2, tit. 2, ley 22. *Obreption* (a creeping upon secretly) refers to actions determined without sufficient consultation, and *subreption* to misrepresentation of essential facts.

5. T. Esquivel Obregón, *Apuntes para la história del derecho en México* (México, 1938), p. 92.

6. John Preston Moore, *The Cabildo in Peru under the Hapsburgs: A Study of the Origins and Power of the Town Council in the Viceroyalty of Peru, 1530-1700* (Durham, 1954), pp. 198, 202, 204. Julio Alemparte, *El cabildo en Chile colonial*, 2d ed. (Santiago, 1966), p. 107.

7. *Recopilación*, lib. 3, tit. 3, ley 19.

8. Juan Bromley, "Recibimiento de virreyes en Lima," *Revista histórica* (1953), p. 88. John Preston Moore, *The Cabildo in Peru under the Bourbons* (Durham, 1966), pp. 88, 105, 124.

9. Rafael Altamira y Crevea, *Historia de España y de la civilización española*, 3d ed. (Barcelona, 1913), vol. 3, pp. 477-480.

10. The extent to which Fernando Cortés followed philosophical guidelines is indicated in Cecilia Barba, "Francisco Vitoria y Hernán Cortés: Teoría y práctica del derecho internacional en el siglo XVI," *Memoria del II congreso de historia del derecho mexicano* (México, 1980), pp. 125-131. Elliot suggests that Cortés responded not out of a deep knowledge, but from the standpoint of an educated individual. He sprinkled his communications with the appropriate phrases indicating cultural allegiance. J. H. Elliott, "The Mental World of Hernán Cortés," *Transactions of the Royal Historical Society*, Fifth Series, vol. 17 (London, 1967), pp. 41-58. Frankl asserted that Cortés had a perfect knowledge of the judical-political tradition and acted on it. Victor Frankl, "Hernán Cortés y la tradición de las siete partidas,"*Revista de história de America* (January-December, 1962), p. 12.

11. Jaime Eyzaguirre, *Ideario y ruta de la emancipación chilena*, 2d ed. (Santiago, 1957), p. 28. In Chile the Crown viewed Santiago's cabildo as representing all Chilean cities. Meza Villalobos, p. 42.

12. Solórzano y Pereyra, lib. 5, cap. 1, num. 3. As an example, Havana's council represented the people during the British occupation (1762-1763) and was recognized as the legitimate representative. O. Carlos Stoetzer, *The Scholastic Roots of the Spanish American Revolution* (New York, 1979), p. 10.

13. Ruben Vargas Ugarte, *Historia general del Perú*, (Lima, 1966), vol. 1, p. 243.

14. Adalberto López, *The Revolt of the Comuneros, 1721-1745: A Study of the Colonial History of Paraguay* (Cambridge, Mass., 1976), pp. 7-8. Manuel J. Cibils, *Anarquía y revolución en el Paraguay* (Buenos Aires, 1757), p. 35. The municipal council served as the major political center of Paraguay until the eighteenth century. Rafael Eladio Velázquez, *El cabildo comunero de Asunción* (Asunción, 1961), pp. 6-7.

15. Guillermo Lohmann Villena, "El corregidor de Lima: estudio-histórico-jurídico," *Anuario de estudios americanos* (Sevilla, 1952), pp. 131, 171.

16. Not broadly representative, as the following statement by the Cuzco Cabildo in 1696 indicates: "This Illustrious Cabilo and each Councilman of it

shall not attend the burial of any nonillustrious person nor of ordinary people as it would be improper to do so." Quoted in Donald Lloyd Gibbs, "Cuzco, 1680-1710: An Andean City Seen Through Its Economic Activities," Ph.D. dissertation, University of Texas, 1979, p. 149.

17. *Recopilación*, lib. 4, tit. 11, ley 2.

18. *Colección de documentos inéditos relativos al descubrimiento, conquista y colonización de las posesiones españoles en América y Oceanía* (Madrid, 1864-1884), vol. 8, pp. 227-228.

19. Bromley, pp. 21, 69.

20. Quoted in Mark A. Burkholder, *Politics of a Colonial Career: José Baquíjano and the Audiencia of Lima* (Albuquerque, 1980), p. 97.

21. Horacio H. Urteaga and Carlos A. Romero, eds., *Colección de libros y documentos referentes a la historia del Perú*, 2 vols. (Lima, 1916-1917), vol. 2, pp. 133-176, and *Colección de documentos...en América y Oceanía*, vol. 7, pp. 451-495.

22. Richard Konetzke, *Colección de documentos para la historia de la formación social de Hispanoamerica, 1493-1810*, (Madrid, 1953), vol. 1, pp. 340-357.

23. *Recopilación*, lib. 4, tit. 8, ley 2. Colin M. MacLachlan and Jaime E. Rodríguez O., *The Forging of the Cosmic Race: A Reinterpretation of Colonial Mexico* (Berkeley, 1980), p. 110.

24. The viceroy may have withheld labor in order to force cooperation. J. I. Israel, *Race, Class and Politics in Colonial Mexico, 1610-1670* (Oxford, 1975), p. 180.

25. Ibid., pp. 99, 194-195.

26. Fred Bonner, "La union de las armas en el Perú: aspectos politicolegales," *Anuario de estudios americanos* (Sevilla, 1967), p. 1171.

27. Ibid., p. 1138. Local officials including the viceroy were denounced for placing other interests over that of the Crown. Kenneth J. Andrien, *Crisis and Decline: The Viceroyalty of Peru in the Seventeenth Century* (Albuquerque, 1985), p. 148. In fact that was their accepted philosophical role.

28. Ibid., p. 1157.

29. Ibid., p. 1168.

30. Frederick B. Pike, "The Municipality...in Spanish America," p. 152.

31. The placing of the aboriginal population within a perceived political structure was linked to Christianization. To be a Christian, one had to live in an orderly (political) fashion, unlike an animal. Temporal order reflected the divine; missionaries spent as much time on political organization as on spiritual matters. Magnus Mörner, *La corona española y los foraneos en los pueblos de Indios de America* (Stockholm, 1970), p. 18. The strength of this notion should not be confused with a simple desire to force Indians to be Spaniards. Nancy M. Farriss, *Maya Society Under Colonial Rule* (Princeton, 1984), p. 91.

32. *Recopilación*, lib. 5, tit. 2, ley 22.

33. Indian legal tradition failed to have more than limited local importance, as demonstrated by the lack of a separate criminal code in the Indies. Although Carlos II asserted that the Recopilación had been formulated to bring together all dispositions that favored and protected the Indians, it remained

supplementary. *Recopilación*, lib. 2, tit. 1, ley 5. Castilian law applied in spite of cultural differences. The Recopilación referred judges to the *Nueva recopilación de Castilla* (1519) and subsequently to other Spanish codes. *Recopilación*, lib. 5, tit. 2, ley 24.

34. The Crown reminded viceroys to be available to petitioners. Solórzano y Pereyra noted that viceroys should be "affable, benevolent, forebearing and provide ready access to the common people." Solórzano y Pereyra, lib. 5, cap. 2, num. 22. With some justification, Stern observed that with the creation of this artificial body, the aboriginal population finally became "Indians." Steve J. Stern, *Peru's Indian Peoples and the Challenge of Spanish Conquest: Huamanga to 1640* (Madison, 1982), p. 80.

35. *Recopilación*, lib. 5, tit. 10, ley 11. Dispensing with procedure in certain instances, and for particular groups, had Roman roots in the *cognito summaria* that allowed direct administrative intervention to rectify a situation; Pope Clement V defined and set its limits. Woodrow Borah, *Justice By Insurance: The General Indian Court of Colonial Mexico and the Legal Aides of the Half-Real* (Berkeley, 1983), pp. 13-14.

36. Henry Stevens, ed., 1543 facsimile edition, *The New Laws and Ordinances of His Majesty Emperor Charles the Fifth* (London, 1893).

37. Silvio A. Zavala, *Las instituciones jurídicas en la conquista de America*, 2d ed. (Mexico, 1971), p. 72.

38. As Góngora observed, the Castilian monarchy's proprietorship made the introduction of Castilian law both natural and legal. Mario Góngora, *El estado en el derecho indiano: época de fundación, 1492-1570* (Santiago, 1951), p. 37. *Colección de documentos inéditos para la historia de Hispanoamérica*, 14 vols. (Madrid, 1927-1932), vol. 8, p. 13. Borah, pp. 94-95.

39. J. Lloyd Mecham, *Church and State in Latin America: A History of Politico-Ecclesiastical Relations* (Chapel Hill, 1966), p. 10.

40. W. Eugene Shiels, *King and Church: The Rise and Fall of the Patronato Real* (Chicago, 1961), p. 18.

41. For the text of the Bull of Granada, see Shiels, pp. 66-70.

42. It would not achieve the same formal and universal power in Spain until 1753. Ibid., pp. 18, 19.

43. Zavala, *Las instituciones*, p. 488.

44. Juan Manzano Manzano, *La incorporación de las Indias a la corona de Castilla* (Madrid, 1948), pp. 43-46, provides the text of the requerimiento. For a review of its critics, see Lewis Hanke, "The 'Requerimiento' and Its Interpreters," *Revista de Historia de America* (March 1938), pp. 25-34.

45. An agent of Pedrarias Dávila reported that the Indians of Castillo del Oro (Darien), responding to the requerimiento, declared that while the theological aspects appeared sound, the pope could not give away what he did not possess. Moreover, if the captain tried to take it, he ran the risk of having his head grace the end of a pole. Silvio Zavala, *New Viewpoints on the Spanish Colonization of America* (Philadelphia, 1943), p. 10. The Indians thus claimed the right to resist force with force.

46. Peggy K. Liss, *Mexico Under Spain, 1521-1556: Society and the Origins of Nationality* (Chicago, 1975), p. 22.

47. Even avid defenders of the Indians accepted the notion of harsh punishment, including enslavement, for such acts of treason. Jaime Eyzaguirre, *Ideario y ruta de la emancipación chilena* (Santiago, 1957), p. 25.

48. Juan de Solórzano y Pereyra, lib. 4, cap. 2 and 3. *Recopilación*, lib. 1, tit. 6, ley 1-4.

49. *Novísima recopilación de las leyes de España*, 6 vols. (Madrid, 1805-1829), lib. 2, tit. 2, ley 17, provided general and interpretive guidelines in case of *recurso de fuerza* as follows: 1. Cognizance of a clearly secular matter. 2. Ignoring method and form prescribed in the laws and in canon law. 3. Refusal to permit legally provided appeals.

50. *Recopilación*, lib. 2, tit. 2, ley 4.

51. José Toribio Medina, *Historia del tribunal del santo oficio de la inquisición en Lima* (Santiago, 1890), vol. 1, pp. 182-187.

52. *Recopilación*, lib. 1, tit. 7, ley 47.

53. For details, see Israel, pp. 135-160.

54. As Carrillo wrote the Council of the Indies concerning the Archbishop, "I do not believe that his Majesty in his holy zeal would wish to have recorded in writing particulars likely to bring the reputation and authority of a prelate of the Church into disrepute, however true and justified they may be." Quoted in Israel, p. 173.

55. Custom carried over from Visigothic tribal practices required a semblance of consultation. The *Siete Partidas* noted the use of advisors out of necessity because the king could not see or decide everything. Such individuals employed power received from the king. *Las siete partidas del rey Alfonso El Sabio contejadas con varios codices antiguos por la real academia de la historia* (Madrid, 1972), pt. 2, tit. 1, ley 3.

56. Richard L. Kagan, *Students and Society in Early Modern Spain* (Baltimore, 1974), pp. 94-95, 97.

57. Quoted in A. W. Lovett, *Philip II and Mateo Vázquez de Leca: The Government of Spain, 1572-1592* (Geneva, 1977), p. 29. Vázquez de Leca received the appointment on March 13, 1573.

58. See, for example, the "Instrucción a Luis de Velasco" (1607) and "Instrucción al Marqués de Cerralvo" (1624), in Lewis Hanke and Celso Rodríguez, eds., "Los virreyes españoles en América durante el gobierno de la casa de Austria," *Biblioteca de autores españoles* (Madrid, 1976-1978), vol. 3, pp. 11-12, 265.

59. Goode suggests that, in certain cases, the absolute lack of substance serves to make those who accept or pursue such honors ridiculous and results in disesteem. William J. Goode, *The Celebration of Heroes: Prestige as a Social Control System* (Berkeley, 1978), pp. 151-180.

60. Arthur Franklin Zimmerman, *Francisco de Toledo, Fifth Viceroy of Peru, 1569-1581* (New York, 1968), p. 270.

61. Lewis Hanke and Celso Rodríguez, eds., "Los virreyes españoles en América durante el gobierno de la casa de Austria," *Biblioteca de autores españoles* (Madrid, 1978-1980), vol. 4, p. 243. Kenneth J. Andrien, "The Sale of Fiscal Offices and the Decline of Royal Authority in the Viceroyalty of Peru, 1633-1700," *Hispanic American Historical Review* (February 1982), pp. 49-71. See

John H. Parry, *The Sale of Public Office in the Spanish Indies Under the Hapsburgs* (Berkeley, 1953), for a discussion.

62. Kagan, p. 92.
63. Mariano Cuevas S. J., ed., *Documentos inéditos del siglo XVI para la historia de Mexico* (Mexico, 1914), p. 119.
64. *Recopilación*, lib. 3, tit. 2, ley 27, 30. Bronner found that many viceregal retainers had been pushed on that official by others. Acceptance established a bond of mutual obligation between the original patron and the viceroy.
65. J. Ignacio Rubio Mañé, *Introducción al estudio de los virreyes de Nueva España, 1535-1746* (Mexico, 1955), pp. 207-214. William L. Sherman, *Forced Labor in Sixteenth-Century Central America* (Lincoln, 1979), p. 345. Ulses Rojas, *Corregidores y justicias mayores de Tunja y su provincia desde la fundación de la ciudad hasta 1817* (Tunja, 1962), pp. 303, 500. Juan Matienzo, *Gobierno del Perú* (Buenos Aires, 1910), p. 117.
66. Stern, p. 97. Manuela Christina García Bernal, "El gobernador de Yucatán, Rodrigo Flores y Aldana," *Homenaje al Dr. Muro Orejón* (Sevilla, 1979), vol. 1, pp. 123,153. Charles Gibson, *The Aztecs Under Spanish Rule: A History of the Indians of the Valley of Mexico* (Stanford, 1964), pp. 58-97. See also Brian R. Hamnett, *Politics and Trade in Southern Mexico, 1750-1821* (Cambridge, 1971). Guillermo Lohmann Villena, *El corregidor de indios en el Perú bajo los Austrias* (Madrid, 1957).
67. Stafford Poole, "Institutionalized Corruption in the Letrado Bureaucracy: The Case of Pedro Farfán (1568-1588)," *The Americas* (October 1981), pp. 149-171.
68. Sherman, p. 138.
69. John Leddy Phelan, *The Kingdom of Quito in the Seventeenth Century: Bureaucratic Politics in the Spanish Empire* (Madison, 1967), pp. 161, 163.
70. Peter Marzahl, *Town in the Empire: Government, Politics, and Society in Seventeenth-Century Popayán* (Austin, 1978), p. 112.
71. Information on the residencia is presented in José María Mariluz Urquijo, *Ensayo sobre los juicios de residencia indianos* (Sevilla, 1952) and the historical antecedents in Luis García de Valdeavellano, "'Las Partidas y los orígenes medievales del juicio de residencia," *Boletín de la real academia de historia* (1963), pp. 205-246.
72. Zimmerman, p. 119.
73. Sherman, p. 141.
74. Poole, pp. 168-169. Poole noted that the case brought into question the Crown's commitment to honesty in government, and also suggested the acceptance of the inevitability of corruption. Ibid., p. 171.
75. Martin de Mencos, president of Guatemala 1659-1668, admitted trading in Dutch contraband, pleaded poverty, escaped judgment and ended his life as a respected consultant to the Council of the Indies while drawing a royal pension. Miles L. Wortman, *Government and Society in Central America, 1680-1840* (New York, 1982), p. 36.
76. *Nueva collección de documentos de España y de sus Indias* (Madrid, 1892-1896), vol. 7, pp. 139-165. Ernst Shäfer, *El consejo real y supremo de las Indias* (Sevilla, 1935-1947), vol. 1, pp. 43-45. José de Torralva (c. 1666-1736)

provides another example. As a member of the Audiencia of Manila, he persecuted his colleagues and engaged in blackmail and extortion. Eventually imprisoned, he died a beggar. Mark A. Burkholder and D. S. Chandler, *Biographical Dictionary of Audiencia Ministers in the Americas, 1678-1821* (Westport, 1982), pp. 328-329.

77. Shäfer, vol. 2, p. 280.

78. Gregorio Martín de Guijo, *Diario, 1648-1664* (Mexico, 1952), vol. 2, p. 61. For details, see Israel, pp. 161-189.

79. *Recopilación*, lib. 5, tit. 2, ley 9. Moore, *The Cabildo under the Hapsburgs*, p. 136. Marzahl, p. 64.

80. Conflict between a forceful Pedro de Alvarado and the weaker Francisco de Montejo, as well as the achievements of Alonso López Cerrato in Central America, provide examples. Sherman, p. 180.

81. *Colección de documentos inéditos...en América y Oceanía*, vol. 8, pp. 225-226. In 1780 Túpac Amaru asserted that he carried secret orders from the king and the Church to rebel against a corrupt colonial regime. Leon G. Campbell, "Social Structure of the Túpac Amaru Army in Cuzco, 1780-81," *Hispanic American Historical Review* (Nov. 1981), p. 683.

82. Hanke and Rodríguez, eds., "Los virreyes españoles en América durante el gobierno de la casa de Austria," vol. 3, pp. 9-10. José María Mariluz Urquijo, *Orígenes de la burocracia rioplatense* (Buenos Aires, 1974), p. 93. Pension funds to provide for dependent survivors (*montepíos*) were established from the 1760s and functioned with limited success.

83. Solórzano y Pereyra and contemporary scholars found it difficult to define jurisdictions precisely. Lohmann Villena, pp. 309-316. *Recopilación*, lib 5, tit. 2, ley 30. In jurisdictional disputes, the king became the ultimate judge and only after his will became known did all discussion cease. Solórzano y Pereyra, lib. 5, cap. 3, num. 44.

84. Between 1620 and 1670, six viceroys in New Spain lost effective political control. Israel suggests that the principal cause of unrest stemmed from the fact that viceroys had a financial interest in maintaining the status quo. Israel, p. 268.

85. John E. Phelan, "Authority and Flexibility in the Spanish Imperial Bureaucracy," *Administrative Science Quarterly* (June 1960), p. 50.

86. He issued his rules before leaving Spain. Zimmerman, p. 54.

87. Leon G. Campbell, "A Colonial Establishment: Creole Domination of the Audiencia of Lima During the Late Eighteenth Century," *Hispanic American Historical Review* (February 1972), p. 5. When a doctor of civil laws entered a courtroom, the presiding judge arose and offered him a seat on the bench. Symbolic formality reenforced the status and cohesiveness of the judicial and legal fraternity. John Tate Lanning, *Academic Culture in the Spanish Colonies* (Oxford, 1940), p. 9.

88. Walter Ullmann, *A History of Political Thought: The Middle Ages* (Middlesex, 1970), p. 30.

89. The same impulse may be identified in the *Livro da virtuosa bemfeitoria* of the Infante of Portugal, Dom Pedro (1392-1449). Greenfield views it as a system of patron client exchanges that integrates the state with its corporate parts. Sidney M. Greenfield, *The Patrimonial State in Patron-Client Relations*

in *Iberia and Latin America: Sources of "the System" in Fifteenth Century Writings of the Infante D. Pedro of Portugal*, Program in Latin American Studies, Occasional Papers, series No. 1 (Amherst, 1976), p. 3.

90. Ruben Vargas Ugarte, *Historia general del Perú* (Lima, 1966), vol. 1, p. 243.

91. Israel, p. 173.

92. Henry Kamen, *Spain in the Later Seventeenth Century, 1665-1700* (London, 1980), p. 159. William B. Taylor, *Drinking, Homicide, and Rebellion in Colonial Mexican Villages* (Stanford, 1979), pp. 113-151. For example, in spite of Crown responsibility for levying taxes, both Indians and Spaniards tended to blame local officials for their fiscal burdens. Liss, p. 130.

93. The notion that willful disrespect constituted an assult on divine authority was present in Visigothic theory. P. D. King, *Law and Society in the Visiogothic Kingdom* (Cambridge, Massachusetts, 1972), p. 43.

94. Bodin stressed the monarch's responsibility to uphold private property rights and maintained that a ruler was bound by contracts. Jean Bodin, *The Six Books of the Commonweal* (Cambridge, Mass., 1967), pp. 11, 106.

95. José María Ots Capdequí, *España en America: el régimen de tierras en la época colonial* (Buenos Aires, 1959), p. 37. *Recopilación*, lib. 4, tit. 12, ley 19. Individual Indians as well as communities used the device to protect and extend their holdings. Metztitlán (New Spain) secured a comprehensive composición in 1695 on its communal land for a fee of fifty pesos, on the basis of which the Audiencia upheld its claims. Wayne S. Osborn, "Indian Land Retention in Colonial Metztitlán," *Hispanic American Historical Review* (May, 1973), pp. 219, 227. For the role of legal documentation see Bernardo Pérez Fernández del Castillo, *Historia de la escribanía en la Nueva España y el notariado en México* (México, 1983).

96. Walter Howe, *The Mining Guild of New Spain and Its Tribunal General, 1770-1821* (New York, 1968), pp. 19, 296-297.

97. MacLachlan and Rodriguez, p. 215. For information on foreigners in the first half of the eighteenth century, see Charles F. Nunn, *Foreign Immigrants in Early Bourbon Mexico, 1700-1760* (Cambridge, 1979).

98. Enrique Torres Saldamando, "Reparto y composición de tierra en el Perú," *Revisita peruana* (1879), p. 33. In the 1640s in the Lima district alone supplied 586,000 pesos and the amount for the entire viceroyalty probably exceeded two million pesos. Andrien, pp. 158-159.

99. José Varallanos, *Historia de Huánuco: introducción para el estudio de la vida social de una región del Peru desde la era prehistórica a nuestro días* (Buenos Aires, 1959), pp. 280-284.

3: Philosophy in Practice

1. John Lynch, *Spain Under the Habsburgs* (Oxford, 1964), vol. I, pp. 152-154.

2. Ernest Shäfer, *El consejo real y supremo de las Indias*, 2 vols. (Sevilla, 1935-1947), provides an account of the organization and its activities.

3. The president of the Council of State could establish ad hoc juntas to discuss American affairs then he referred the decision to the Council of the Indies. For example, Cardinal Diego de Espinosa, president of the Council of State,

created one in 1598. The junta, which included the president of the Council of the Indies, convened at his home. Among other things, the junta drew up the preliminary instructions issued to Francisco de Toledo, viceroy of Peru (1569-1581). A. W. Lovett, "A Cardinal's Papers: The Rise of Mateo Vázquez de Leca," *The English Historical Review* (April 1973), pp. 246, 256.

4. Charles H. Carter, "The Nature of Spanish Government After Philip II," *Historian* (November 1963), pp. 1-18, and "The Informational Base of Spanish Policy, 1598-1625," *Cahiers D'Histoire Mondiale* (1964), pp. 149-159. For a brief discussion of the governing structure, see Henry Kamen, *Spain in the Later Seventeenth Century 1665-1700* (London, 1980), pp. 1-38.

5. H. Keniston, *Francisco de los Cobos, Secretary of the Emperor Charles V* (Pittsburgh, 1960), pp. 99-103.

6. A. W. Lovett, *Philip II and Mateo Vázquez de Leca: The Government of Spain, 1572-1592* (Geneva, 1977), pp. 33-34.

7. Francisco Tomás y Valiente, *Los validos en la monarquía española del siglo XVIII* (Madrid, 1963), pp. 35-55. Williams noted that Felipe III knew how to delegate. His own deficiencies led him to rely upon a "fully" autonomous administration. Patrick Williams, "Philip III and the Restoration of the Spanish Government, 1598-1603," *The English Historical Review* (October 1973), p. 751.

8. José Antonio Escudero, *Los secretarios de estado y del despacho* (Madrid, 1969), I, 253.

9. Liss observed that the Hapsburg state was not a corporate one in a rigid sense but a mental organization of diversity. Peggy K. Liss, *Mexico under Spain, 1521-1556* (Chicago, 1975), p. 145. Erasmus advised a prince to avoid every novel idea "for even if conditions are bettered thereby, the very innovation is a stumbling block." Erasmus, p. 211. Montaigne also equated a lust for innovation with tyranny and injustice. Albert W. Levi, *Humanism and Politics: Studies in the Relationship of Power and Value in the Western Tradition* (Bloomington, 1969), p. 54.

10. Land becomes alienable and a commodity under the impact of commercialization, as in the case of Greece, Rome, the Chinese Empire, and medieval Europe. John H. Kantsky, "The Question of Peasant Revolts in Traditional Empires," *Studies in Comparative International Development* (Fall-Winter 1981), p. 15. Incipient commercialization in the Aztec Empire was reflected in the movement toward private landholdings. Colin M. MacLachlan and Jaime E. Rodríguez O., *The Forging of the Cosmic Race: A Reinterpretation of Colonial Mexico* (Berkeley, 1980), p. 55.

11. Rafael Altamira, "El texto de los Leyes de Burgos de 1512," *Revista de historia de America* (1938), no. 4, pp. 5-79.

12. Mendoza to the Audiencia of Mexico, October 28, 1548, Vasco de Puga, *Provisiones, cédulas, instrucciones de su Magestad* (Madrid, 1945), vol. 2, pp. 8-13. At the close of the Hapsburg era, Bishop-Viceroy Juan de Ortega Montañés expressed the same opinion in his instructions (1697) to the Count of Moctezuma, his successor in the Mexican viceregal post. Norman F. Martin, ed., *Instrucción reservada que el obispo-virrey Juan de Ortega Montañés dio a su sucesor en el mando, el Conde de Moctezuma* (México, 1965), pp. 65-66. Cunningham noted the same situation. Charles Henry Cunning-

ham, *The Audiencia in the Spanish Colonies As Illustrated by the Audiencia of Manila* (1583-1800) (Berkeley, 1919), p. 99.

13. Arthur S. Aiton, *Antonio de Mendoza, First Viceroy of New Spain* (Durham, 1927), p. 94.

14. S. Lorente, ed., *Relaciones de los virreyes y audiencias que han gobernado el Perú* (Lima, 1867), vol. 1, pp. 37-38. Steve J. Stern, *Peru's Indian Peoples and the Challenge of Spanish Conquest, Huamanga to 1640* (Madison, 1982), p. 121.

15. Donald Lloyd Gibbs, "Cuzco, 1680-1710: An Andean City Seen through Its Economic Activities," Ph.D. dissertation, University of Texas, 1979, p. 22.

16. Wayne S. Osborn, "Indian Land Retention in Colonial Metztitlán," *Hispanic American Historical Review* (May 1973), p. 237.

17. Peter Marzahl, *Town in the Empire: Government, Politics, and Society in Seventeenth-Century Popayán* (Austin, 1978), p. 48. Stern, *Peru's Indian Peoples*, p. 31.

18. Nicholas P. Cushner, *Lords of the Land: Sugar, Wine, and Jesuit Estates of Coastal Peru, 1600-1767* (Albany, 1980), pp. 15, 18, 44.

19. José María Chacón y Calvo, *Cedulario cubano: los orígines de la colonización* (1493-1512) (Madrid, n.d.), p. 429.

20. Joaquín Pacheco, Francisco de Cárdenas, and Luis Torres de Mendoza, eds., *Colección de documentos inéditos relativos al descubrimiento, conquista y organización de las antiguas posesiones españolas de America y Oceanía*, 42 vols. (Madrid, 1864-1889), vol. 31, pp. 209-212.

21. Liss, p. 172.

22. The encomienda placed Indians under an encomendero to whom they owed tribute; in return, the encomendero offered spirital and material guidance. Its roots go back to the *behetría*, an association of lesser nobles (*infanzones*) and urban centers who jointly commended themselves (*behetría colectiva*) to a magnate to whom they paid tribute, receiving protection in return. Many became hereditary lordships that could be divided among heirs. Some retained their power to commend themselves to any lord of their choice. They could also be created by royal grant (encomienda). The encomienda represented a feudal layer between the king and his subjects. Heinrich Mitters, *The State in the Middle Ages: A Comparative Constitutional History of Feudal Europe* (Amsterdam, 1975), p. 380.

23. Otis H. Green, *Spain and the Western Tradition: The Castilian Mind in Literature from El Cid to Calderón* (Madison, 1964), vol. 2, p. 193.

24. Ibid.

25. Ibid., p. 154. The Jesuits in particular took to the notion. For a discussion, see Pedro S. Achútegui, *La universalidad del conocimiento de Dios en los paganos, según los primeros teólogos de la Compañia de Jesús, 1534-1648* (Pamplona, 1951).

26. Alfonso de la Torre in *Visión delectible* (ca. 1440) noted an inferiority based on climate where individuals in such climates and regions of "evil complexion" have weak reason, lack understanding, and are natural slaves of those who dwell in countries of good climate and complexion where reason abounds. Green, pp. 154-155.

27. Lewis Hanke, *The Spanish Struggle for Justice in the Conquest of America* (Philadelphia, 1949), p. 86.

28. Juan López de Palacios Rubios, *De las islas del mar océano*, Fray Matías de Paz, *Del dominio de los reyes de España sobre los indios*, ed. Silvio Zavala and Agustín Millares Carlos (Mexico, 1954), pp. 258-259.

29. Palacios Rubios, pp. 39-43.

30. Altamira, pp. 5-79. Lewis Hanke, "Las Leyes de Burgos en 1512 y 1513," *Anuario de historia argentina* (1942), pp. 33-56. Lesley B. Simpson provides an English translation in *The Laws of Burgos* (San Francisco, 1960).

31. Las Casas received a Cuban encomienda in 1511, the year after he entered the priesthood. In 1514 he renounced it and began his efforts on behalf of the Indians. He died in Madrid in 1566.

32. Manuel Giménez Fernández, *Bartolomé de Las Casas: delegado de Cisneros para la reformación de las Indias (1516-1517)* (Sevilla, 1953), p. 97.

33. Manuel Giménez Fernández, "Fray Bartolomé de Las Casas: A Biographical Sketch," in Juan Friede and Benjamin Keen, eds, *Bartolomé de Las Casas in History: Towards an Understanding of the Man and His Work* (De Kalb, 1971), pp. 75-76.

34. Marcel Bataillon, "The Clerigo Casas, Colonist and Colonial Reformer," in Friede and Keen, *Bartolomé de Las Casas in History*, pp. 367-372.

35. Giménez Fernández, in Friede and Keene, *Bartolomé de Las Casas in History*, pp. 76-77.

36. Bataillon, p. 384. Luis Alonso Getino, *Influencia de los dominicos en las leyes nuevas* (Sevilla, 1945), p. 69, made the point that long before Las Casas entered the battle many others were involved, even while "Licenciado Las Casas" enjoyed his encomienda. He credits Montesinos, who accompanied Las Casas on his first trip to Spain, with introducing him to the Archbishop of Seville, a close friend of the king, and helping him obtain letters of recommendation.

37. Juan Friede, "Las Casas and Indigenism in the Sixteenth Century," in Friede and Keen, *Bartolomé de Las Casas in History*, p. 142.

38. Bartolomé de Las Casas, *Historia de las Indias* (Madrid, 1951), pp. 3, 170.

39. Keniston, p. 55.

40. Friede, "Las Casas and Indigenism," p. 143.

41. On at least one occasion, officials entertained the idea of moving the Council of the Indies to the New World as a means of remedying the lack of first-hand knowledge. Lovett, *Philip II*, p. 22.

42. Hanke provides a summary in *The Spanish Struggle for Justice*, pp. 66-68.

43. Beatriz Arteaga Garza and Guadalupé Pérez San Vicente, eds. *Cedulario cortesiano* (México, 1949), pp. 54-55.

44. Friede, "Las Casas and Indigenism," p. 145.

45. *Instrucciones que los vireyes de Nueva España dejaron a sus sucesores* (México, 1867-1873), vol. 1, p. 23.

46. The Crown, aware of its debt, reluctantly indicated its willingness to consider permitting the encomienda to become a permanent institution— although by 1530 the inability of the conquistadors to establish harmony

and stability undermined their claim to special privileges. MacLachlan and Rodríguez O., pp. 88-89.

47. The reformed Audiencia received secret orders to incorporate encomiendas stripped from Cortés's followers by Nuño de Guzmán, as president of the first Audiencia, as well as those distributed by Guzmán. Reincorporated encomiendas were to be placed under royal officials. Simpson, p. 85.

48. John H. Parry, *The Spanish Theory of Empire in the Sixteenth Century* (Cambridge, 1940), p. 28.

49. Ibid., p. 29. *Sublimis Deus* remained in force. A later example of papal pressure was Pope Pius V's letter to Francisco de Toledo on his appointment as viceroy of Peru, offering congratulations and a reminder of the importance of converting the Indian. *Colección de documentos inéditos relativos al descubrimiento, conquista, y colonización de las posesiones españoles de América y Oceanía*, vol. 8, pp. 215-216.

50. Friede, p. 168.

51. Demetrio Ramos Pérez, "La etapa lascasiana de la presion de conciencias," *Anuario de estudios Americanos* (1967), pp. 882-883.

52. Ibid., pp. 875, 881.

53. Agustín Yañez, ed., *Doctrina de fray Bartolemé de Las Casas* (Mexico, 1941), pp. 55-83.

54. Bartolomé de Las Casas, *Brevisima relación de la destrucción de las Indias* (Buenos Aires, 1953), p. 28.

55. Ibid., p. 43.

56. Ibid., p. 49.

57. Ibid., p. 100.

58. Ibid., p. 102.

59. Alonso de la Santa Cruz, *Crónica del emperador Carlos V*, 5 vols. (Madrid, 1920-1925), vol. 4, pp. 217-221. This was essentially the same three-pronged attack as Las Casas mounted in 1516, in which one memorial outlined the problem, another suggested the solution, and a third attacked the responsible officials. In this instance, Giménez Fernández posits the existence of a yet to be discovered memorial charging administrators with misconduct. Giménez Fernández, p. 95.

60. Giménez Fernández, p. 96.

61. Henry Stevens, ed., 1543 facsimile edition, *The New Laws and Ordinances of His Majesty Emperor Charles the Fifth* (London, 1893).

62. Las Casas, *Brevisima relación*, p. 72.

63. Hanke, *The Spanish Struggle*, p. 91.

64. Ibid., p. 97.

65. Motolinía, a dedicated protector of Indians, believed that Las Casas disrupted race relations. He urged a balanced approach and attempted to blunt Las Casas's efforts to create the overwhelming pressure needed to force a response. He accused Las Casas of using Indian porters to transport his anti-Spanish documentation and then failing to pay them. Fr. Toribio Motolinía, *Carta al emperador: refutatión a las casas sobre la colonización española* (México, 1949).

66. Liss, p. 79.
67. Hanke, *The Spanish Struggle*, p. 96.
68. Puga, vol. I, pp. 472-475. *Recopilación de leyes de los reynos de las Indias* (Madrid, 1791), lib. 6, tit. 8, ley 4.
69. Puga, vol. I, pp. 479-480. Mendoza took steps to inventory individuals and villages preliminary to a new distribution. Instead, the Crown extended encomienda titles for additional lifetimes. In some cases, titles were renewed up to five times.
70. J. Ignacio Rubio Mané, *Introducción al estudio de los virreyes de Nueva España, 1535-1746* (México, 1955), p. 209. Ignacio Bejarano, ed., *Actas de cabildo de la ciudad de México*, 12 vols. (Mexico, 1889-1900), vol. 5, p. 162.
71. Hanke, *The Spanish Struggle*, p. 119.
72. Ibid., p. 121.
73. Ricardo Smith, *Un humanista al servicio del imperialismo: Juan Ginés de Sepúlveda (1490-1573)* (Córdoba, 1942), p. 37.
74. Richard Konetzke, ed., *Colección de documentos para la historia de la formación social de Hispanoamérica, 1493-1810* (Madrid, 1953), vol. 1, pp. 326-328, 330.
75. Silvio A. Zavala, *La encomienda indiana* (Madrid, 1935), pp. 205-206.
76. *Documentos para la historia de la formación social*, vol. 1, pp. 340-358.
77. Roberto Levillier, ed., *Audiencia de Lima, correspondencia de presidentes y oidores* (Madrid, 1922), vol. 1, pp. 198-201. Fernando de Santillán, *Origen, descendencia política y gobierno de las Incas* (Lima, 1927), pp. 112-113; Juan Matienzo, *Gobiero de Perú* (Buenos Aires, 1910), pp. 57-62.
78. Joaquín García Icazbalceta, ed., *Nueva colección de documentos para la historia de México* (México, 1941), vol. 2, pp. 231-237. Carlos A. Romero, "Breves apuntes sobre perpetuidad de las encomiendas en el Perú," *Revista inca* (Lima, 1923), p. 688.
79. For a discussion, see Marvin Goldwert, "The Struggle for the Perpetuity of Encomiendas in Viceregal Peru, 1550-1600," M.A. thesis, University of Texas, 1958.
80. William L. Sherman, *Forced Labor in Sixteenth-Century Central America* (Lincoln, 1979), p. 133. For a discussion of Cerrato's reforms, see Sherman, pp. 129-188.
81. Gibson quoted disillusioned caciques and principales (secondary chiefs) who wrote Felipe II in 1570 that "the royal cédulas favor us, but they are not obeyed here." Charles Gibson, "Caciques in Postconquest and Colonial Mexico," in Ronald Dolkart and Robert Kern, *The Caciques* (Albuquerque, 1973), p. 20. Early in the seventeenth century, the Araucanians recognized the same phenomenon. They told Valdivia that the "king is very good and his commands just...but your captains and governors do not obey his will." Quoted in Eugene H. Korth, *Spanish Policy in Colonial Chile: The Struggle for Social Justice, 1537-1700* (Stanford, 1968), p. 119.
82. Las Casas, *Opúsculos*, p. 450b. From 1543 on, Las Casas's goal became the restoration of Indian Republics governed by their natural lords and subject only to the Castilian monarch. He believed that only in this fashion could Indian society be protected from the Europeans. Friede, pp. 176-177.

83. Korth, pp. 59-77.

84. Luis de Valdivia, in a letter (March 15, 1617) to Felipe III reporting the death of Governor Alonso de Ribera, described the political process. He predicted that with the governor's death the flow of reports and objections would cease, and the political consensus of the municipal council, religious orders, and military, so tirelessly maintained by the governor to justify his failure to obey royal wishes and instructions, would fall apart. For details of the struggle between Valdivia and Ribera, see Korth, pp. 139-157.

85. An acculturated, technically and residentially integrated urban Indian society emerged in spite of attempts to segregate ethnic groups. For a view of Lima in 1613 based on the elaborate census of that year, see Paul J. Charney, "The Urban Indian: A Case Study of the Indian Population of Lima in 1613," M.A. thesis, University of Texas, 1980.

86. Sherman, p. 208.

87. Ibid., pp. 187, 201. The inability of Indian villages to protect their members from Spanish demands may have made wage labor relatively more attractive. Murdo J. MacLeod, *Spanish Central America: A Socioeconomic History, 1520-1720* (Berkeley, 1973), p. 226.

88. Experimentation with the temporary assignment of labor (*Indios de servicio*) during the establishment of the European settlement of Puebla opened the way for limited, controlled, and temporary assignment of labor under the *repartimiento* system in the latter half of the sixteenth century. Julia Hirschberg, "An Alternative to Encomienda: Puebla's Indios de Servicio, 1531-45," *Journal of Latin American Studies* (November 1979), pp. 241-264.

89. The sequence of institutions (encomienda, repartimiento, and independent labor) implies defined stages rather than an actual overlapping. Charles Gibson, *The Aztecs under Spanish Rule: A History of the Indians of the Valley of Mexico, 1519-1810* (Stanford, 1964), p. 346.

90. Steve J. Stern, "The Rise and Fall of Indian-White Alliances: A Regional View of 'Conquest' History," *Hispanic American Historical Review* (August 1981), p. 469.

91. Peter J. Bakewell, *Silver Mining and Society in Colonial Mexico: Zacatecas, 1546-1700* (Cambridge, 1971), p. 225. Humboldt, at the end of the eighteenth century, observed that Mexican miners received the best pay. Alejandro de Humboldt, *Ensayo político sobre el reino de la Nueva España* (México, 1966), p. 399. In Peru wage labor constituted over half the labor force in the mines by 1600 and the trend continued. Peter J. Bakewell, *Miners of the Red Mountain: Indian Labor in Potosí* (Albuquerque, 1984), pp. 181, 185.

92. In the eighteenth century, a classic case of misjudgment caused the 1766 strike in Real del Monte. The Conde de Regla's efforts to cut costs and increase profits led to disputes over the *partido* (share) and, along with other complaints (in particular the conduct of those who rounded up workers to staff the shifts), triggered a strike. The miners argued that Regla acted unjustly and subsequently appealed to the viceroy to settle the issue. Failure to resolve their grievances led to mob violence. In the end, the workers' demands had to be met, at least in part, and the Conde de Regla went into a self-imposed eight-year exile. Noblet Barry Danks, "Revolts in 1766 and

1767 in Mining Communities in New Spain," Ph.D. dissertation, University of Colorado, 1979, pp. 131-201.

93. Friede noted that under Felipe II the Council of the Indies became less interested in Indian problems. Friede, p. 196.

94. Recopilación, lib. 6, tit. 6, ley 3. John Preston Moore, *The Cabildo in Peru under the Hapsburgs: A Study in the Origins and Power of the Town Council in the Viceroyalty of Peru, 1530-1700* (Durham, 1954), p. 234. *Recopilación*, lib. 2, tit. 24, ley 27.

95. For the text, see José Toribio Medina, *Biblioteca hispano-chilena, 1523-1817* (Santiago, 1963), vol. 2, pp. 5-20. For its importance, see Korth pp. 84-91. Korth dates the document 1599, while Medina suggests 1601.

96. Quentin Skinner, *The Foundation of Modern Political Thought* (Cambridge, 1978), vol. 2, p. 352.

97. Menéndez Pidal identified, yet found it difficult to appreciate, Las Casas's "intolerant convictions, aggressiveness, egocentric vanity, intellectual and moral delirium, excessive exaggeration, contagious passion, and propagandistic repetition," which made him a political force. Ramón Menéndez Pidal, *El padre Las Casas: su doble personalidad* (Madrid, 1963), pp. 388-389.

98. Sherman, p. 330. An example of hyperbole is provided by a Dominican friar in Lima who, reporting to the Council of the Indies in 1553 on conditions in Chile, writes that Indian workers who concealed a "single grain" of gold suffered the loss of their nose and ears. With overstatement and hearsay, the friar pressured the council to act against real abuses. Diego Barros Arana, *Historia jeneral de Chile* (Santiago, 1884-1913), vol. I, pp. 412-413.

99. Miranda noted that the rapid transformation in Mexico evident by 1560 would have surprised, perhaps even shocked, a returning conquistador. Change occurred at a different rate in marginal areas. José Miranda, *España y Nueva España en la época de Felipe II* (México, 1962), pp. 61-62.

100. Differing explanations are offered by Moreno, who viewed violation of the law as a consequence of the lack of coercive force, and Phelan, who suggested that intentional conflicting standards gave colonial officials flexibility and made them more dependent on the monarch's indulgence. Frank Jay Moreno, "The Spanish Colonial System: A Functional Approach," *The Western Political Quarterly* (June 1967), p. 310. John E. Phelan, "Authority and Flexibility in the Spanish Imperial Bureaucracy," *Administrative Science Quarterly* (June 1960), pp. 47-65.

4: *The Governing Ideology of the Bourbon State*

1. The period between 1500 and 1740 in Europe may be divided into two major epochs. The first emphasized organization and regulation of consumption, and the second stressed production and the stimulation of consumption. Marc Raeff, *The Well-Ordered Police State: Social and Institutional Change Through Law in the Germanies and Russia, 1600-1800* (New Haven, 1983), p. 14. Such a schema appears applicable to Spain. Intent on a new economic order, reformers subordinated everything, including cultural reforms. Vicente Palacio Atard, *Los españoles de la ilustración* (Madrid, 1964), p. 33.

2. John Laures, *The Political Economy of Juan de Mariana* (New York, 1928), pp. 89, 96, 100.

3. Thomas K. Niehaus, "Population Problems and Land Use in the Writings of the Spanish 'Arbitristas': Social and Economic Thinkers, 1610-1650." Ph.D. dissertation, University of Texas, 1976, pp. 112, 173. The arbitristas reacted to the national crisis and disillusionment of the period. John H. Elliot, *Imperial Spain, 1469-1716* (London, 1963), pp. 294-295.

4. Muñoz Pérez distinguished eighteenth-century *proyectismo* from *arbitrismo* as a utilitarian, rational, and methodical application of knowledge designed to resolve concrete questions with an understanding of their connection with the general situation. José Muñoz Pérez, "Los proyectos de España e Indias en el siglo XVIII: el proyectismo como género," *Revista de estudios políticos* (Mayo-Junio 1955), pp. 169-195.

5. Majorie Grice-Hutchinson, *Early Economic Thought in Spain, 1177-1740* (London, 1978), pp. 156-160. Demetrio Iparraguire, "Los antiguos economistas españoles y el desarrollo económico de España," *Boletín de estudios económicos* (Enero-Abril 1963), pp. 99-108.

6. Juan de Cabrera, *Crisis política. Determina el más florido imperio y la mejor institución de principes y ministros* (Madrid, 1719), p. 151.

7. Ibid., p. 159.

8. Gaspar Melchor de Jovellanos, "Discurso sobre los medios de promover la felicidad del Principado," *Biblioteca de autores españoles*, vol. 50, p. 439.

9. Marcia D. Davidson, "Three Spanish Economists of the Enlightenment: Campomanes, Jovellanos, Florez Estrada," Ph.D dissertation, Duke University, 1962, p. 120.

10. Otis H. Green, *Spain and the Western Tradition: The Castilian Mind in Literature from El Cid to Calderón* (Madison, 1964), vol. 2, pp. 14-15. The directive nature of the notion of the Great Chain of Being is evident in Ignatius de Loyola's declaration that "man is created to praise, revere, and serve God our Lord...and all other things on the face of the earth are created for man, to help him achieve the purpose for which he is created." José Rocafull Gallegos, *La experiencia de Dios en los místicos españoles* (México, 1945), p. 18.

11. Richard Herr, *The Eighteenth-Century Revolution in Spain* (Princeton, 1958), p. 39.

12. Benito Jerónimo Feijóo, *Teatro crítico universal* (Madrid, 1941), I. pt. 4, par. 43.

13. According to Feijóo, "This is what constitutes a great and glorious king, one who does not strike his neighbors or destroy their walls and the field with blood." "Carta a Don Agustín de Hordeñana," *Escritos políticos de Feijóo* (Madrid, 1947), p. 535.

14. For a review of Feijóo's political thought, see Luis Sánchez Agesta, *El pensamiento político del despotismo ilustrado* (Madrid, 1953), pp. 48-69.

15. Bailyn characterized the power of such a peculiar configuration of ideas as an "intellectual switchboard wired so that certain combinations of events would activate a distinct set of signals." Bernard Bailyn, *The Ideological Origins of the American Revolution* (Cambridge, 1967), p. 23.

16. Melchor de Macanaz, "Auxilios para bien gobernar una monarquía católica," *Semanario erudito* (Madrid, 1780), vol. 5, p. 235.

17. Ibid., p. 244.

18. Bernardo Francisco Aznar, *Discurso que formó tocante a la Real Hacienda y administración de ella* (Madrid, 1727), p. 175.

19. Ibid.

20. Callahan noted that this constituted an essentially conservative modification of traditional theories on the nobility's social function. William J. Callahan, *Honor, Commerce and Industry in Eighteenth-Century Spain* (Boston, 1972), p. 12. The long-range implications appear more radical.

21. Valentín de Foronda, "Disertación sobre lo honroso que es la profesión del comercio," *Miscelánea o colección de varios discursos* (Madrid, 1793).

22. Callahan, p. 35.

23. Francisco Puy, *El pensamiento tradicional en la España del siglo XVIII* (Madrid, 1966), pp. 55-56.

24. Gerónimo de Uztáriz, *Teórica y práctica de comercio y de marina en diferentes discursos y calificados ejemplares...*, 3d ed. (Madrid, 1757), pp. 320-325, 330.

25. Ibid., pp. 89, 90.

26. Ibid., pp. 391-396. Gaspar Melchor de Jovellanos, "Introducción a un discurso sobre el estado de la economía civil," *Biblioteca de autores españoles*, vol. 87, no. 10, p. 9. Posada also noted the two types. Eduardo Arcila Farias, *Reformas económicas de siglo XVIII en Nueva España* (Mexico, 1974), p. 20.

27. Uztáriz, p. 412.

28. Clement G. Motten, *Mexican Silver and the Enlightenment* (Philadelphia, 1950), p. 30. For an institutional study, see Thomas A. Brown, *La academia de San Carlos de la Nueva España*, 2 vols. (México, 1976). Uztáriz had a broad influence. An English translation of his work published in 1751 provided Adam Smith with material for his *Wealth of Nations*. In 1753 a French edition appeared, and four years later a third Spanish edition. Uztáriz's son published a revised edition of the *Teórica* (1783), and translations enjoyed wide distribution.

29. Bernardo de Ulloa, *Restablecimiento de las fábricas y comercio español* (Madrid, 1740), pp. 92-98. Vicens Vives estimated that in 1686 illegal trade accounted for two-thirds of colonial commerce. Jaime Vicens Vives, *Manuel de historia económica de España* (Barcelona, 1967), p. 371. Robert J. Shafter, *The Economic Societies in the Spanish World (1763-1821)* (Syracuse, 1958), p. 9.

30. José del Campillo y Cossío, *Lo que hay de más y de menos en España para que sea lo que debe ser y no lo que es* (Madrid, 1798).

31. José del Campillo y Cossío, *Nuevo sistema de gobierno económico para la América* (Madrid, 1787), p. 9.

32. Ibid.

33. Campillo's work influenced the Marqués de Pombal and his ministers. In Portuguese America, the Indian Directorate in 1757 changed the physical surroundings and dress of Amazonian Indians in an attempt to transform them into a productive peasantry. Colin M. MacLachlan, "The Indian Directorate: Forced Acculturation in Portuguese America (1757-1799)," *The Americas* (April 1972), pp. 369-392.

34. Campillo y Cossío, *Nuevo sistema*, p. 18. John H. Parry, *The Spanish Seaborne Empire* (London, 1966), p. 315. Josefina Cintrón Tiryakian, "Campillo's Pragmatic New System: A Mercantile and Utilitarian Approach to Indian Reform in Spanish Colonies of the Eighteenth Century," *History of Political Economy* (1978), p. 237, suggests the importance of English thought in molding Campillo's approach. On this issue, see Polt's work on the English sources of Jovellanos. John H. R. Polt, *Gaspar Melchor de Jovellanos* (New York, 1971).

35. Miguel Artola, "Campillo y Las Reformas de Carlos III," *Revista de Indias* (October-December 1952), pp. 711-712.

36. John Lynch, *Spanish Colonial Administration, 1782-1810: The Intendant System in the Viceroyalty of the Rio de la Plata* (London, 1958), pp. 18-19.

37. Francisco Roma y Rosell, *Las señales de la felicidad de España y medios de hacer las eficaces* (Madrid, 1768), pp. 313-315.

38. Bernardo Ward, *Proyecto económico en que se proponen varios providencias, dirigidas á promover los intereses de España* (Madrid, 1779), p. xxii.

39. Ibid., pp. xvi, 127. The distinction between money and real wealth can be traced back to Aristotle, as can such other economic concepts as the connection between supply, demand, and value.

40. Ward, p. 264. This same conclusion had been reached earlier by many seventheenth-century intellectuals, including Quevedo. Juan Marichal, "Quevedo: El escritor como 'espejo' de su tiempo," *La voluntad de estilo* (Barcelona, 1957), pp. 149-162, Francisco de Quevedo Villegas, *Política de Dios y govierno de Christo*, ed. James O. Crosby (Madrid, 1966).

41. Ward, p. 277.

42. El virrey Amat da cuenta al rey de los defectos y vicios de organización del virreinato del Perú—1762," *Revista de la biblioteca nacional* (Buenos Aires, 1942), pp. 349-350. Fisher notes that a corrupt Amat purposely cultivated the senior judge and thus escaped censure. J. R. Fisher, *Government and Society in Colonial Peru: The Intendant System, 1784-1814* (London, 1970), p. 10.

43. Prólogo de la Memoria del virrey Amat," *Revista chilena de historia y geografía* (1951), p. 45. Miguel Feyjóo de Sosa probably authored the report. He served as corregidor of Quispicanchi and Trujillo and retired as contador mayor of the Tribunal de Cuentas. In 1763 he published *Relación description de la ciudad y provincia de Trujillo*. Ibid., pp. 43-44.

44. Jorge Juan and Antonio de Ulloa, *Discourse and Political Reflections on the Kingdoms of Peru*, ed. John J. Tepaske (Norman, 1978), pp. 3-33.

45. Endorsement of an active government is evident in the prologue: "To be successful he [the king] must plan unexpected, quick action along whatever lines wisdom may dictate. To forestall future problems he must apply preventive measures...to restore [damage already done] to a condition where justice based on reason ought to prevail without interruption." Ibid., p. 38.

46. Ibid., pp. 51-53.

47. Ibid., p. 69.

48. Ibid., pp. 96, 161. The frequency of revolts in Peru is examined in Leon G. Campbell, "Social Structure of the Túpac Amaru Army in Cuzco, 1781-81,"

Hispanic American Historical Review (November 1981), pp. 675-693. See also Oscar Cornblit, "Levantamiento de masas de Perú y Bolivia durante el siglo dieciocho," in Tulio Halperín Donghi, ed., *El ocaso del orden colonial en Hispanoamérica* (Buenos Aires, 1978), pp. 60-61.

49. Juan and Ulloa, pp. 248, 272. *The Gaceta de Lima* (1743), responding to the traditional perception of politics, almost invariably commenced with news of the health of the king, followed by similar information on the viceroy and the archbishop. Ella Dunbar Temple, *La gaceta de Lima del siglo XVIII: facsimiles de seis ejemplares raros de este periódico* (Lima, 1965).

50. Pedro Rodríguez de Campomanes, *Discurso sobre la educación popular de los artesanos y su fomento; y apéndice a la educación popular* (Madrid, 1775), appendix XXVII.

51. Davidson, p. 39.

52. Campomanes, *Discurso*, pp. 129-132, 274-275.

53. José Muñoz Pérez, "La idea de America en Campomanes," *Anuario de estudios Americanos* (1953), p. 245.

54. O. Carlos Stoetzer, *The Scholastic Roots of the Spanish American Revolution* (New York, 1979), pp. 66-67. Jovellanos to Campomanes, 1777, published in *El Español* (12 February 1836).

55. Gaspar Melchor de Jovellanos, "Introducción a un discurso sobre el estado de la economía civil," *Biblioteca de autores españoles*, vol. 87. Written in 1776, it reflected Jovellanos's belief in education and the totally interdependent nature of the economy.

56. Jovellanos to Rafael Floranes, 23 July 1800, *Biblioteca de autores españoles* (Madrid, 1956), vol. 86, p. 231.

57. Jovellanos asserted that the "continual conflict of interests that agitated men among themselves, naturally established an equilibrium which laws could never establish." Gaspar Melchor de Jovellanos, *Informe de la Sociedad Económica de esta corte al real y supremo consejo de Castilla en el expediente de ley agraria...* (Madrid, 1795), pp. 8-9.

58. Luis Miguel Enciso Recio, *Nipho y el periodismo español del siglo XVIII* (Valladolid, 1956), p. 153.

59. A "directive elite" sought to influence public opinion. Newspaper editors, such as Nipho, constituted an important secondary level, popularizing and simplifying "information" for the literate but non-elite strata. Vicente Palacio Atard, *Los españoles de la ilustración* (Madrid, 1964) p. 37. Enciso Recio noted that newspapers supplied a "bridge between the elites and the masses." Enciso Recio, *Nipho*, p. 333.

60. For a review of the periodical literature, see Jaime Carrera Pujal, *Historia de la economía española* (Barcelona, 1945), vol. 3, pp. 455-457, and Herr, pp. 183-200. An indication of the distribution within Spain and in the empire is suggested in Luis Miguel Enciso Recio, *La gaceta de Madrid y el mercurio histórico y politico, 1756-1781* (Valladolid, 1957).

61. José Torre Revello, *El libro, la imprenta y el periodismo en America durante la dominación española* (Buenos Aires, 1940), p. 174.

62. José Antonio de Alzate y Ramírez, *Obras: periódicos*, ed. Roberto Moreno (Mexico, 1980), vol. 1, p. xiii. José Ignacio Bartolache, *Mercurio volante*, ed. Roberto Moreno (Mexico, 1979)

63. The editors of the *Correo mercantil de España y sus Indias* (1797) published information on weather, harvests, prices, agricultural innovations, physical and geographical features, cattle, factories and machines, price histories, markets, new commercial houses, general economic problems, shipwrecks, crime, freight charges, books, ship arrivals, and everything else that shed light on commerce. Luis Miguel Enciso Recio, *Prensa económica del XVIII: el correo mercantil de España y sus Indias* (Valladolid, 1958), pp. 89-91. José M. Mariluz Urquijo, *Noticias del correo mercantil de España y sus Indias: sobre la vida económica del virreinato del Río de la Plata* (Buenos Aires, 1977), pp. 16-17.

64. Alzate, *Obras: Periódicos* vol. 1, pp. xiii, 52-58. Roberto Moreno, *Un eclesiástico criollo frente al estado borbón* (México, 1980), pp. 32-33, 58. José Antonio de Alzate, *Memoria sobre la naturaleza, cultivo y beneficio de la grana*, ed. Roberto Moreno (México, 1981).

65. Enciso Recio, *Nipho*, pp. 144-145. Voltaire, himself a journalist, considered newspaper writers to be "the insects of literature."

66. Eduardo Arcila Farías, *El pensamiento económico Hispanoaméricano en Baquíjano y Carrillo* (Caracas, 1976), pp. 32-40. See also José Ignacio López Lorea, *El pensamiento de José Baquíjano y Carrillo* (Lima, 1970).

67. *Papel periódico de la ciudad de Santafé de Bogotá 1791-1797* (facsimile edition, Bogotá, 1978), vol. 1, pp. 31-32. Mark A. Burkholder, *Politics of a Colonial Career: José Baquíjano and the Audiencia of Lima* (Albuquerque, 1980), pp. 84, 86.

68. Alzate, *Obras: periódicos*, vol. 1, p. 61.

69. The influence on policy of Adam Smith's *Wealth of Nations* (1776) is difficult to determine. Many of his ideas had already been expressed by Spanish political economists. The first Spanish edition appeared in 1792, but it is evident many had already read the English or French edition. Robert S. Smith, "The Wealth of Nations in Spain and Hispanic America, 1780-1830," *Journal of Political Economy* (April 1957), pp. 104-125. Even the translator of the 1792 edition, Carlos Martínez de Irujo, did not support the notion of open trade, although he advocated the use of neutral shipping during wartime. Carlos Martínez de Irujo, *Observations on the Commerce of Spain with Her Colonies in Time of War* (Philadelphia, 1800).

70. Consisting of letters written between 1787 and 1789 to the Count of Lerena, Secretary of Finance, by an unknown high official, it is often attributed to Campomanes, Cabarrus, and others without convincing evidence. Sánchez Agesta, pp. 305-308.

71. Marcelo Bitar Letayf, *Los economistas españoles del siglo XVIII y sus ideas sobre el comercio con Las Indias* (México, 1975), p. 39.

72. Antonio Rodríguez Villa, ed., *Cartas político-económicas* (Madrid, 1878), p. 156. Periodicals such as *El espiritu de los mejores diarios* (1787-91) and *El correo de los ciegos* (1787) carried articles on Rousseau. After the 1799 Spanish edition of the *Social Contract*, his work enjoyed wider circulation. J. R. Spell, "Rousseau in Spanish America," *Hispanic American Historical Review* (May 1935), pp. 261, 263.

73. Sánchez Agesta, p. 90. Juan Manuel Herrero, "Notas sobre la ideología del burgués español del siglo XVIII," *Anuario de estudios Americanos* (Sevilla, 1952), p. 302. In a similar manner in the late sixteenth and seventeenth

centuries Montaigne and his successor among the *libertines* supported the political order in France while they mocked it among themselves. Nannerl O. Keohane, *Philosophy and the State in France: The Renaissance to the Enlightenment* (Princeton, 1980), p. 19.

74. James Clayburn La Force, Jr., *The Development of the Spanish Textile Industry, 1750-1800* (Berkely and Los Angeles, 1965), pp. 154-166. For university reforms, see Luis Sala Babust, *Visitas y reformas de los colegios mayores de Salamanca en el reinado de Carlos III* (Valladolid, 1958); George M. Addy, *The Enlightenment in the University of Salamanca* (Durham, 1966), includes the text of the 1771 university reform plan; see also Antonio Alvarez de Morales, *La "ilustracion" y la reforma de la universidad en la España del siglo XVIII* (Madrid, 1971). The resurgence of university training must be kept in perspective. Only a small number of students evidenced interest in the new science. Richard L. Kagan, *Students and Society in Early Modern Spain* (Baltimore, 1974), pp. 227-230.

75. La Force, p. 31.

76. Ibid., p. 50.

77. For an institutional history, see Walter Howe, *The Mining Guild of New Spain and Its Tribunal General, 1770-1821* (New York, 1968).

78. John H. Elliot, *Imperial Spain, 1469-1716* (London, 1963), p. 373.

79. Gisela Morazzani de Pérez Enciso, *La intendencia en España y America* (Caracas, 1966), p. 27. Navarro García noted that Carlos II's appointment of a superintendent-general of the treasury in 1687, and in 1691 the appointment of superintendents in the Castilian provinces, foreshadowed the intendant system. Luis Navarro García, *Intendencias en Indias* (Sevilla, 1959), pp. 7-8.

80. Pérez Enciso, p. 34.

81. Eleazon Cordova-Bello, *Las reformas del despotismo ilustrado en America* (Caracas, 1975), p. 40. Gildas Bernard, *Le secretariat d'état et le conseil espagnol des Indies, 1700-1808* (Genève-Paris, 1972), pp. 31, 33. Luis Navarro García, *Hispanoamérica en el siglo XVIII* (Sevilla, 1975), pp. 57-58.

82. Gildas Bernard, pp. 21, 25.

83. Antonio Ferrer Del Río, "Obras originales del Conde de Floridablanca, y escritas referentes a su persona," *Biblioteca de Autores Españoles* (Madrid, 1924), p. 343.

84. Ibid.

85. José Miranda and Pablo González Casanova, eds., *Sátira anónima del siglo XVIII* (Mexico, 1953), p. 15. Jovellanos eulogy for Carlos III stressed the deceased monarch's economic achievements and gave him full credit for a depersonalized "science of economics." This was rational praise very different from the emotional and spiritual eulogies of the previous century. Mario Rodríguez, *The Cádiz Experiment in Central America, 1808 to 1826* (Berkeley, 1978), pp. 1-3.

86. Manuel Herrero, p. 306. In Chile a subtle change concerning royal service occurred as the elite responded to the materialism of the ideology. Jacques A. Barbier, "Elites and Cadres in Bourbon Chile," *Hispanic American Historical Review* (August 1972), p. 427.

87. Ramón de Posada, *Informe sobre el comercio de harina* (1781), quoted in

Eduardo Arcila Farías, *Reformas económicas del siglo XVIII en Nueva España* (México, 1974), vol. 1, p. 18.

88. Pedro Rodríguez de Campomanes, *Apéndice a la educación popular*, 4 vols. (Madrid, 1775-1776), I. pt. 1.

89. Miranda and González Casanova, p. 131.

90. Philip Louis Astuto, *Eugenio Espejo (1747-1795) reformador ecuatoriano de la ilustración* (Mexico, 1969), pp. 62-63.

91. Palacio Atard, *Los Españoles*, pp. 27-29.

92. Vicente Rodríguez Casado, *La política y los políticos en el reinado de Carlos III* (Madrid, 1962), pp. 82-83.

93. Juan Marichal, "From Pistoia to Cádiz: A Generation's Itinerary, 1786-1812." in A. Owen Aldridge, *The Ibero-American Enlightenment* (Urbana, 1971), p. 99. Sánchez Agesta, p. 101. Status as a reward for meritorious service, rather than for personal loyalty, indicated growing professionalism. The Crown established in 1771 the civil Order of Carlos III as a state performance award. Mark A. Burkholder and D. S. Chandler, *From Impotence to Authority: The Spanish Crown and the American Audiencias, 1687-1808* (Columbia, 1977), p. 122.

94. Stanley Payne, *A History of Spain and Portugal* (Madison, 1973), vol. 2, p. 363.

5: *Ideology and Reality*

1. Zorraquín Becú discounts the notion of a simple translation. The French term *domaine de la couronne* was equivalent to the Castilian *realengo*. Ricardo Zorraquín Becú, *La organización política argentina en el período hispánico* (Buenos Aires, 1959), p. 34.

2. Rafael Antúnez y Acevedo, *Memorias históricas sobre la legislación y gobierno del comercio de los españoles con sus colonias en las Indias occidentales* (Madrid, 1797), pp. 298-305.

3. Luis Navarro García, *Intendencias en Indias* (Sevilla, 1959), p. 17.

4. Phelan refused to label innovations "reforms" on the grounds that the King's American subjects viewed them as a new departure. John Leddy Phelan, *The People and the King: The Comunero Revolution in Columbia, 1781* (Madison, 1978), p. 84.

5. Herbert Ingram Priestley, *José de Gálvez, Visitador-General of New Spain, 1765-1771* (Berkeley, 1916), p. 20.

6. W. W. Pierson, "La Intendencia de Venezuela en el régimen colonial," *Boletín de la academia nacional de la historia* (Caracas, 1941), p. 264.

7. John Lynch, *Spanish Colonial Administration, 1782-1810: The Intendant System in the Viceroyalty of the Río de La Plata* (New York, 1969), pp. 59-60.

8. D. A. Brading, *Miners and Merchants in Bourbon Mexico, 1763-1810* (Cambridge, 1970), p. 44.

9. Reformers did not dispense with the old formalities; intendants swore allegiance before a royal representative before assuming their positions.

Gisela Morazzani de Pérez Enciso, *La Intendencia en España y América* (Caracas, 1966), p. 59.

10. Escobedo nominated one criollo as intendant to gain the support of Lima's elite. The Minister of the Indies refused to confirm the appointment. J. R. Fisher, *Government and Society in Colonial Peru: The Intendant System, 1784-1814* (London, 1970), p. 38.

11. The telescoping of Campillo's two-stage plan into one may account for the reaction. Phelan, p. 33.

12. Fisher, p. 33.

13. For a discussion of French manipulations, see Geoffrey J. Walker, *Spanish Politics and Imperial Trade, 1700-1789* (Bloomington, 1979), pp. 19-33.

14. Raymond De Roover, "Scholastic Economics: Survival and Lasting Influence from the Sixteenth Century to Adam Smith," *Quarterly Journal of Economics* (May 1955), p. 186.

15. Roland D. Hussey, *The Caracas Company, 1728-1784: A Study in the History of Spanish Monopolistic Trade* (Cambridge, Massachusetts, 1934), pp. 21-22. In 1624 the Junta de Comercio attacked the notion of a private company on the grounds it would injure many and benefit few. Ibid., p. 11.

16. Ibid., p. 41. This view was shared by Uztáriz. Geronimo de Uztáriz, *Teórica y práctica de comercio, y marina...* (Madrid, 1757), pp. 89, 90. Daubeton recommended abolition of the fleet systm and open colonial commerce by all Spanish subjects, as well as breaking the power of the Seville Consulado. His advice foreshadowed José del Campillo's recommendations. E. W. Dahlgren, *Les Relations Commerciales et Maritimes entre la France et Côtes de l'Océan Pacifique* (Paris, 1909), pp. 256-257.

17. Preference for simple partnerships, following Italian forms of commercial contracts, may also have discouraged the organization of massive amounts of capital needed to form a comprehensive trading company. André E. Sayous, "Partnerships in the Trade Between Spain and America and also in the Spanish Colonies in the Sixteenth Century," *Journal of Economic and Business History* (February 1929), pp. 282-301.

18. Hussey, p. 38.

19. Ibid., p. 61.

20. For examples of the type and extent of privileges conceded, see the case of the Casa de Uztáriz Hermanos of Cádiz, in Eduardo Arcila Farías, *Reformas económicas del Siglo XVIII en Nueva España* (México, 1974), vol. 1, pp. 40-42.

21. Hussey, p. 223.

22. Arcila Farias, *Reformas*, vol. 1, p. 130.

23. The regulations of 1778, issued in the king's name by José de Gálvez, stated that "only free commerce between Spaniards and Americans could revitilaze agriculture, industry," *Reglamento y aranceles reales para el comercio libre de España a Indias de 12 de octubre de 1778* (Madrid, 1778), p. 1.

24. Quoted in Vicente Palacio Atard, *Los españoles de la ilustración* (Madrid, 1964), p. 89.

25. Bibiano Torres Ramírez, "Alejandro O'Reilly en Cuba," *Anuario de estudios Americanos* (1967), pp. 1357-1368. Allan J. Kuethe and G. Douglas Inglis,

"Absolutism and Enlightened Reforms: Charles III, The Establishment of the Alcabala and Commercial Reorganization in Cuba," *Past and Present* (November, 1985), pp. 118-143.

26. Morazzani de Pérez Enciso, p. 37. For the text of the 1764 regulation, see ibid., pp. 252-274.

27. Allan J. Kuethe, "The Development of the Cuban Military as a Sociopolitical Elite, 1763-83," *Hispanic American Historical Review* (November, 1981), pp. 695-704. Defense industries also boosted the Cuban economy, especially shipbuilding. As early as 1702, a plan had been developed, and shortly thereafter yards were established in Coatzacoalcos (Mexico) and in Havana. The Cuban yard proved successful and constructed "navios criollos" to meet the need, as expressed by Secretary Arriaga, for "ships, ships, ships that are flying fortresses" (*fortalezas volantes*). Guayaquil and Manila supplied needs in the Pacific. Luis Navarro García, *Hispanoamerica en el Siglo XVIII* (Sevilla, 1975), p. 63.

28. Ricardo Rees Jones, *El despotismo ilustrado y los intendentes de la Nueva España* (México, 1979), pp. 80-81. Morazzani de Pérez Enciso, p. 38.

29. María del Pópulo Antolín Espino, "El virrey Marqués de Cruillas," in José Antonio Calderón Quijano, ed., *Los virreyes de Nueva España en el reinado de Carlos III* (Sevilla, 1967), vol. 1, p. 133, noted the differing tone of the two sets of instructions. She observed that the council's instructions appear vague and uninformed, whereas Arriaga makes concrete references. Priestly, pp. 404-417, appends copies of the instructions.

30. This is true of both the 14 March and 16 March 1765 instructions to Gálvez issued by the Council. Priestley, pp. 413-417.

31. Arcila Farías suggests that officials without American experience generalized Spain's decadence to the entire Spanish world. Arcila Farías, *Reformas* vol. 1, pp. 11-12.

32. José de Gálvez, "Plan de intendencia (1768)," in Navarro García, *Intendencias* pp. 164-176. Rees Jones, p. 83.

33. Gálvez's actions resulted in the capture of the English frigate Nancy and the Triton, a French sloop, and imposition of fines and imprisonment of local officials and merchants. Calderón Quijano, vol. I, p. 146.

34. Priestly, p. 161.

35. Luis Navarro García, "El virrey Marqués de Croix, 1766-1771," in Calderón Quijano, vol. I, pp. 163, 165. Marqués de Croix, *Correspondence du Marquis de Croix* (Nantes, 1891), pp. 195-199. Gálvez initially received the appointment of judicial reviewer (*juez de residencia*) of ex-viceroy Cruillas's term in office, but the order was subsequently countermanded. Calderón Quijano, vol. I, p. 155.

36. Priestly, p. 171. Christon I. Archer, *The Army in Bourbon Mexico, 1760-1810* (Albuquerque, 1977), p. 116.

37. The term *Jesuitphobia*, applied by Dauril Alden in *Royal Government in Colonial Brazil* (Berkeley, 1968) to describe the official reaction, indicates the psycho-political role into which the Society was forced during the eighteenth century in countries struggling to reorder their perception of reality.

38. Colin M. MacLachlan and Jaime E. Rodríguez O., *The Forging of the Cosmic Race: A Reinterpretation of Colonial Mexico* (Berkeley, 1981), pp. 265-270.

39. Priestly, p. 183.

40. Rees Jones, p. 95.

41. Brading, p. 52.

42. Lillian Estelle Fisher, *The Intendant System in Spanish America* (Berkeley, 1929), p. 16.

43. Vicente Palacio Atard, *Areche y Guirior: observaciones sobre el fracaso de una visita al Perú* (Sevilla, 1946), p. 7.

44. For a discussion, see Guillermo Cespedes del Castillo, *Lima y Buenos Aires: repercusiones económicas y políticas de la creación del virreinato del Plata* (Sevilla, 1947).

45. Sergio Villalobos R., *El comercio y la crisis colonial: un mito de la independencia* (Santiago, 1968), p. 222.

46. Kendall Walker Brown, "The Economic and Fiscal Structure of Eighteenth-Century Arequipa," Ph.D. dissertation, Duke University, 1979, p. 179.

47. Atard, p. 19.

48. Ibid., p. 9.

49. Ruben Vargas Ugarte, *Historia del Perú: virreinato (siglo XVIII) 1700-1790* (Lima, 1956), pp. 379-380.

50. Quoted in J. R. Fisher, p. 12.

51. Atard, p. 24. Areche characterized Lima as a "Babylon" presided over by the viceroy and his wife and manipulated by the elite. Leon G. Campbell, "A Colonial Establishment: Creole Domination of the Audiencia of Lima during the Late Eighteenth Century," *Hispanic American Historical Review* (February 1972), p. 8.

52. Ibid., p. 32.

53. Ibid., p. 34.

54. Ugarte, pp. 398-399. See O. Carlos Stoetzer, *The Scholastic Roots of the Spanish American Revolution* (New York, 1979), p. 119, for a list of viceroys with military backgrounds.

55. Mark A. Burkholder, *Politics of a Colonial Career: José Baquíjano and the Audiencia of Lima* (Albuquerque, 1980), pp. 60-68.

56. While in Lima in 1777 he attended philosophical discussions at the university and also informed the viceroy of mita problems. Lillian Estelle Fisher, *The Last Inca Revolt, 1780-1783* (Norman, 1966), p. 35.

57. Magnus Mörner, *Perfil de la sociedad rural del Cuzco a fines de la colonia* (Lima, 1977), pp. 104-132.

58. Leon G. Campbell, "Social Structure of the Túpac Amaru Army in Cuzco, 1780-81," *Hispanic American Historical Review* (November 1981), pp. 675-693.

59. John Fisher, "Regionalism and Rebellion in Late Colonial Peru: The Aguilar-Ubalde Conspiracy of 1805," *Biblioteca Americana* (September 1982), p. 49. Campbell, "A Colonial Establishment," p. 17.

60. The repartimiento had been legalized in 1751 in a vain effort to control abuses as well as raise revenue. J. R. Fisher, pp. 14, 21.

61. Campbell, "Social Structure," p. 691.

62. J. R. Fisher, p. 24.

63. Ibid., p. 26.

64. Ibid., p. 28.

65. Ibid., p. 26.

66. Campbell characterized the effect of such commissions as the development of an "interlocking directorate." Campbell, "A Colonial Establishment," p. 15.

67. "Home rule" meant access to the fruits of their own kingdoms, including officeholding, but not in a direct political fashion. Mark A. Burkholder and D. S. Chandler, *From Impotence to Authority: The Spanish Crown and the American Audiencias, 1687-1808* (Columbia, Missouri, 1977), p. vii.

68. Ibid., p. 8.

69. Juan de Solórzano y Pereyra, "Política indiana," *Biblioteca de autores españoles* (Madrid, 1978), lib. 5, cap. 4, num. 29 and 30.

70. Hereditary transferable offices (*oficios vendible y renunciables*), essentially minor posts in municipal service or permitting the collection of fees, had been sold as early as 1559. Systematic sale of treasury posts began in 1633, vending of corregidor and alcalde mayor positions in 1678, and Audiencia positions in 1667.

71. Burkholder and Chandler, p. 43.

72. Ibid., pp. 97, 99, 104. Subsequently, those who traced the causes of the independence movements assigned the issue of jobs a major role. By excluding Americans many of the most illustrious families had been alienated. Michael P. Costeloe, *Response to Revolution: Imperial Spain and the Spanish American Revolutions, 1810-1840* (Cambridge, 1986), pp. 178-179.

73. Rees Jones, p. 98.

74. Lynch, *Spanish Colonial Administration*, pp. 93-94.

75. J. R. Fisher, p. 49. José M. Mariluz Urquijo, *Origenes de la burocracia Rioplatense: La secretaria del virreinato* (Buenos Aires, 1974), pp. 21-22.

76. María Luisa Rodríguez Baena, "Manuel Antonio Florez (1787-1789)," in José Antonio Calderón Quijano, ed., *Los virreyes de Nueva España en el reinado de Carlos IV* (Sevilla, 1972), vol. 1, pp. 6-7. Phelan, p. 30.

77. Phelan, p. 33.

78. J. R. Fisher, pp. 58-59. Escobedo foresaw conflict between the superintendents and the viceroys. Ibid., p. 31.

79. Jaime Eyzaguirre, *Ideario y ruta de la emancipación chilena* (Santiago, 1957), p. 50.

80. J. R. Fisher, pp. 83-84.

81. Bernard E. Bobb, *The Viceregency of Antonio María Bucareli in New Spain, 1771-1779* (Austin, 1962), p. 32. José Joaquín Real Díaz and Antonia M. Heredia Herrera, "Martín de Mayorga (1779-1783)," in José Antonio Calderón Quijano, ed., *Los virreyes de Nueva España en el reinado de Carlos III*, 2 vols. (Sevilla, 1967), vol. 1, p. 9, notes that Bucareli represented the last viceroy able to maintain a traditional concept of his role, whereas Mayorga served as the connection between Bucareli and the Gálvez era.

82. María Lourdes Díaz-Trechuelo Spínola, "Don Antonio María Bucareli y Ursúa (1771-1779)," in Calderón Quijano, *Virreyes en el reinado de Carlos III*, vol. 1, pp. 496, 502.

83. Brian R. Hamnett, *Politics and Trade in Southern Mexico, 1750-1821* (Cambridge, 1971), p. 43.

84. Carta de Pedro Muñoz de Villavicencio al virrey, 28 February 1773. W. B. Stephens Collection 1934 Benson Latin American Collection, University of Texas, Austin.

85. José Joaquin Real Díaz and Antonia M. Heredia Herrera, "Martín de Mayorga (1779-1783)," in Calderón Quijano, *Virreyes en al reinado de Carlos III*, vol. 1, pp. 64-68.

86. Adolfo Rubio G. I., "Alonso Nuñez de Haro (1787)," in Calderon Quijano, *Virreyes en el reinado de Carlos III*, vol. 2, pp. 374-375.

87. *Justa repulsa del reglamento de intendencias...* forms part of a larger work, *México enfermedades políticas*, often attributed to Hipólito Villarroel. Rees Jones disputes Villarroel's authorship and provides the text of the Justa Repulsa. Rees Jones, pp. 220-284.

88. *Instrucciónes que los virreyes de Nueva España dejaron a sus sucesores* (Mexico, 1867-73), vol. 2. p. 46. Flores struggled with excessive demands on the treasury. During his term, expenditures far outstripped revenue. Prudently, Flores did not favor innovation in the midst of a financial crisis. Rodríguez Baena, p. 78.

89. Born in Havana, he grew up in a Mexico governed by his father, and returned as viceroy in 1789. For a discussion, see María Lourdes Díaz-Trechuelo Spínola, et al., "El Virrey Don Juan Vicente de Güemes Pacheco, Segundo Conde de Revillagigedo (1789-1794)," in Calderón Quijano, *Virreys en el reinado de Carlos III*, vol. 1, pp. 87-311, and James Manfred Manfredini, *The Political Role of the Count of Revillagigedo, Viceroy of New Spain, 1789-1794* (New Brunswick, 1949).

90. Díaz-Trechuelo Spinola, pp. 358-361.

91. Revillagigedo, *Instrucción reservada*, arts. 14 and 46-50 and p. 210.

6: *A Faltering Ideology*

1. Roberto Levillier, *Gobernantes del Perú: cartas y papeles* (Madrid, 1925), vol. 8, pp. 400-406.

2. Alfredo Moreno Cebrian, *El corregidor de indios y la economía peruana del siglo XVIII* (Madrid, 1977), pp. 317-354.

3. Brian R. Hamnett, *Politics and Trade in Southern Mexico, 1750-1821* (Cambridge, 1971), p. 23.

4. Moreno Cebrian, p. 464. Javier Ortíz de la Tabla Ducasse, *Comercio exterior de Veracruz, 1778-1821: crisis de dependencia* (Sevilla, 1978), p. 27.

5. A discussion of the pro-repartimiento argument is presented in Hamnett, pp. 45-56.

6. *Informe general...entregó el Exmo. Señor Marqués de Sonora...al...Virrey Frey Dr. Antonio Bucareli y Ursúa* (December 1771), p. 41. Genaro García Collec-

tion, G 206-0, Benson Latin American Collection, University of Texas, Austin.

7. Moreno Cebrian, pp. 175, 178, 181, 184.

8. Quoted in Eduardo Arcila Farías, *Reformas económicas del siglo XVIII en Nueva España* (México, 1974), vol. 1, p. 26. Posada was the nephew of Ana de Zayas, wife of Gálvez's brother, Matías de Gálvez. A former *alcalde del crimen* in Lima, he was appoiinted fiscal of the Mexican Audiencia by Gálvez and assumed office in 1781. José Joaquin Real Díaz and Antonia M. Heredia Herrera, "Martín de Mayorga (1779-1783)," in José Antonio Calderón Quijano, ed., *Los virreyes de Nueva España en el reinado de Carlos III* (Sevilla, 1968), vol. 1, pp. 124-125.

9. Eric Mack, "Distributive Justice and the Tensions of Lockeanism," *Social Philosophy and Policy* (Fall 1983), p. 132.

10. María Lourdes Díaz-Trechuelo Spínola, "Don Antonio María Bucareli y Ursua 1771-1779," in Calderón Quijano, *Los virreyes en el reinado de Carlos III*, vol. 1, p. 498, notes that his opposition stemmed in part from an authoritarian character, conservatism, horror of innovation, and the belief that it weakened his viceregal powers. As a politican, he became a popular viceroy.

11. John Fisher, *Government and Society in Colonial Peru: The Intendant System (1784-1814)*, pp. 89, 99. Moreno Cebrian, p. 637. Timothy E. Anna, *The Fall of the Royal Government in Peru* (Lincoln, 1979), pp. 1-25, 78-79.

12. Moreno Cebrian, p. 639.

13. Hamnett, p. 91.

14. Arcila Farías, vol. 2, pp. 187-188.

15. Richardo Rees Jones, *El despotismo ilustrado y los intendentes de la Nueva España* (México, 1979), p. 169.

16. Hamnett, p. 83.

17. Economic development required credit, which in turn had to be secured. Credit inevitably brought restrictions that conflicted with individual freedom. The attempt to find a middle ground is demonstrated by the conditions under which the Crown granted the Philippine Company a monopoly on cotton in 1791. The company had to advance money to farmers, mutually arrive at a fair price, and finally buy all the cotton produced. Arcila Farías, vol. I, p. 47.

18. Hamnett, pp. 87-88.

19. Mark A. Burkholder, "The Council of the Indies in the Late Eighteenth Century: A New Perspective," *The Hispanic American Historical Review* (August 1976), pp. 404-423.

20. The new Ordinance of Intendants in 1803 provided for an adequate salary and prohibited the repartimiento, but because of costs and opposition it never went into effect. Hamnett, p. 93.

21. Moreno Cebrian, p. 177.

22. Fisher, p. 97.

23. Jacques A. Barbier, "Tradition and Reform in Bourbon Chile: Ambrosio O'Higgins and Public Finances," *The Americas* (January 1978), pp. 381-399.

24. Antonio Muró Orejón, "Estudio general del nuevo código de leyes de Indias," in Luis Navarro García, ed., *Homenaje al Dr. Muró Orejón* (Sevilla, 1979), vol. 2, pp. 51-52.

25. Walter Howe, *The Mining Guild of New Spain and Its Tribunal General, 1770-1821* (New York, 1968), pp. 205-208, 307, 367. The tribunal has received a mixed assessment. Humboldt appears impressed, whereas Lucas Alamán, a graduate of the school, sees the tribunal as a burden. Howe observes that the ordinance remained the basis of mining law until Porfirio Díaz, and influenced codes throughout the empire and in the American southwest. With the 1849 California gold rush, an English edition appeared in San Francisco. Motten credits the tribunal with providing the push necessary to introduce new technology. Izquierdo notes that it represented the institutionalization of the new science in New Spain and that alone constituted a significant step. Alexandro de Humboldt, *Ensayo político sobre el reino de la Nueva España* (México, 1966), p. 399. Lucas Alamán, *Historia de México*, 5 vols. (México, 1942), vol. I, p. 67. Howe, p. 447. Clement G. Motten, *Mexican Silver and the Enlightenment* (Philadelphia, 1950), p. 36. José Joaquin Izquierdo, *La primera casa de las ciencias en México: El real seminario de minería (1792-1811)* (México, 1958), p. 256.

26. German O. E. Tjarks, *El consulado de Buenos Aires y sus proyecciones en la historia del Río de La Plata* (Buenos Aires, 1973), p. 46.

27. *Reglamento*, arts., 53, 54. Humberto Tandron, *El real consulado de Caracas y el comercio exterior de Venezuela* (Caracas, 1976), p. 81.

28. *Real cédula de su Majestad para la erección del consulado de la muy noble y muy leal ciudad de Veracruz de orden de su junta de gobierno*, ed. Leonardo Pasquel (México, 1959), arts. 10, 21. Ortíz de la Table Ducasse, p. 79.

29. Ralph Lee Woodward, *Class Privilege and Economic Development: The Consulado de Comercio of Guatemala, 1793-1871* (Chapel Hill, 1966), pp. 5-8.

30. For the traditional consulados, see Robert S. Smith, *The Spanish Guild Merchants: A History of the Consulado, 1250-1700* (Durham, 1940). For Lima, see María Encarnación Rodríguez Vicente, *El tribunal del consulado de Lima en la primera mitad del siglo XVIII* (Madrid, 1960).

31. Branciforte is often dismissed as corrupt and reactionary, a view challenged in Luis Navarro García and María del Pópulo Antolín Espino, "El Virrey Marqués de Branciforte (1794-1798)," in José Antonio Calderón Quijano, *Virreyes de Nueva España en el reinado de Carlos IV* (Sevilla, 1972), vol. 1, pp. 369-371. Mark A. Burkholder, *Politics of a Colonial Career: José Baquíjano and the Audiencia of Lima* (Albuquerque, 1980), p. 50.

32. Woodrow Borah, *Justice By Insurance: The General Indian Court of Colonial Mexico and the Legal Aides of the Half-Real* (Berkeley, 1983), p. 389. Article 248 of the constitution of 1812 abolished the Indian court along with other special courts. *Constitución política de la monarquía Española* (Madrid, 1820), art. 284.

33. Navarro García and Pópulo Antolín Espino, p. 381.

34. Ibid., p. 383.

35. María del Carmen Galbis Díaz, "Miguel José de Azanza (1798-1800)," in Calderón Quijano, *Virreyes en el reinado de Carlos IV*, vol. 2, pp. 28-29.

36. Howe, p. 376.

Conclusion

1. Anderson used the terms "power contenders" and "power capability." Charles W. Anderson, *Politics and Economic Change in Latin America* (Princeton, 1967), p. 91.

2. Even in late eighteenth-century Mexico, when population pressure and scarce resources resulted in contests over land, Indians forced favorable decisions. Eric Van Young, *Hacienda and Market in Eighteenth-Century Mexico: The Rural Economy of the Guadalajara Region, 1675-1820* (Berkeley, 1981), pp. 315-342. The same process is demonstrated in William B. Taylor, *Drinking, Homicide, and Rebellion in Colonial Mexican Villages* (Stanford, 1979), pp. 113-151.

3. Such a process did not exclude radical departures. For example, the creation of a police organization, the Acordada, in New Spain in 1710 broke with the traditional jurisdictional practices. Colin M. MacLachlan, *Criminal Justice in Eighteenth-Century Mexico: The Tribunal of the Acordada* (Berkeley, 1974). José de Gálvez, ignoring the method of its establishment, referred to it as a "modern and extremely useful" organization—unintended acknowledgment that a rational response could result from traditional consensus decision-making. *Informe general...entregó el Exmo Señor Marqués de Sonora...at...virrey frey Dr. Antonio Bucareli y Ursúa* (December 1771), p. 41. Genaro García Collection, G206-0, Benson Latin American Collection, University of Texas, Austin.

4. Susan M. Socolow, *The Merchants of Buenos Aires, 1778-1810: Family and Commerce* (Cambridge, 1978), p. 111.

5. R. K. Merton, "Role of the Intellectual in Public Bureaucracy," *Social Forces* 23 (1945): 405-415. Merton provides a suggestive model.

6. This situation is analogous to Mannheim's view of modern Europe when stress, induced by the movement from laissez-faire to rational planning, introduced a similar sense of maladjustment. Karl Mannheim, *Man and Society in an Age of Reconstruction* (London, 1940), pp. 6-15.

7. José María Ots Capdequí, *Instituciones* (Barcelona, 1959), p. 539.

8. The economic power of Mexican plutocrats, merchants, manufacturers, and others, is noted in Doris M. Ladd, *The Mexican Nobility and Independence, 1780-1826* (Austin, 1976), pp. 25-52, and John E. Kicza, *Colonial Entrepreneurs: Families and Business in Bourbon Mexico City* (Albuquerque, 1983).

9. Julio Alemparte, *El cabildo en Chile colonial* 2d ed. (Santiago, 1966), p. 353. Jorge Basadre, "Notas sobre la experiencia histórica peruana," *Revista histórica* (1952), p. 22.

10. Conde de Revillagigedo, "Informe sobre el estado del comercio de Nueva España, Agosto 31, 1793," *Boletín del archivo general de la nación* (November-December 1930 and January-February 1931). The merchant-trader dealt with an increased volume of contraband, and an improved flow of legal goods. On occasion, excess supply ruined the less nimble. See Sergio Villalobos, *Comercio y contrabando en el Río de la Plata y Chile 1700-1811* (Buenos Aires, 1965).

11. Javier Ortíz de la Tabla Ducasse, *Comercio exterior de Veracruz, 1778-1821: crisis de dependencia* (Sevilla, 1978), p. 101. Juan Manuel Herrero, "Notas sobre la ideología del burgués espanol del siglo XVIII," *Anuario de estudios americanos* (Sevilla, 1952), p. 300. José María Quirós, "Reflexiones sobre el comercio libre de las Americas," *Boletín del archivo general de la nación* (April-June 1948), pp. 179-189.

12. John Fisher, *Commercial Relations Between Spain and Spanish America in the Era of Free Trade, 1778-1796* (Liverpool, 1985), pp. 87-90.

13. John L. Phelan, *The People and the King: The Comunero Revolution in Colombia, 1781* (Madison, 1978), pp. 212-217.

14. Europeans viewed the Old World as inherently superior, if flawed. The New World, when not portrayed as inferior, might be presented as brashly immature. Americans found themselves in an intellectually defensive position. Bernabé Navarro B., *Cultura Mexicana moderna en el siglo XVIII* (México, 1964), pp. 45-61.

15. Even in the underpopulated and new Viceroyalty of La Plata, the number of new offices was impressive. For a partial list, see Ricardo Zorraquín Becú, *La organización política argentina en el periodo hispánico* (Buenos Aires, 1959), pp. 249-250.

16. An attempt to distinguish the role of bureaucrats from that of politicians is provided in Joel D. Aberbach, Robert D. Putnam, and Bert A. Rockman, *Bureaucrats and Politicians in Western Democracies* (Cambridge, Massachusetts, 1981). For the structure, internal organization, and operation of the late eighteenth-century colonial bureaucracy, see Linda J. Arnold, "Bureaucracy and Bureaucrats in Mexico City: 1742-1835," Ph.D. dissertation, University of Texas, Austin, 1982.

17. Jacques A. Barbier, "Elites and Cadres in Bourbon Chile," *Hispanic American Historical Review* (August 1972), pp. 418, 433. Brading noted the stress caused by the perceived distinction between office and influence characteritistic of the formative stage of bureaucratic development. D. A. Brading, *Miners and Merchants in Bourbon Mexico, 1763-1810* (Cambridge, 1970), p. 239.

18. The number of Americans receiving Audiencia appointments declined to 13 percent between 1751 and 1775, then 9 percent in 1776-77, before reversing in 1778-1808 with 30 percent, followed in 1809 with 52 percent. See Table 1, Mark A. Burkholder and D. S. Chandler, *Biographical Dictionary of Audiencia Ministers in the Americas, 1687-1821* (Westport, 1982), p. xviii.

19. Mark A. Burkholder, *Politics of a Colonial Career: José Baquíjano and the Audiencia of Lima* (Albuquerque, 1980), pp. 102, 116, 126. Baquíjano subsequently (1814) accused the liberal cortes of engaging in "anti-political conduct." Timothy E. Anna, "Spain and the Breakdown of the Imperial Ethos: The Problem of Equality," *Hispanic American Historical Review* (May 1982), p. 265. Eduardo Arcila Farías, *El pensamiento económico hispanoamericano en Baquíjano y Carrillo* (Caracas, 1976), p. 29.

20. John Preston Moore, *The Cabildo in Peru Under the Bourbons* (Durham, 1966), pp. 184, 185, 188. Costeloe observed that the decision-making process between 1810 and 1824, whether under the liberals or the restored monarchy was a labyrinth that produced decisions already overtaken by events and could not supply a coherent policy. Michael P. Costeloe, *Response*

to Revolution: Imperial Spain and the Spanish American Revolutions, 1810-1840 (Cambridge, 1986), pp. 10-13.

21. The intellectual depth of the Mexican Enlightenment is demonstrated in Roberto Moreno, *Ensayo biobibliográfico de Antonio de León y Gama* (México, 1969) and his *Joaquin Velázquez de León y sus trabajos científicos sobre el valle de México* (México, 1977).

22. Ladd, pp. 68-69. Tutino states that a single elite culture emerged based on intermarriage and other ties. John M. Tutino, "Creole Mexico: Spanish Elites, Haciendas and Indian Towns, 1750-1810," Ph.D. dissertation, University of Texas, Austin 1976, p. 98. On the other hand elite economic and status competition may have led to internal differentiation and conflict within the elite as proposed by Jorge I. Domínguez, *Insurrection or Loyalty: The Breakdown of the Spanish American Empire* (Cambridge, Mass., 1980), p. 115. Shared perceptions as to how a political system should function may have been the one area that united the elite, while actual competition over its benefits resulted in differentiation and conflict.

23. Guillermo Furlong, *Nacimiento y desarrollo de la filosofía en el Río de la Plata, 1536-1810* (Buenos Aires,, 1952), p. 400. O. Carlos Stoetzer, *The Scholastic Roots of the Spanish American Revolution* (New York, 1979), pp. 134-135.

24. José María Álvarez, *Instituciones de derecho real de Castilla y de Indias*, Estudio preliminar por Jorge Mario García Laguardia y María del Refugio González, 2 vols. (México, 1982), Vol. 1, pp. 105-146.

25. Anna, "Spain and the Breakdown...," p. 268. Spanish liberals also found the issue of equality a difficult one. While acceptible in theory they resisted it in fact. Marina Volio, *Costa Rica en las cortes de Cádiz* (San Jose, 1980), pp. 129-31. Mario Rodríguez, *The Cadiz Experiment in Central America, 1808-1826* (Berkeley, 1978), pp. 89-95.

26. The Viceroyalty of La Plata (1776) came close to being a purely economic creation. Manfred Kossok, *El virreynato del Río de la Plata: su estructura económica-social* (Buenos Aires, 1959).

27. Jaime E. Rodríguez O. *The Emergence of Spanish America: Vicente Rocafuerte and Spanish Americanism 1808-1832* (Berkeley, 1975), pp. 27-30. The realization of their worst fears is documented in the brilliant study by Jaime E. Rodríguez O. *Down from Colonialism* (Los Angeles, 1983) and by the same author *Estudios sobre Vicente Rocafuerte* (Guayaquil, 1975), Timothy E. Anna, *The Fall of the Royal Government in Peru* (Lincoln, 1979), pp. 99-103.

28. W. Woodrow Anderson, "Reform As a Means to Quell Revolution," in Nettie Lee Benson, ed., *Mexico and the Spanish Cortes, 1810-1822* (Austin, 1966), pp. 185-207. William Spence Robertson, "The Policy of Spain Towards Its Revolted Colonies, 1820-1823," *Hispanic American Historical Review* (February-August 1926), p. 26.

29. Victoriano de Villava, Apuntamientos para la reforma del reino España e Indias," in Ricardo Levine, *Vida y escritos de Victoriáno de Villava* (Buenos Aires, 1946), pp. 103-112. Peggy K. Liss, *Atlantic Empries: The Network of Trade and Revolution, 1713-1826* (Baltimore, 1983), pp. 172-173.

30. E. Bradford Burns, *The Poverty of Progress* (Berkeley and Los Angeles, 1980), pp. 132-154.

Works Cited

Abellán, José Luis. *El Erasmismo Español: Una historia de la otra España*. Madrid, 1976.

Achútegui, Pedro S. *La univeralidad de conocimiento de Dios en los paganos, según los primeios teólogos de la Compañía de Jesus, 1534-1648*. Pamplona, 1951.

Addy, George M. *The Enlightenment in the University of Salamanca*. Durham, 1966.

Adorno, Roléna. "Las otras fuentes de Guaman Poma: sus lecturas castellañas," *Histórica* (Lima, Dic., 1978) pp. 137-58.

Aiton, Arthur S. *Antonio de Mendoza, First Viceroy of New Spain*. Durham, 1927.

Alamán, Lucas. *Historia de México*, 5 vols. Mexico, 1942.

Alden, Dauril. *Royal Government in Colonial Brazil*. Berkeley, 1968.

Alemparte, Julio. *El cabildo en Chile colonial*, 2nd. ed. Santiago, 1966.

Alonso Getino, Luis. *Influencia de los Dominicos en las Leyes Nuevas*. Sevilla, 1945.

Alonso Getino, Luis. *Reccliónes telógicas de Maestro Fray Francisco de Vitoria*, 3 vols. Madrid, 1933-1936.

Altamira, Rafael. "El texto de los Leyes de Burgos de 1512," *Revista de historia de America* (1938) pp. 5-79.

Altamira, Rafael. *Historia de España y de la civilización española*, 3rd. ed., 4 vols. Barcelona, 1913.

Álvarez de Morales, Antonio. *La "ilustracion" y la reforma de la universidad en la España del siglo XVIII*. Madrid, 1971.

Álvarez, José María. *Instituciones de derecho real de Castilla y de Indias*. Estudio preliminar por Jorge Mario García Laguardia y María del Refugio González, 2 vols. México, 1982.

Alzate y Ramírez, José Antonio de. *Memoria sobre la naturaleza, cultivo y beneficio de la grana*. Roberto Moreno, ed. México, 1981.

Alzate y Ramírez, José Antonio de. *Obras: Periódicos*. Robero Moreno, ed. Mexico, 1980.

Amat, Manuel de. "El Virrey Amat da cuenta El Rey de los defectos y vicios de organización del virreinato del Perú—1762," *Revista de la biblioteca nacional* (Buenos Aires) (1942) pp. 345-50.

Anderson, Charles A. *Politics and Economic Change in Latin America*. Princeton, 1967.

Anderson Imbert, Enrique. *Spanish American Literature: A History*. Detroit, 1963.

Anderson, W. Woodrow. "Reform As a Means to Quell Revolution." Nettie Lee Benson, ed. *Mexico and the Spanish Cortes, 1810-1822*. Austin, 1966.

Andrien, Kenneth J. *Crisis and Decline: The Viceroyalty of Peru in the Seventeenth Century*. Albuquerque, 1985.

Andrien, Kenneth J. "The Sale of Fiscal Offices and the Decline of Royal Authority in the Viceroyalty of Peru, 1633-1700," *Hispanic American Historical Review* (February, 1982) pp. 49-71.

Anna, Timothy E. "Spain and the Breakdown of the Imperial Ethos: The Problem of Equality," *Hispanic American Historical Review* (May, 1982) pp. 254-72.

Anna, Timothy E. *The Fall of the Royal Government in Peru*. Lincoln, 1979.

Archer, Christon I. *The Army in Bourbon Mexico, 1760-1810*. Albuquerque, 1977.

Arcila Farias, Eduardo. *El pensamiento económico Hispanoamericano en Baquíjano y Carrillo*. Caracas, 1976.

Arcila Farias, Eduardo. *Reformas económicas del siglo XVIII en Nueva España*. México, 1974.

Arnold, Linda J. "Bureaucracy and Bureaucrats in Mexico City: 1742-1835." Ph.D. Dissertation, University of Texas. Austin, 1982.

Arteaga Garza, Beatriz and Pérez San Vicente, Guadalupé. Comp. *Cedulario cortesiano*. México, 1949.

Artola, Miguel, "Campillo y las reformas de Carlos III," *Revista de Indias*, (October-December, 1952) pp. 685-714.

Astuto, Philip Louis. *Eugenio Espejo (1747-1795) Reformador Ecuatoriano de la ilustración*. México, 1969.

Aznar, Bernardo Francisco. *Discurso que formó tocante a la Real Hacienda y administración de ella*. Madrid, 1727.

Bailyn, Bernard. *The Ideological Origins of the American Revolution*. Cambridge, 1967.

Bakewell, Peter J. *Miners of the Red Mountain: Indian Labor in Potosí*. Albuquerque, 1984.

Bakewell, Peter J. *Silver Mining and Society in Colonial Mexico: Zacatecas, 1546-1700*. Cambridge, 1971.

Barba, Cecilia. "Francisco Vitoria y Hernán Cortés: Teoría y práctica del derecho internacional en el siglo XVI," *Memoria del II congreso de historia del derecho mexicano*. México, 1980, pp. 125-31.

Barbier, Jacques A. "Tradition and Reform in Bourbon Chile: Ambrosio O'Higgins and Public Finances," *The Americas* (January, 1978) pp. 381-99.

Barbier, Jacques A. "Elites and Cadres in Bourbon Chile," *Hispanic American Historical Review* (August, 1972) pp. 416-35.

Barros Arana, Diego. *Historia jeneral de Chile*, 16 vols. Santiago, 1884-1902.

Basadre, Jorge. "Notas sobre la experiencia histórica peruana," *Revista histórica* (1952) pp. 5-40.

Bejarano, Ignacio, Ed. *Actas de cabildo de la ciudad de México*, 12 vols. México, 1889-1900.

Benert, Richard R. "Lutheran Resistance Theory and the Imperial Constitution," *Il Pensiero Politico* (1973), pp. 17-36.

Benson, Nettie Lee. *Mexico and the Spanish Cortes, 1810-1822.* Austin, 1968.

Bernard, Gildas. *Le Secretariat D'etat et le Conseil Espagnol des Indies, 1700-1808.* Geneva, Paris, 1972.

Boase, T.S.R. *Boniface VIII.* London, 1933.

Bobb, Bernard E. *The Viceregency of Antonio María Bucareli in New Spain, 1771-1779.* Austin, 1962.

Bodin, Jean. *The Six Books of the Commonweal.* Trans. Beatrice Reynolds. Kenneth D. McFae, ed. Cambridge, Mass., 1967.

Borah, Woodrow. "Legacies of the Past: Colonial," *Contemporary Mexico: Papers of the IV International Congress of Mexican History.* James W. Wilkie, Michael C. Meyer, Edna Monzón de Wilkie, eds. Los Angeles, 1976.

Borah, Woodrow W. *Justice By Insurance: The General Indian Court of Colonial Mexico and the Legal Aides of the Half-Real.* Berkeley, 1983.

Brading, D.A. *Miners and Merchants in Bourbon Mexico, 1763-1810.* Cambridge, 1970.

Braybrooke, David. "Ideology," *The Encyclopedia of Philosophy*, 8 vols. New York, 1967.

Bromley, Juan. "Recibimiento de virreyes en Lima," *Revista histórica* (1953) pp. 5-108.

Bronner, Fred. "La unión de las armas en el Perú: aspectos politico-legales," *Anuario de estudios americanos.* Sevilla, 1967, pp. 1133-1176.

Brown, Kendall Walker. "The Economic and Fiscal Structure of Eighteenth-Century Arequipa." Ph.D. Dissertation. Duke University, 1979.

Brown, Thomas A. *La academia de San Carlos de la Nueva España*, 2 vols. México, 1976.

Burkholder, Mark A. "The Council of the Indies in the Late Eighteenth Century: A New Perspective," *Hispanic American Historical Review* (August, 1967) pp. 404-423.

Burkholder, Mark A. *Politics of a Colonial Career: José Baquíjano and the Audiencia of Lima.* Albuquerque, 1980.

Burkholder, Mark A. and Chandler, D.S. *From Impotence to Authority: The Spanish Crown and the American Audiencias, 1687-1808.* Columbia, 1977.

Burkholder, Mark A. and Chandler, D.S. *Biographical Dictionary of Audiencia Ministers in the Americas, 1687-1821.* Westport, 1982.

Burns, E. Bradford. *The Poverty of Progress.* Berkeley and Los Angeles, 1980.

Bury, J.B. *The Idea of Progress: An Inquiry into Its Growth and Origin.* New York, 1955.

Cabrera, Juan de. *Crisis política. Determina el más florido imperio y la mejor institución de principes y ministros.* Madrid, 1719.

Calderón Quijano, José Antonio, ed. *Los virreyes de Nueva España en el reinado de Carlos III.* 2 vols. Sevilla, 1967.

Calderón Quijano, José Antonio. ed. *Los virreyes de Nueva Espana en el reinado de Carlos IV.* Sevilla, 1972.

Callahan, William J. *Honor, Commerce, and Industry in Eighteenth-Century Spain.* Boston, 1972.

Campbell, Leon G. "A Colonial Establishment: Creole Domination of the Audiencia of Lima During the Late Eighteenth Century," *Hispanic American Historical Review* (February, 1972) pp. 1-25.

Campbell, Leon G. "Social Structure of the Túpac Amaru Army in Cuzco, 1780-81." *Hispanic American Historical Review* (November, 1981) pp. 675-93.

Campillo y Cossío, José del. *Lo que hay de más y de menos en España para que sea lo que debe ser y no lo que es.* Madrid, 1798.

Campillo y Cossío, José del. *Nuevo sistema de gobierno económico para la América.* Madrid, 1787.

Campomanes, Pedro Rodríguez de. *Apéndice a la educación popular.* 4 vols. Madrid, 1775-1776.

Campomanes, Pedro Rodríguez de. *Discurso sobre la educación popular de los artesanos y su formento; y apéndice d la educación popular.* Madrid, 1775.

Canovan, Margaret. *G. K. Chesterton: Radical Populist.* New York, 1977.

Carrera Pujal, Jaime. *Historia de la economía española.* 5 vols. Barcelona, 1943-1947.

Carta de Pedro Muñoz de Villavicencio al virrey (Feb. 28, 1773) W. B. Stephens Collection 1934 Benson Latin American Collection, University of Texas, Austin.

Carter, Charles H. "The Informational Base of Spanish Policy, 1598-1625," *Cahiers D'Histoire Mondiale* (1964) pp. 149-59.

Carter, Charles H. "The Nature of Spanish Government after Philip II," *Historian* (November, 1963) pp. 1-18.

Castrillo, Alonso de. *Tratado de república.* Madrid, 1958.

Castillo de Bobadilla, Jerónimo. *Política para corregidores y señores de vasallos en tiempo de paz y de guerra.* Madrid, 1775.

Cespedes del Castillo, Guillermo. *Lima y Buenos Aires: Repercusiones económicas y políticas de la creación del virreinato del Plata.* Sevilla, 1947.

Chacón y Calvo, José María. *Cedulario Cubano: Los orgínes de la colonización (1493-1512).* Madrid, n.d.

Chamberlain, Robert S. "The Concept of the Señor Natural as Revealed by Castilian Law and Administrative Documents," *Hispanic American Historical Review* (May, 1939) pp. 130-137.

Charney, Paul J. "The Urban Indian: A Case Study of the Indian Population of Lima in 1613," M.A. Thesis, University of Texas, 1980.

Chesterton, G. K. *Chaucer.* London, 1959.

Cibils, Manuel J. *Anarquía y revolución en el Paraguay.* Buenos Aires, 1957.

Colección de documentos inéditos para la historia de Hispano-America. 14 vols. Madrid, 1927-1932.

Constitución política de la monarquia Española. Madrid, 1820.

Cordova-Bell, Eleazon. *Las reformas del despotismo ilustrado en America.* Caracas, 1975.

Cornblit, Oscar. "Levantamiento de masas de Perú y Bolivia durante el siglo dieciocho," *El ocaso del orden colonial en Hispanoamérica.* Tulio Halperín Donghi, ed. Buenos Aires, 1978.

Costeloe, Michael P. *Response to Revolution: Imperial Spain and the Spanish American Revolutions, 1810-1840.* Cambridge, 1986.

Croix, Marqués de. *Correspondence du Marquis de Croix.* Nantes, 1891.

Crozier, Brian. *A Theory of Conflict.* London, 1974.

Cuevas, Mariano, ed. *Documentos inéditos del siglo XVI para la historia de México.* México, 1941.

Cunningham, Charles Henry. *The Audiencia in the Spanish Colonies As Illustrated by the Audiencia of Manila* (1593-1800). Berkeley, 1919.

Cushner, Nicholas P. *Lords of the Land: Sugar, Wine, and Jesuit Estates of Coastal Peru, 1600-1767*. Albany, 1980.

Dahlgren, E. W. *Les Relations Commerciales et Maritimes entre la France et Côtes de l'Ocean Pacifique*. Paris, 1909.

Danks, Noblet Barry, "Revolts in 1766 and 1767 in Mining Communities in New Spain," Ph.D. Dissertation, University of Colorado, 1979.

Davidson, Marcia D. "Three Spanish Economists of the Enlightenment: Campomanes, Jovellanos, Florez Estrada," Ph.D. Dissertation, Duke University, 1962.

Díaz Thomé, Jorge Hugo. "Francisco Cervantes de Salazar y su cronica de la Conquista de Nueva España," *Estudios de historiógrafia de la Nueva España*. México, 1945. pp. 15-47.

Domínguez, Jorge I. *Insurrection or Loyalty: The Breakdown of the Spanish American Empire*. Cambridge, Mass., 1980.

Domínguez, Ortíz Antonio. "Ventas y exenciones de lugares durante el reinado de Felipe IV," *Anuario de historia del derecho español*. Madrid, 1964. pp. 163-207.

Doyle, Phyllis. *A History of Political Thought*. London, 1963.

Eladio Velázquez, Rafael. *El cabildo comunero de Asunción*. Asunción, 1961.

Elliott, John H. *Imperial Spain, 1469-1716*. London, 1963.

Elliott, John H. "The Mental World of Hernán Cortés," *Transactions of the Royal Historical Society*. 5th ser. Vol. 17. London, 1967. pp. 41-58.

El Sabio, Alfonso. *Las Siete Partidas del Rey Alfonso El Sabio contejados con varios codices antiguos por la Real Academia de la Historia*. Madrid, 1972.

Enciso Recio, Luis Miguel. *La Gaceta de Madrid y El Mercario Histórico y Politico, 1756-1781*. Valladolid, 1957.

Enciso Recio, Luis Miguel. *Prensa económica del XVIII: El Correo Mercantil de España y Las Indias*. Valladolid, 1958.

Enciso Recio, Luis Miguel. *Nipho y el periodismo español del siglo XVIII*. Valladolid, 1956.

Erasmus, Desiderius. *The Education of a Christian Prince*. Trans. Lester K. Born. New York, 1936.

Escudero, José Antonio. *Los secretarios de estado y de despacho*. 2 vols. Madrid, 1969.

Esqivel Obregón, T. *Apuntes para la história del derecho en México*. México, 1938.

Eyzaguirre, Jaime. *Ideario y ruta de la emancipación chilena*. 2nd ed. Santiago, 1957.

Farriss, Nancy M. *Maya Society Under Colonial Rule: The Collective Enterprise of Survival*. Princeton, 1984.

Feijóo, Benito Jerónimo. *Escritos políticos de Feijóo*. Madrid, 1947.

Feijóo, Benito Jerónimo. *Teatro critico universal*. Madrid, 1941.

Fernández del Castillo, Bernardo Pérez. *Historia de la escribania en la Nueva España y el notariado en México*. México, 1983.

Fernández-Santamaria, J. H. *The State, War and Peace: Spanish Political Thought in the Renaissance, 1516-1559*. Cambridge, 1977.

Feyjóo de Sosa, Miguel. "Prologo de la memoria del virrey Amat," *Revista Chilena de historia y geografía* (1951), pp. 42-64.

Fisher, John R. *Commercial Relations Between Spain and Spanish America in the Era of Free Trade, 1778-1796*. Liverpool, 1985.

Fisher, John R. *Government and Society in Colonial Peru: The Intendant System, 1784-1814*. London, 1970.

Fisher, John R. "Regionalism and Rebellion in Late Colonial Peru: The Aguilar-Ubalde Conspiracy of 1805," *Biblioteca Americana* (September, 1982), pp. 45-59.

Fisher, Lillian Estelle. *The Intendant System in Spanish America*. Berkeley, 1929.

Fisher, Lillian Estelle. *The Last Inca Revolt, 1780-1783*. Norman, 1966.

Font Ruis, José María. *Instituciónes-medievales Españolas: La organización política, economica y social de los reinos cristianos de la reconquesta*. Madrid, 1949.

Foronda, Valentín de. "Disertación sobre lo honroso que es la profesión de comercio," *Miscelánea o colección de varios discursos*. Madrid, 1793.

Frankl, Victor. "Hernán Cortés y la tradición de las Siete Partidas," *Revista de história de America* (Enero-Dic, 1962) pp. 9-74.

Friede, Juan. "El privilegio de vasallos otorgado a Hernán Cortés," *Historia y Sociedad en el mundo de habla española: Homenaje a José Miranda*. Bernardo García Martínez et al., eds. Mexico, 1970.

Friede, Juan and Keen, Benjamin, Eds. *Bartolomé de Las Casas in History: Towards an Understanding of the Man and His Work* (DeKalb, 1971).

Furlong, Guillermo. *Nacimiento y desarrollo de la filosofía en el Río de la Plata, 1536-1810*. Buenos Aires, 1952.

Gallegos Rocafull, José. *La experiencia de Dios en los místicos españoles*. México, 1945.

Gallegos Rocafull, José. *El hombre y el mundo de los teologos españoles de los siglos de oro*. México, 1946.

Gálvez, José de. Informe general...entregó el Exmo. Señor Marqués de Sonora...al Virrey Frey Dr. Antonio Bucareli y Ursua. (Dic, 1771) Genero García Collection, 6206-0, Benson Latin American Collection, University of Texas, Austin.

García Bernal, Manuela Cristina. "El gobernador de Yucatán, Rodrigo Flores de Aldona," *Homenaje al Dr. Muró Orejón*. 2 vols. Sevilla, 1979. Vol. 1, 123-172.

García de Valdeavellano, Luis. "Las Partidas y los origenes medievales del juicio de residencia," *Boletín de la real academia de historia* (1963) pp. 205-246.

García Icazbalceta, Joaquín. Ed. *Nueva colección de documentos para la historia de México*. 5 vols. México 1886-1892.

Garcilaso de la Vega, El Inca. *Royal Commentaries of the Incas and General History of Peru*. Trans. Harold V. Livermore. Austin, 1966.

Gibbs, Donald L. "Cuzco, 1680-1710: An Andean City Seen Through Its Economic Activities," Ph.D. dissertation. University of Texas, 1979.

Gibson, Charles. "Caciques in Postconquest and Colonial Mexico," *The Caciques*. Robert Kern and Ronald Dolkart, eds. Albuquerque, 1973, pp. 18-26.

Gibson, Charles. *The Aztecs Under Spanish Rule: A History of the Indians of the Valley of Mexico*. Stanford, 1964.

Gibson, Etienne. *Dante the Philosopher*. London, 1948.

Gilbert, Allan H. *Machiavelli's Prince and Its Forerunners: "The Prince" as a Typical Book "de Regimine Principum."* Durham, 1938.

Gimenez Fernández, Manuel. *Bartolomé de las Casas: Delegado de Cisneros para la reformación de las Indias (1516-1517)*. Sevilla, 1953.

Gínes de Supúlveda, Juan. *Democrates segundo o de las justas causas de la guerra contra los Indios*. Madrid, 1951.

Goldwert, Marvin. "The Struggle for the Perpetuity of Encomiendas in Viceregal Peru, 1550-1600," M.A. Thesis, University of Texas, 1958.

Góngora, Mario. *El estado en el derecho indiano: Epoca de fundación, 1492-1570*. Santiago, 1951.

Goode, William J. *The Celebration of Heroes: Prestige as a Social Control System*. Berkeley, 1978.

Gravelle, Sarah Stever. "Humanist Attitudes to Convention and Innovation in the Fifteenth Century," *The Journal of Medieval and Renaissance Studies* (Fall, 1981) pp. 193-209.

Green, Otis H. *Spain and the Western Tradition: The Castilian Mind in Literature from El Cid to Calderón*. 4 vols. Madison, 1963.

Greenfield, Sidney M. *The Patrimonial State in Patron-Client Relations in Iberia and Latin America: Sources of the "System" in Fifteenth Century Writings of the Infante D. Pedro of Portugal*. Amherst, 1976.

Grice-Hutchinson, Marjorie. *Early Economic Thought in Spain, 1170-1740*. London, 1978.

Hamilton, Bernice. *Political Thought in Sixteenth Century Spain: A Study of the Political Ideas of Vitoria, Soto, Suárez, and Molina*. Oxford, 1963.

Hamnett, Brian R. *Politics and Trade in Southern Mexico, 1750-1821*. Cambridge, 1971.

Hanke, Lewis. "Las leyes de Burgos in 1512 y 1513," *Anuario de historia Argentina* (1942) pp. 33-56.

Hanke, Lewis. "The 'Requerimiento' and Its Interpreters," *Revista de historia de America* (Marzo, 1938) pp. 25-34.

Hanke, Lewis. *The Spanish Struggle for Justice in the Conquest of America*. Philadelphia, 1949.

Hanke, Lewis and Rodríguez, Celso, Eds. Los virreyes españoles en America durante el gobierno de la casa de Austria, *Biblioteca de autores españoles*. 6 vols. Madrid, 1978-1979.

Haring, Clarence. "Early Spanish Colonial Exchequer," *American Historical Review* (1917-1918) pp. 779-796.

Harth Terre, Emilio. *Negros e indios: un estamento social ignorado del Perú colonial*. Lima, 1973.

Haskins, Charles Homer. *The Renaissance of the Twelfth Century*. Cambridge, Mass., 1927.

Herr, Richard. *The Eighteenth-Century Revolution in Spain*. Princeton, 1958.

Herrero, Juan Manuel. "Notas sobre la ideología del burgués español del siglo XVIII," *Anuario de estudios americanos*. Sevilla, 1952.

Hintze, Otto. "The Origins of the Modern Ministerial System: A Comparative Study," *Historical Essays of Otto Hintz*, ed. Felix Gilbert. New York, 1975.

Hirschberg, Julia. "An Alternative to Encomienda: Puebla's Indios de Servicio, 1531-45," *Journal of Latin American Studies* (November, 1979) pp. 241-64.

Howe, Walter. *The Mining Guild of New Spain and Its Tribunal General, 1770-1821*. New York, 1968.

Huamán Poma de Ayala, Felipe. *Letters to a King*. Ed. Trans. Christopher Dilke. New York, 1978.

Hudson, Winthrop S. *John Ponet (1516?-1556), Advocate of Limited Monarchy*. Chicago, 1942.

Humboldt, Alejandro de. *Ensayo político sobre el reino de la Nueva España*. México, 1966.

Hussey, Roland D. *The Caracas Company, 1728-1784: A Study in the History of Spanish Monopolistic Trade*. Cambridge, Mass., 1934.

Instruciónes que los virreys de Nueva España dejaron a sus sucessores. 2 vols. México, 1867-1873.

Iparraguire, Demetrio. "Los antiguos economistas españoles y el desarrollo económico de España," *Boletín de estudios económicos* (Enero-Abril, 1963) pp. 99-108.

Israel, J. I. *Race, Class and Politics in Colonial Mexico, 1610-1670*. Oxford, 1975.

Izquierdo, José Joaquín. *La primera casa de las ciencias en Méxcio: El real seminario de mineria (1792-1811)*. México, 1958.

Jago, Charles. "Habsburg Absolutism and the Cortes of Castile," *The American Historical Review* (April 1981) pp. 307-326.

Javier de Ayala, F. *Ideas politicas de Juan de Solórzano*. Sevilla, 1946.

Jovellanos, Gaspar Melchor de. "Discurso sobre los medios de promover la felicidad del Principado," *Biblioteca de autores Españoles*. Vol. 50. Madrid.

Jovellanos, Gaspar Melchor de. *Informe de la Sociedad Económica de esta corte al real y supremo consejo de Castilla en el expediente de ley agraria...* Madrid, 1795.

Jovellanos, Gaspar Melchor de. "Introducción a un discurso sobre el estado de la económia civil," *Biblioteca de autores españoles*. Vol. 87.

Juan, Jorge and Ulloa, Antonio de. *Discourse and Political Reflections on the Kingdoms of Peru*. John J. Tepaske, Ed. Norman, 1978.

Kagan, Richard L. *Students and Society in Early Modern Spain*. Baltimore, 1974.

Kamen, Henry. *Spain in the Later Seventeenth Century, 1665-1700*. London, 1980.

Kamen, Henry. *The Spanish Inquisition*. New York, 1965.

Kantsky, John H. "The Question of Peasant Revolts in Traditional Empires," *Studies in Comparative International Development*, (Fall-Winter, 1981) pp. 3-34.

Keniston, H. *Francisco de los Cobos, Secretary of the Emperor Charles V.* Pittsburg, 1960.

Keohane, Nannerl O. *Philosophy and the State in France: The Renaissance to the Enlightenment*. Princeton, 1980.

Kicza, John E. *Colonial Entrepreneurs: Families and Business in Bourbon Mexico City*. Albuquerque, 1983.

King, P. D. *Law and Society in the Visigothic Kingdom*. Cambridge, Mass., 1972.

Knowles, David. *The Evolution of Medieval Thought*. London, 1962.

Kolakowski, Leszek. *Marxism and Beyond: On Historical Understanding and Individual Responsibility*. London, 1968.

Konetzke, Richard. Ed. *Colección de documentos para la historia de la formación social de Hispanoamerica, 1493-1810*. 3 vols. Madrid, 1953.

Korth, Eugene H. *Spanish Policy in Colonial Chile: The Struggle for Social Justice, 1537-1700*. Stanford, 1968.

Kossok, Manfred. *El virreynato del Río de la Plata: Su estructura económica-social*. Buenos Aires, 1959.

Krieger, Leonard. "The Idea of Authority in the West," *The American Historical Review* (April, 1977), pp. 249-270.

Kuethe, Allan J. and Inglis, G. Douglas. "Absolutism and Enlightened Reform: Charles III, the Establishment of the Alcabala, and Commercial Reorganization in Cuba," *Past and Present: A Journal of Historical Studies* (November, 1985) pp. 118-143.

Kuethe, Allan J. "The Development of the Cuban Military as a Sociopolitical Elite, 1763-83," *Hispanic American Historical Review* (November, 1981) pp. 695-704.

Ladd, Doris M. *The Mexican Nobility and Independence, 1780-1826*. Austin, 1976.

LaForce, James Clayburn Jr. *The Development of the Spanish Textile Industry, 1750-1800*. Berkeley and Los Angeles, 1965.

Lanning, John Tate. *Academic Culture in the Spanish Colonies*. Oxford, 1940.

Larruga, Eugenio. *Historia de la real y general junta de comercio, moneda, y minas*. 12 vols. Madrid, 1779-1789.

Las Casas, Bartolomé de. *Brevisma relación de la destruccion de las Indias*. Buenos Aires, 1953.

Las Casas, Bartolomé de. *Historia de las Indias*. Madrid, 1951.

Laures, John. *The Political Economy of Juan de Mariana*. New York, 1928.

León Cazares, María del Carmen, et al., eds. *Carta-relación, Relacion y Forma de Diego García de Palacio, Oidor de la real Audiencia de Guatemala*. México, 1983.

Leonard, Irving A. *Books of the Brave: Being an Account of Books and of Men in the Spanish Conquest and Settlement of the Sixteenth-Century New World*. New York, 1964.

Letayf, Marcelo Bitar. *Los economistas españoles del siglo XVIII y sus ideas sobre el comercio con las Indias*. México, 1975.

Levi, Albert William. *Humanism and Politics: Studies in the Relationship of Power and Value in the Western Tradition*. Bloomington, 1969.

Levillier, Roberto. Ed. *Audiencia de Lima, correspondencia de presidentes y oidores*. Madrid, 1922.

Levillier, Roberto. *Don Francisco de Toledo, supremo organizador del Perú: Su vida su obra (1515-1582)*. 2 vols. Buenos Aires, 1935-1942.

Levillier, Roberto. *Gobernantes del Perú. Cartas y Papeles*. 14 vols. Madrid, 1921-1926.

Levine, Ricardo. *Las Indias no erán colonias*. Buenos Aires, 1951.

Levine, Ricardo. *Vida y escritos de Victoriáno de Villava*. Buenos Aires, 1946.

Lewy, Guenter. *Constitutionalism and Statecraft During the Golden Age of Spain: A Study of the Political Philosophy of Juan de Mariana, S.J.* Geneva, 1960.

Linehan, Peter. *The Spanish Church and the Papacy in the Thirteenth Century*. Cambridge, 1971.

Linz, Juan J. "Intellectual Roles in Sixteenth and Seventeenth-Century Spain." *Daedalus* (Summer, 1972), pp. 59-108.

Liss, Peggy K. *Atlantic Empires: The Network of Trade and Revolution, 1713-1826*. Baltimore, 1983.

Liss, Peggy K. *Mexico Under Spain, 1521-1556: Society and the Origins of Nationality*. Chicago, 1975.

Lockhart, James, et al. Eds. *The Tlaxcalan Actas: A Compendium of the Records of the Cabildo of Tlaxcala (1545-1627)*. Salt Lake City, 1986.

Lohmann Villena, Guillermo. *El Corregidor de indios en el Perú bajo los Austrias*. Madrid, 1957.

Lohmann Villena, Guillermo. "El corregidor de Lima: Estudio-historico-juridico," *Anuario de estudios americanos*. Sevilla, 1952, pp. 131-171.

López, Adalberto. *The Revolt of the Comuneros, 1721-1735: A Study in the Colonial History of Paraguay*. Cambridge, Mass., 1976.

Lorente, Sebastián, ed. *Relaciones de los virreyes y audiencias que han gobernado el Perú*. Lima, 1867.

Losada, Angel. "Hernán Cortés en la obra del cronista Sepúlveda," *Estudios cortesiano*. Madrid, 1948.

Lovett, A. W. *Philip II and Mateo Vázquez de Leca: The Government of Spain 1572-1592*. Geneva, 1977.

Lovett, A. W. "A Cardinal's Papers: The Rise of Mateo Vázquez de Leca," *The English Historical Review* (April, 1973) pp. 5-20.

Lynch, John. "Philip II and the Papacy," *Transactions of the Royal Historical Society*. 5th series, vol. II (1961) pp. 23-42.

Lynch, John. *Spanish Colonial Administration, 1782-1810: The Intendant System in the Viceroyalty of the Río de la Plata*. London, 1958.

Lynch, John. *Spain Under the Habsburgs*. 2 vols. Oxford, 1964.

Macanaz, Melchor de. "Auxilios para bien gobernar una monarquía católica," *Semanario erudito*. Madrid, 1720.

Machiavelli, Niccolò. *The Discourses*. Trans. Leslie J. Wilkes. Harmondsworth, 1970.

Mack, Eric. "Distributive Justice and the Tensions of Lockeanism," *Social Philosophy and Policy* (Autumn, 1983) pp. 132-150.

MacLachlan, Colin M. *Criminal Justice in Eighteenth-Century Mexico: The Tribunal of the Acordada*. Berkeley and Los Angeles, 1974.

MacLachlan, Colin M. and Rodríguez O., Jaime E. *The Forging of the Cosmic Race: A Reinterpretation of Colonial Mexico*. Berkeley, 1980.

MacLachlan, Colin M. "The Indian Directorate: Forced Acculturation in Portuguese America, 1757-1799," *The Americas* (April, 1972) pp. 369-392.

MacLeod, Murdo J. *Spanish Central America: A Socioeconomic History, 1520-1720*. Berkeley, 1973.

Madariaga, Salvador de. *El auge del imperio español en America*. Buenos Aires, 1955.

Manfredini, James Manfred. *The Political Role of the Count of Revillagigedo, Viceroy of New Spain, 1789-1794*. New Brunswick, 1949.

Mannheim, Karl. *Man and Society in an Age of Reconstruction*. London, 1940.

Manuel, Juan. *Libro de los estados*. R. B. Tate and I. R. MacPherson, eds. Oxford, 1974.

Manzano, Juan M. *La incorporación de las Indias a la corona de Castilla*. Madrid, 1948.

Mariana, Juan de. "Obras del Padre Juan de Mariana," *Biblioteca de autores Españoles*. Vol. 2. Madrid, 1909.

Marichal, Juan. "From Pistoia to Cádiz: A Generation's Itinerary, 1786-1812," A. Owen Aldridge, ed. *The Ibero-American Enlightenment*. Urbana, 1971, pp. 97-110.

Mariluz Urquijo, José María. *Ensayo sobre los juicios de residencia indianos*. Sevilla, 1952.

Mariluz Urquijo, José María. *Origenes de la burocracia Rioplatense: La secretaria del virreinato*. Buenos Aires, 1974.

Mariluz Urquijo, José María. *Noticias del correo mercantil de España y sus Indias: Sobre la vida ecónomica del virreinato de Río de la Plata*. Buenos Aires, 1977.

Marley, David. ed. Documentos varios para la historia de la Ciudad de Mexico a fines de la época colonial (1769-1815). México, 1983.

Marsiglio of Padua. *The Defender of Peace*. New York, 1956.

Martin de Guijo, Gregorio. *Diario, 1648-1664*. 2 vols. México, 1952.

Martin, Norman F. ed. *Instrucción reservada que el obispo-virrey Juan de Ortega Montañés dio a su sucesor en el mando, el Conde de Moctezuma*. México, 1965.

Martínez de Irujo, Carlos. *Observations on the Commerce of Spain with Her Colonies in Time of War*. Philadelphia, 1800.

Marzahl, Peter. *Town in the Empire: Government, Politics, and Society in Seventeenth-Century Popayán*. Austin, 1978.

Matienzo, Juan. *Gobierno del Perú*. Buenos Aires, 1910.

McGrade, Arthur S. *The Political Thought of William of Ockham*. Cambridge, 1974.

Mecham, J. Lloyd. *Church and State in Latin America: A History of Politico-Ecclesiastical Relations*. Chapel Hill, 1966.

Medina, José Toribio. *Biblioteca hispano-chilena, 1523-1817*. 3 vols. Santiago, 1897-1899.

Medina, José Toribio. *Historia del tribunal del santo oficio de la inquisición en Lima*. 2 vols. Santiago, 1890.

Menéndez Pidal, Ramon. *El padre Las Casas: Su doble personalidad*. Madrid, 1963.

Merton, R. K. "Role of the Intellectual in Public Bureaucracy," *Social Forces* 23 (1945) pp. 405-415.

Miranda, José. *España y Nueva España en la época de Felipe II*. México, 1962.

Miranda, José. *La función económica del encomendero en los orígenes del régimen colonial* (Nueva España, 1525-1531). México, 1965.

Miranda, José and González Casanova, Pablo, Eds. *Sátira anónima del siglo XVIII*. México, 1953.

Mitters, Heinrich. *The State in the Middle Ages: A Comparative Constitutional History of Feudal Europe*. Amsterdam, 1975.

Montaigne, Michel de. "Essays," *The Complete Works of Montaigne*. Trans. Donald M. Frame. London, 1957.

Moore, John Preston. *The Cabildo in Peru Under the Bourbons*. Durham, 1966.

Moore, John Preston. *The Cabildo in Peru Under the Habsburgs*. Durham, 1954.

Morazzani de Pérez Enciso, Gisela. *La intendencia en España y America*. Caracas, 1966.

Moreno Cebrian, Alfredo. *El corregidor de indios y la economia peruana del siglo XVIII*. Madrid, 1977.

Moreno, Frank Jay. "The Spanish Colonial System: A Functional Approach," *The Western Political Quarterly* (June, 1968) pp. 308-320.

Moreno de los Arcos, Roberto. *Ensayo biobibliográfico de Antonio de León y Gama*. México, 1969.

Moreno de los Arcos, Roberto. *Joaquín Velázquez de León y sus trabajos cientificos sobre el valle de México*. México, 1977.

Moreno de los Arcos, Roberto. "Las instituciones de la industria minera Novohispaña," *La minería en Mexico: Estudios sobre su desarrollo histórico*. México, 1978.

Moreno, de los Arcos, Roberto. *Un eclesiástico criollo frente al estado Borbón*. México, 1980.

Mörner, Magnus, *La corona española y los foraneos en los pueblos de Indios de America*. Stockholm, 1970.

Mörner, Magnus. *Perfil de la sociedad rural del Cuzco a fines de la colonia*. Lima, 1977.

Morse, Richard M. "The Heritage of Latin America," *The Founding of New Societies*. Louis Hartz, ed. New York, 1964, pp. 123-177.

Motolinía, Fr. Toribio. *Carta al Emperador: Refutación a Las Casas sobre la colonización española*. México, 1949.

Motten, Clement G. *Mexican Silver and the Enlightenment*. Philadelphia, 1950.

Muñoz Pérez, José. "La idea de America en Campomanes," *Anuario de estudios Americanos* (1953) pp. 209-264.

Muñoz Pérez, José. "Los proyectos de España e Indias en el siglo XVIII: El projectismo como género," *Revista de estudios políticos* (Mayo-Junio, 1955) pp. 169-195.

Navarro B., Bernabé. *Cultura Mexicana moderna en el siglo XVIII*. México, 1964.

Navarro B., Bernabé. *La introducción de la filosofia moderna en México*. México, 1948.

Navarro García, Luis. *Hispanoamerica en el siglo XVIII*. Sevilla, 1975.

Navarro García, Luis, ed. *Homenaje al Dr. Muró Orejón*. 2 vols. Sevilla, 1979.

Navarro García, Luis. *Intendencias en Indias*. Sevilla, 1959.

Niehaus, Thomas K. "Population Problems and Land Use in the Writings of the Spanish 'Arbitristas': Social and Economic Thinkers, 1610-1650," Ph.D. Dissertation. University of Texas, 1976.

Novísma recopilación de las leyes de España. 6 vols. Madrid, 1805-1829.

Nueva colección de documentos de España y de sus Indias. 6 vols. Madrid, 1892-1896.

Nunn, Charles F. *Foreign Immigrants in Early Bourbon Mexico, 1700-1760*. Cambridge, 1979.

Ockham, William of. *Opera Politica*. Manchester, 1940.

O'Gorman, Edmundo. *The Invention of America*. Bloomington, Ind., 1961.

Ortíz Domínguez, Antonio. "Ventas y exenciones de lugares durante el reinado de Felipe IV," *Anuario de historia del derecho Espanol*. Madrid, 1964.

Osborn, Wayne S. "Indian Land Retention in Colonial Metztitlán," *Hispanic American Historical Review* (May, 1973) pp. 217-238.

Ots Capedequí, José María. *España en America: El régimen de tierras en la época colonial*. Buenos Aires, 1959.

Ots Capedequí, José María. *Instituciones*. Barcelona, 1959.

Pacheco, Joaquín, et al, eds. *Colección de documentos inéditos relativos al descubrimiento, conquista y organización de las antiguas posesiones españoles de America y Oceanía*. 42 vols. Madrid, 1864-1889.

Palacio Atard, Vicente. *Areche y Guirior. Observaciones sobre el fracaso de una visita al Perú*. Sevilla, 1946.

Palacio Atard, Vicente. *Los españoles de la ilustración*. Madrid, 1964.

Papel periodico de la Ciudad de Santafé de Bogotá, 1791-1797 (edicion facsimilar) 6 vols. Bogotá, 1978.

Parry, John H. *The Sale of Public Office in Spanish Indies Under the Habsburgs*. Berkeley, 1953.

Parry, John H. *The Spanish Seaborne Empire*. London, 1966.

Parry, John H. *The Spanish Theory of Empire in the Sixteenth Century*. Cambridge, 1940.

Pasquel, Leonardo, Ed. *Real cédula de su Majestad para la erección del consulado de la muy noble y muy leal ciudad de Veracruz de orden de su junta de gobierno*. México, 1959.

Payne, Stanley G. *A History of Spain and Portugal*. 2 vols. Madison, 1973.

Phelan, John Leddy. "Authority and Flexibility in the Spanish Imperial Bureaucracy," *Administrative Science Quarterly* (June, 1960) pp. 47-65.

Phelan, John Leddy, *The People and the King: The Comunero Revolution in Columbia, 1781*. Madison, 1978.

Phelan, John Leddy. *The Kingdom of Quito in the Seventeenth Century: Bureaucratic Politics in the Spanish Empire*. Madison, 1967.

Pierson, W. W. "La intendencia de Venezuela en el régimen colonial." *Boletín de la academia nacional de la historia* (Caracas, 1941) pp. 259-275.

Pike, Frederick B. "The Municipality and the System of Checks and Balances in Spanish America," *The Americas* (October, 1958) pp. 139-158.

Polt, John H. R. *Gaspar Melchor de Jovellanos*. New York, 1971.

Poole, Stafford. "Institutionalized Corruption in the Letrado Bureaucracy: The Case of Pedro Farfán 1568-1588," *The Americas* (October, 1981) pp. 149-171.

Priestley, Herbert Ingram. *José de Gálvez, Visitador-General of New Spain, 1765-1771*. Berkeley, 1916.

Puga, Vasco de. *Provisiones, cédulas, instrucciones de su Magestad*. 3 vols. Madrid, 1945.

Putnam, Robert D. and Rockman, Bert A. *Bureaucrats and Politicians in Western Democracies*. Cambridge, Mass., 1981.

Puy, Francisco. *El Pensamiento tradicional en la España del siglo XVIII*. Madrid, 1966.

Quevedo Villagas, Francisco de. *Política de Dios y govierno de Christo*. James O. Crosby, Ed. Madrid, 1966.

Quirós, José María. "Refleciones sobre el comercio libre de las Americas," *Boletín del archivo general de la nación* (Abril, mayo, junio, 1948) pp. 179-189.

Raeff, Marc. *The Well-Ordered Police State: Social and Institutional Change Through Law in the Germanies and Russia, 1600-1800*. New Haven, 1983.

Ramos, Pérez, Demetrio. "La etapa lascasiana de la presion de conciencias," *Anuario de estudios Americanos* (1967), pp. 861-954.

Recopilación de leyes de los reynos de las Indias. Madrid, 1791.

Redmond, Walter Bernard. *Bibliography of Philosophy in the Iberian Colonies of America*. The Hague, 1972.

Rees Jones, Ricardo. *El despotismo ilustrado y los intendentes de la Nueva España*. México, 1979.

Rees Jones, Ricardo, ed. *Real ordenanza para el establecimiento e instrucción de intendentes de ejercito y provincia en el reino de la Nueva España, 1786*. México, 1984.

Reglamento y arancles reales para el comercio libre de España a Indias de 12 de Octobre de 1778. Madrid, 1778.

Revillagigedo Conde de. "Informe sobre el estado del comercio de Nueva España (Agosto 31, 1793)," *Boletín del archivo general de la nación* (Nov.-Dic., 1930 and Enero-Feb., 1931) pp. 192-211.

Robertson, William Spence. "The Policy of Spain Towards Its Revolted Colonies, 1820-1823," *Hispanic American Historical Review* (Feb.-Aug., 1926) pp. 21-46.

Rodrígues Casado, Vicente. *La política y los políticos en el reinado de Carlos III*. Madrid, 1962.

Rodríguez, Linda A. *The Search for Public Policy: Regional Politics and Government Finance in Ecuador, 1830-1940*. Berkeley and Los Angeles, 1985.

Rodríguez O., Jaime E. *Down From Colonialism: Mexico's Nineteenth-Century Crisis*. Los Angeles, 1983.

Rodríguez O., Jaime E. *The Emergence of Spanish America: Vicente Rocafuerte and Spanish Americanism, 1808-1832*. Berkeley and Los Angeles, 1975.

Rodríguez, Mario. *The Cádiz Experiment in Central America, 1808 to 1826*. Berkeley, 1978.

Rodríguez Vicente, María Encarnación. *El tribunal de consulado de Lima en la primera mitad del siglo XVIII*. Madrid, 1960.

Rodríguez Villa, Antonio, ed. *Cartas politico-económicas*. Madrid, 1878.

Rojos, Ulses. *Corregidores y justicias mayores de Tunja y su provincia desde la fundación de la ciudad hasta 1817*. Tunja, 1962.

Roma y Rosell, Francisco. *Las señales de la felicidad de España y medios de hacer las eficaces*. Madrid, 1768.

Romero, Carlos A. "Breve apuntes sobre perpetuidad de las encomiendas en el Perú," *Inca: revista trimestral de estudios antropologicos* (1923) pp. 676-689.

Rubio Mañe, J. Ignacio. *Introducción al estudio de los virreyes de Nueva España, 1535-1746*. México, 1955.

Sala Babust, Luis. *Visitas y reformas de la colegios mayores de Salamanca en el reinado de Carlos III*. Valladolid, 1958.

Sánchez Agesta, Luis. *El concepto del estado en el pensamiento Español del siglo XVI*. Madrid, 1959.

Sánchez Agesta, Luis. *El pensamiento político del despotismo ilustrado*. Madrid, 1953.

Santa Cruz, Alonso de la. *Crónica del emperador Carlos V*. 5 vols. Madrid, 1920-1925.

Santillán, Fernando de. *Historia de los Incas y relación del origen, descendencia, política y gobierno de los Incas*. Lima, 1927.

Sawyer, P. H., and Woods, I. N., eds. *Early Medieval Kingship*. Leeds, 1977.

Sayous, André E. "Partnerships in the Trade Between Spain and America and also the Spanish Colonies in the Sixteenth Century," *Journal of Economic and Business History* (February, 1929) pp. 282-301.

Schwerin, Karl H. "The Anthropological Antecedents: Caciques, Cacicazgos, and Caciquismo," *The Caciques*. Robert Kern and Ronald Dolkart, Eds. Albuquerque, 1973, pp. 5-17.

Sexton, James D., Ed. *Son of Tecún Umán: A Maya Indian Tells His Life Story*. Tucson, 1981.

Shäfer, Ernst. *El consejo real y supremo de las Indias*. 2 vols. Sevilla, 1935-1947.

Shäfter, Robert J. *The Economic Societies in the Spanish World, 1763-1821*. Syracuse, 1958.

Sherman, William L. *Forced Labor in Sixteenth-Century Central America*. Lincoln, 1979.

Shiels, Eugene W. *King and Church: The Rise and Fall of the Patronato Real*. Chicago, 1961.

Shils, Edward. *Tradition*. London, 1981.

Simpson, Lesley B. *The Laws of Burgos*. San Francisco, 1960.

Skinner, Quentin. *The Foundations of Modern Political Thought*. 2 vols. Cambridge, 1978.

Smith, Ricardo. *Un humanista al servicio del imperialismo: Juan Ginés de Sepúlveda (1490-1573)*. Córdoba, 1942.

Smith, Robert S. "Sales Taxes in New Spain, 1595-1700," *Hispanic American Historical Review* (February, 1948) pp. 2-37.

Smith, Robert S. *The Spanish Guild Merchants: A History of the Consulado 1250-1700*. Durham, 1940.

Smith, Robert S. "The Wealth of Nations in Spain and Hispanic America, 1780-1830," *Journal of Political Economy* (April, 1957) pp. 104-125.

Soberanes Fernández, José Luis. *Los Tribunales de la Nueva España*. Mexico, 1980.

Socolow, Susan M. *The Merchants of Buenos Aires, 1778-1810: Family and Commerce*. Cambridge, 1978.

Solórzano y Pereyra, Juan de. "Política indiana," *Biblioteca de autores españoles*. Madrid, 1978.

Spalding, Karen. "Indian Rural Society in Colonial Peru: The Example of Huarochiri," Ph.D. Dissertation. University of California, Berkeley, 1967.

Spell, J. R. "Rousseau in Spanish America," *Hispanic American Historical Review* (May, 1935) pp. 260-267.

Stern, Steve J. *Peru's Indian Peoples and the Challenge of Spanish Conquest: Huamanga to 1640*. Madison, 1982.

Stern, Steve J. "The Rise and Fall of Indian-White Alliances: A Regional View of 'Conquest' History," *Hispanic American Historical Review* (August, 1981) pp. 461-491.

Stevens, Henry, ed. *The New Laws and Ordinances of His Majesty Emperor Charles the Fifth*. Facsimile ed. London, 1893.

Stoetzer, O. Carlos. *The Scholastic Roots of the Spanish American Revolution*. New York, 1979.

Suárez, Francisco. *Selection from Three Works*. Trans. G. L. Williams. 2 vols. Oxford, 1944.

Tabla Ducasse, Javier Ortíz de la. *Comercio exterior de Veracruz, 1778-1821: Crisis de dependencia*. Sevilla, 1978.

Tandron, Humberto. *El real consulado de Caracas y el comercio exterior de Venezuela*. Caracas, 1976.

Taylor, William B. *Drinking, Homicide, and Rebellion in Colonial Mexican Villages*. Stanford, 1979.

Temple, Ella Dunbar. *La gaceta de Lima del siglo XVIII: Facsímiles de seis ejemplares raros de este periódico*. Lima, 1965.

Thompson, E. A. *The Goths in Spain*. Oxford, 1969.

Tiryakian, Josefina Cintrón. "Campillo's Pragmatic New System: A Mercantile and Utilitarian Approach to Indian Reform in Spanish Colonies of the Eighteenth Century," *History of Political Economy* (1978) pp. 233-257.

Tjarks, German O. *El consulado de Buenos Aires y sus proyecciones en la historia del Río de la Plata*. Buenos Aires, 1973.

Tomás y Valiente, Francisco. *Los validos en la monarquía española del siglo XVIII*. Madrid, 1963.

Torre Revello, José. *El libro, la imprenta y el periodismo en America durante la dominación española*. Buenos Aires, 1940.

Torres Ramírez, Bibiano. "Alejandro O'Reilly en Cuba," *Anuario de estudios Americanos*, (1967) pp. 1357-1368.

Torres Saldamando, Enrique. "Reparto y composción de tierra en el Perú," *Revista peruana* (1879) pp. 28-34.

Tutino, John M. "Creole Mexico: Spanish Elites, Haciendas and Indian Towns, 1750-1810" Ph.D. Dissertation, University of Texas. Austin, 1976.

Ullman, Walter. *A History of Political Thought: The Middle Ages*. Middlesex, 1970.

Ulloa, Bernardo de. *Restablecimiento de las fabricas y comercio español*. Madrid, 1740.

Urteaga, Horacio H. and Romero Carlos A. eds. *Colección de libros y documentos referentes a la historia del Perú*. 2 vols. Lima, 1916-1917.

Uztariz, Gerónimo de. *Teórica y práctica de comercio y marina en diferentes discursos y calificados ejemplares...* Madrid, 1757.

Van Aken, Mark. "The Lingering Death of Indian Tribute in Ecuador," *Hispanic American Historical Review* (August, 1981), pp. 429-459.

Van Kleffens, E. N. *Hispanic Law Until the End of the Middle Ages*. Edinburgh, 1968.

Van Young, Eric. *Hacienda and Market in Eighteenth-Century Mexico: The Rural Economy of the Guadalajara Region, 1675-1820*. Berkeley, 1981.

Varallanos, José. *Historia de Huánuco*. Buenos Aires, 1959.

Vargas Ugarte, Ruben. *Historia general del Perú*. 10 vols. Lima, 1966.

Vargas Ugarte, Ruben. *Historia del Perú: Virreinato (Siglo XVIII) 1700-1790*. Lima, 1956.

Vargas, José María. *La economía política del Ecuador durante la colonia*. Quito, 1957.

Varner, John Grier. *El Inca, the Life and Times of Garcilasco de la Vega*. Austin, 1968.

Varon Gabai, Rafael. *Curacas y encomenderos: acomadomiento nativo en Huáraz, siglos XVI y XVII*. Lima, 1980.

Véliz, Claudio. *The Centralist Tradition of Latin America*. Princeton, 1980.

Vicens Vives, Jaime. *Manuel de historia económica de España*. Barcelona, 1967.

Villalobos, Nestor Meza. *La conciencia política chilena durante la monarquía*. Santiago, 1958.

Villalobos, Sergio. *Comercio y contrabando en el Río de la Plata y Chile, 1700-1811*. Buenos Aires, 1965.

Villalobos, Sergio. *El comercio y la crisis colonial: Un mito de la independencia*. Santiago, 1968.

Vitoria, Francisco de. *Relecciones de indios y del derecho de la guerra*. Madrid, 1928.

Walker, Geoffrey J. *Spanish Politics and Imperial Trade, 1700-1789*. Bloomington, 1979.

Ward, Bernardo. *Projecto económico en que se proponen varios providencias, dirigidas á promover los intereses de España*. Madrid, 1779.

Watt, John A. *The Theory of Papal Monarchy in the Thirteenth Century*. Cambridge, 1971.

Wilenius, Reijo. *The Social and Political Theory of Francisco Suárez*. Helsinki, 1963.

Wilks, Michael. *The Problem of Sovereignty in the Later Middle Ages*. Cambridge, 1963.

Williams, Patrick. "Philip III and the Restoration of the Spanish Government, 1598-1603," *The English Historical Review* (October 1973) pp. 751-769.

Woodward, Ralph Lee. *Class Privilege and Economic Development: The Consulado de Comercio de Guatemala, 1793-1871*. Chapel Hill, 1966.

Wortman, Miles L. *Government and Society in Central America, 1680-1840*. New York, 1982.

Yañez, Augustín, ed. *Doctrina de fray Bartolomé de Las Casas*. México, 1941.

Zavala, Silvio and Millares, Augustín Carlos, eds. *De las islas del mar océano* (Juan López de Palacios Rubios) *Del dominio de los reyes de España sobre los indios* (Fray Matias de Paz). México, 1954.

Zavala, Silvio A. *La encomienda indiana*. Madrid, 1935.

Zavala, Silvio A. *Las instituciónes jurídicas en la conquista de America*. 2nd. ed. Mexico, 1971.

Zavala, Silvio A. *New Viewpoints on the Spanish Colonization of America*. Philadelphia, 1943.

Zimmerman, Arthur Franklin. *Francisco de Toledo, Fifth Viceroy of Peru, 1569-1581*. New York, 1968.

Zorraquín Becú, Ricardo. *La organización política argentina en el período hispánico*. Buenos Aires, 1959.

Index

24; salary of, 35; attack on by Amat, 76; portrayal of in report of Juan and Ulloa, 77; portrayal of by Areche and Gálvez, 100

Corruption: as a question of degree, 37; portrayal of in report of Juan and Ulloa, 77

Cortés, Fernando: and municipal council of Veracruz, 23; ignores instructions on encomienda, 54

Cortes: relationship of with monarchy, 9; of Burgos, 10; calling of in Peru, 21, 61; rejection of autonomy by, 134

Council of State: functions of, 46-47; ordered to hear Las Casas, 58

Council of the Indies: on issue of *encomiendas*, 26; responsibility of for American appointments, 33; opposition of to sale of office by, 34; establishment of, 45; structure of, 46; early attitude of toward encomienda, 54; ordered to hear Las Casas, 58; opinion of on perpetuity of encomiendas, 60-61; functions of in eighteenth century, 85; hostility of toward trading companies, 91; instruction of to Gálvez, 95; opposition of to Gálvez's fiscal reforms, 98; instructions of to Areche, 100; elevation of to same status as Council of Castile, 104; Escobedo appointed to, 106; opposition of to any modification of repartimiento de comercio, 118; order of to eliminate exclusion of women by guild regulations in New Spain, 122

Crime, political approach toward, 42

Croix, Marqués de: reaction of to Alzate's journalistic efforts, 81-82; appointment of as viceroy, 96; received authority to establish intendancies, 98

Croix, Teodoro de: briefed on Túpac Amaru's revolt, 102; background of, 103; reaction of to intendant system, 106

Cruillas, Marqués de, reaction of to Gálvez's activities, 96

Cuba, reforms in, 93-94

Dante, support of for emperor's authority, 4

Daubenten, Ambrose, opinion of on trading companies, 91

Despacho Universal, creation of, 47

Don Juan Manuel, and worthiness of secular political activities, 4

Ecclesiastical censure, politics of, 32

Ensenada, Marqués de: plans of to reform administrative structure, 88; comments of on Spanish merchants, 93

Erasmus, Desiderius: and humanism in Spain, 5-6; and natural law, 6; on ruler's subordination to law, 14

Escobedo, Jorge: appointment of as visitador, 101; clash of with viceroy over taxes, 106; bitterness of about repartimiento de comercio, 118

Espejo, Eugenio, reaction of to reforms, 87

Estrada, Alvaro Florez, defines monarch's economic role, 69

Exaggeration, use of as a political tool, 65

Falcón, Francisco, 25

Farfán, Pedro, as an example of corruption, 37

Feijóo y Montenegro, Benito Gerónimo, importance of, 69

Felipe II: and mineral rights, 15; *Real Cámara de Castilla* appointed by, 33; and Vázquez de Leca, 33; reliance of on secretaries, 46; receives offer of money to revoke New Law, 59

Felipe III, abuse of appointment process by, 33

Felipe V: innovations of, 84-85; French pressure on to form a joint stock company, 91

Ferguson, Adam, Influence of on Jovellanos, 80

Fernando III, superior position of over Church, 3

Finestrad, Joaquín de, Hobbesian view of, 130

Flores, Manuel Antonio, conflict of with reforms, 106

Floridablanca, Count of: comment of on difficulty of reform, 83; opinion of on *Junta de Estado*, 85

Fonseca, Juan Rodríguez de, reaction of to Las Casas, 52-54

Foronda, Valentín de, views of on ennobling merchants, 72

Fuero Juzgo: and hierocratic benevolence, 2; use of by monarchy, 8; on king's subordination to law, 13

Fuero Real: sense of hierarchy of, 1; use of by monarchy, 8; notion of a monarchy contained within, 9; on king's subordination to law, 13

Gálvez, José de: attack on by Espejo, 87; activities of as visitor in New Spain, 90-91, 94-96; suppression of revolts by, 98; activities of as Secretary of Marine and Indies, 98; opinion on Túpac Amaru rebellion, 102; plan of for New Spain, 108; secret appointments of, 108; family members appointed by, 109; comments of on repartimiento de comercio, 114; general frustration of, 130

Garcilaso de la Vega, the Inca, approach of to Spanish conquest, xii

Gasca, Pedro de la, 23

General Indian Court, establishment of, 29

Gerson, Jean, on proprietary rights, 15

Great Chain of Being, comparison of with eighteenth century notion of intellectual unity, 69

Haro, Alonso Nuñez de: implementation of reforms by, 109; description of Revillagigedo by, 110

Honors, political and socioeconomic use of, 33-34

Huaman Poma: importance of book of, xii; philosophical approach of, 103

Huguenots: impact of on theory of tyrannicide, 11; comparison with, 130

Ignacio de Loyola, Martín, comments of on nature of law, 22

Indians: as a subgroup, 28; and New Laws of 1542, 29; and legal cases, 29; European reaction to, 48-49; willingness of to litigate, 48; and wage labor, 49; within encomienda, 50; acceptance of repartimiento by, 63; Campillo view of, 74; Ward's recommendations on, 75; Juan and Ulloa's recommendations on, 78; response of to repartimiento de comercio, 114-115; ability of to respond to free commerce questioned, 117

Inquisition, control of by political authorities, 32

Intellectuals: exposure of to wide range of political theories, xii; and Inquisition, xii; fear of in eighteenth

century, 12; Rivarola as example of, 132

Intendant System: campillo's support of, 74; introduction of in Spain, 84-85; introduction of in America, 90-91; in Cuba, 94; as a remedy for Túpac Amaru revolt, 102; ordinance of, 104; undermining of traditional structure by, 105; modification of by Toboada y Lemos, 107; attack on in *Justa repulsa*, 109-110; opinion of Revillagigedo of, 110-111; impact of on repartimiento, 115

Jeronymites, mission of in New World, 53

Jesuits: expulsion of from Paraguay, 10; and Indian virtues, 50; as an enlightened target, 97

John, of Paris, views of, 4

Jovellanos, Gaspar Melchor de: definition of happiness by, 69; incorporation of Uztáriz's ideas by, 73; ideas of, 79-80

Juan y Santacilia, Jorge: report of, 76-78; ideas of reflected in Areche's instructions, 100

Judges: duty of to reflect royal compassion, 12; public respect for, 40

Junta de Comercio, opinion of on trading companies, 92

Junta de Estado, establishment of, 85

Jurisdiction: lack of precision of, 40; struggle over between viceroy and Gálvez, 96

Justa repulsa del reglamento de intendencias, importance of, 109-110

Justice: as a demonstration of benevolence, 12; Visigothic notion of, 13; and revocation of law, 13; expectation of, 41

Juzgado de Indios: establishment and function of, 64; possible abolition of, 121

Kingdom: notion of, 25; implied rights of in Peru, 27

Labor: as a socioeconomic problem, 48-49; Las Casas approach to issue of, 52; supposed dependency of missionaries on, 59; compensated, 63; in mines, 63-64; Campomanes portrayal of in Spain, 79

Landazuri, Tomás Ortíz de, comments of on Gálvez's reforms, 98

Las Casas, Bartolomé de: reaction of to *requerimiento*, 31; early political activities of, 52-53; entry of into Dominicans, 54; return of to Spain, 55; mature political style of, 55; use of concept of tyrannicide by, 57; meeting of with Sepúlveda, 60; opinion of on Cerrato, 62; comments of on nature of laws, 62

Laws of Burgos, reaffirmation of Crown's legal presence and involuntary Indian labor by, 52

Leca, Mateo Vázquez de: king's obligation to, 33; functions of, 46

Locke, John: influence of on Jovellanos, 80; ideas of linked to Indian response to repartimiento de comercio, 115

Loyalty: political importance of, 22; as a result of appointment process, 33

Lutheran: attitude of toward natural law, 6; attack of on an orderly hierarchy, 7

Macanaz, Melchor de, 16; views of on monarch's economic role, 70-71; advice of to ennoble merchants, 72

Machiavelli, Niccolò: and natural law, 6; attack on by Feijóo, 70

Madrid, Fernández de, 134

Maldonado, Diego, labor relations of, 63

Mal Lara, Juan de, ideas of, x

Mariana, Juan de: and tyrannicide, 10-11; on subordination of king to law, 14; on proprietary rights, 15; economic notions of, 68

Marichal, Juan, characterization of enlightened officials by, 88

Marsiglio de Padua, attack of on Church authority, 4

Matienzo, Juan: justifies Spain's conquest of Peru, xi; comment of on public office, 35

Mendoza, Antonio de: investments of, 36; view of Indian labor, 48; links revenue to Indian labor, 54; ordered to placate settlers with grants of Indians, 59; suspension of New Laws by, 61

Mendoza, Pedro de: influenced by humanism, 5

Mesta, portrayal of by Campomanes, 79

Metztitlán, as an example of Indian use of legal devices, 48

Mining tribunal, establishment and functioning of, 119

Miralla, José Antonio, 134

Mobilization of Influence, importance of, 35

Mogravejo, Toribio Alfonso, as part of patronage network, 34

Mompó y Zayas, Fernando de, revolt justified by, 11

Monarchy: relations of with clergy, 3; Erasmus' view of, 6; reliance of on philosophical acceptance, 8; and tyrannicide, 11; compassionate impulse of, 12; attitude of toward public office, 35; as source of authority, 38; threat to in Las Casas opinion, 56; economic role of according to Macanaz, 71; view of by enlightened theorists, 83; nature of in eighteenth century, 86; problem of with trading companies, 91

Montesinos, Antonio de, activities of, 51

Morillo, Pablo, 12

Motolinía, Toribio de, defense of encomienda by, 59

Municipal council: need of to justify a new order, xi; and ceremonial loyalty, 22; royal recognition conceded to, 23-25; in marginal areas, 24; role of in Paraguay, 24; and Union of Arms, 26-27; restriction on lobbying by, 28; recognition by of royal appointees, 38; of Mexico on issue of native son appointments, 104; conflict of with Croix, 106

Naranjo y Romero, Gaspar, backing of for establishment of trading companies, 92

Natural Law: x; role of in New World, 28; relative to proprietary rights, 28; as justification for royal appointments, 33; Las Casas refers to, 56

New Laws: approval of, 58; problem-specific nature of, 58-59; watering down of, 59; varied enforcement of, 61

Newspapers: role of, 80; recognition of directive impact of, 82

Nipho, Francisco Mariano, role of in development of newspapers, 81

Novísima Recopilación, 13

Designer: Linda M. Robertson
Compositor: Trigraph Inc.
Text: 10/12 Palatino
Display: Palatino
Printer: Braun-Brumfield, Inc.
Binder: Braun-Brumfield, Inc.